Women of Mexico

The Consecrated and the Commoners
1519-1900

Women of Mexico

The Consecrated and the Commoners
1519-1900

by

Bobette Gugliotta

Floricanto Press

Copyright © 1989 by Bobette Gugliotta.

All rights reserved. Except for brief passages quoted in a review, no part of this book may be reproduced in any form, by photostat, microfilm, xerography, or any other means, or incorporated into any information retrieval system, electronic or mechanical, without the written permission of the copyright owners.

ISBN 0-915745-16-X
Cover illustration by Phyllis Martinez.

Floricanto Press
16161 Ventura Blvd., Suite 830
Encino, CA 91436

Women of Mexico

Acknowledgements

I would like to thank the following people for their help and encouragement. At Stanford University: Cecilia Preciado Burciaga, Associate Dean of Graduate Studies and Director of Summer Session; José Antonio Burciaga, Artist in Residence; Captain Paul Ryan, USN (Ret.), Naval Historian, Hoover Institution; Lee Ziegler, Director, Bechtel International Center. Special thanks to my husband, Captain Guy Gugliotta, USN (Ret.), for undertaking the exacting and difficult jobs of alphabetizing and typing the bibliography and index of this book.

Table of Contents

	Acknowledgements	i
	Introduction	iii
1.	The Conquistadoras	1
2.	Of Tribulations and Trials	32
3.	Practical Nuns and Other Sisters	56
4.	La Decima Musa	71
5.	Freedom Fighters	90
6.	The Lovers	125
7.	Carlota and Company	142
	Bibliography	171
	Index	181

Introduction

Our U.S. population with ancestral Latin American background has been growing by leaps and bounds in the last twenty years and there is every indication that it will continue to do so. Statistics demonstrate this dramatically.

Although Mexico is the Hispanic country most heavily represented in the United States, historical material on Mexican women is lean. To the best of my knowledge a volume of this kind has not been available and educators as well as the general public are ready for more publications. There are studies on the fertility, socioeconomic status, literacy (complete with charts and graphs) about Mexican women. There are also historical novels on some of the better known, colorful and exotic females. In the United States, which is often indifferent to its sister country, all material is to be encouraged, but the work presented here hopes to bridge a gap.

Women of Mexico presents heroines big and small within a framework of available facts and figures, but emphasizes readability rather than encyclopedic format. The book starts with the conquest and ends with the twentieth century because the lack of comprehensive, sequential information is greatest during these four hundred years. The twentieth century, with its speed of communication and abundance of materials, makes it easier for educator and layman to research Mexican women from 1900 on if they have the will and diligence.

I have put in several years of intense effort on this project, but many women who deserve coverage will be left out because no individual can touch all bases no matter how much time is expended. The hope is to stimulate interest and curiosity in people of many backgrounds so that they will become aware of the heroines represented and be on the watch for those still to be unearthed.

This book is not political. Whether we approve of the causes espoused by the females in these pages is unimportant; nor are we concerned with morals. There are saints, sinners, wives, mothers, business women, nuns, politicians and transvestites among them. I have incorporated quotations and translations into the text and eliminated footnotes because they can become a stumbling block in a work that covers many names and places and hopes to reach a general audience.

Historically, the focus of the United States has been on Europe rather than Latin America and the rise of the equal rights movement in our country has not substantially altered that thrust. Since the feminist movement has had comparatively less impact on Hispanics, fall-out from the recent emphasis on women in the United States has not extended to Latinas, their history and special needs. Although my background has included six years residence in the Andean countries of South America, I chose to write about Mexico as a starting point because of the great number of women in the United States who are Mexican American or Mexican born. Also, Americans of other ethnic backgrounds, especially in the western states, are more apt to have had Hispanic travel, if any, in nearby Mexico rather than Bolivia, Ecuador, Venezuela and so forth. People are naturally more interested in the history of a country they have visited or intend to visit.

Outstanding women in Mexican history need to be buttressed by information about their sisters who have also made contributions by sheer courage, independence, cleverness or dogged determination not to be downed. The world is composed of women who are small gems, and can be counted as successes, as well as the sparkling diamonds.

A final word on the composition of *Women of Mexico*. Those not born in the new world are incorporated when their lives affected, or were truly affected by, the country of adoption such as the Carvajal women who died in the Inquisition in Mexico City. Spanish and Indian words are translated in first usage only. The occasional scenes that go into the heads of women, imagining their thoughts, and the bits of dialogue, are the interpretation of the author unless otherwise indicated.

1
The Conquistadoras

Twenty females, to be given as slaves, walked soundlessly behind the male emissaries who headed the delegation laden with gifts for the victors who had slain thousands of their men the previous day, March 25, 1519, at the fierce encounter that history would call the great battle of Tabasco. The young girls, most under fifteen, were an exceedingly pretty lot. Custom demanded that the conquerors receive only the best and common sense dictated that a parcel of ugly women would not placate a victor nor soften his demands for plunder.

In contrast to the bronze-brown skins of the men of the province, the girl's faces were of a light yellow tint achieved by the application of an ointment called axin made from natural clay. Nieces, daughters and favorite chattels of Tabascan nobles, they had delicately rouged cheeks and a few had painted their teeth red with cochineal, a dye made from insects found on nopal cactus. It was a new fashion that came from the Huaxtec and Otomí tribes; now local women were taking it up, especially the *auinime* (courtesans). But the most pleasing of all the girls, the one who headed the group, was not painted with axin and when she smiled her teeth were a natural white. Though her thick, black hair was worn long and loose, except for two little loops above the forehead like horns, she constantly shook it back off her face and from time to time thrust it from her shoulders with impatient hands, making it obvious that this style, also a trademark of the courtesans, was not usual for her.

She walked proudly with shoulders back, head erect. The simple lines of her clothes became her. Her *cueitl* (skirt) consisted of a straight, ankle-length piece of cloth fastened at the waist with a red and green embroidered belt. This was topped by a *huipilli* (overblouse) embroidered around the scooped neck in the same colors. The hem of her skirt was stitched in a gay border of red hearts entwined with green leaves and finished with a fringe that flirted with the graceful movements of her sandaled feet.

The group slowed as it reached the strangely helmeted and armored foreign soldiers whose leader motioned back his men so that he stood alone at the front making it clear that he was the one to parley with and please. The young slave woman stole a glance and noticed that these men had faces of an even lighter color than her girl companions. Some had skins that were yellowish as though they too had used axin, but others were the hue of ivory. Their cheeks and chins were covered with long hair making them look more animal than human, yet they were said to be gods. It was told that they fought with weapons never seen before, tubes that belched fire and lightning and blew men into little bits. The foot soldiers were accompanied by monstrous creatures, half-man, half-beast, that trampled bodies beneath their hoofs with the ease of maize being pounded into tortillas.

The leader of the fair men watched the approaching Indians with a bold, unblinking gaze. His dark hair and beard accented his sallow complexion. He was of medium height, broad of shoulder and deep of chest. His build did not divulge his skill with the sword nor did the slightly bow legs of the horseman disclose that he ranked with the finest as an equestrian. This was Hernán Cortés, leader of these conquistadors, a man attracted to anything that smacked of adventure, competition, money or danger. Affable and controlled on the surface, the angry red scar under his lower lip which he stroked self-consciously, bore testimony to his frequent contests with other men. It was said that he had never lost a sword-fight and had fought a slew of them. There was little at first glance to merit his reputation as a *burlador de maridos* (mocker of husbands), a cuckolder who took his pleasure where he found it. On this day Cortés was fated to start a chapter in history that he might never have finished without the aid of the girl La Malinche, or Doña Marina as the Spaniards would call her, who headed the file of females given as slaves to comfort and appease the conquerors.

Her true name was Malinalli, meaning in Nahuatl, the ancient Mexican language, one grass of penance. The corruption "Malin-che" was the later result of the suffix "che" being used to indicate respect in the mother tongue by the natives. Born at Painalla in the province of Coatzacualco on the southeastern border of the pre-conquest Mexican empire, her turmoil started in early childhood. The daughter of a noble family, she was a little girl when her father died. Perhaps he had been a warrior, a class highly respected in Aztec society, and had lived long enough to impart some of his discipline to his child. This would help account for the valor with which Malinche took to her strenuous and dangerous life with Cortés. There are many dramatic stories of how she came to the province of Tabasco. One version states that during a war she was stolen by merchants because her family was related to the governor of the Coatzacoalcos province. The kidnappers might have planned to use her as a hostage to trade for prisoners of war or merely to fatten their pockets with ransom money.

Malinche's mother, Cimatl, married again. Some historians claim that the mother wanted to be rid of her daughter because Cimatl had borne a son and wished this boy to inherit the estate from her first spouse as well as her second. Others think that the soothsayers, astrologers and magicians who figured so heavily in the superstition-ridden Mexican religion frightened Malinche's mother with their predictions of trouble surrounding the girl. Whatever the cause, Cimatl took advantage of the death of a child of one of her slaves to pretend that the burial was that of her own daughter. Weeping copiously at the funeral, she then spirited Malinche away and either sold or gave her to traders from Xicalanco. But lest we be too hard upon this seemingly heartless lady, let us remember that there could be another interpretation. It is possible that the second husband was so resentful because of the inheritance the girl might claim later on that Cimatl, fearing this man meant to harm her daughter, gave her away as the lesser of two evils.

No matter what story one prefers, eventually the traders sold her to a *cacique* (chief) from Tabasco which is how Malinche came to be part of the line-up of girls given to Cortés and his men. That she was uncommonly pretty, outstandingly brave and highly intelligent, we know first hand from early chronicles. She certainly needed all of these attributes.

During the next few days Cortés took possession of the prosperous province of Tabasco and its port in the name of his monarch, Carlos V of Spain. He also invited the Tabascan nobles and their families to attend mass on Palm Sunday. The locals were impressed with the cross and image of the Virgin with the baby Jesus in her arms and promised to keep the altar clean and in order after Cortés departed. Cortés, satisfied that he had done his best on a higher plane and wanting to get on with his work on a lower plane, ordered his men and the twenty women to board his ships and set sail for the next port up the coast. When he reached San Juan de Ulúa he secretly planned to begin a march into the interior of Mexico which was rumored to drip gold, silver and jewels. He had seen enough evidence in the lavish gifts of the Tabascans to make him eager for more.

As a wise leader he decided to apportion the women to the officers most devoted to him. Cortés, at this time thirty-four years old, had a wife in Cuba, Catalina Xuárez, and an illegitimate daughter by a Cuban Indian woman, Leonor Pizarro, upon whom he had conferred his mother's maiden name. These little family obligations would in no way lie heavily upon any gentleman of the era and Cortés was no exception. But he did not at this moment select any of the girls for his consort, perhaps because he wanted no distractions for the campaign ahead, perhaps because he felt that keeping his army in good spirits was of prime importance. Since these were the only women available, it was prudent of the commanding officer to set an example of self-sacrifice. As with most outstanding leaders, he knew how to inspire love and loyalty in his followers and despite his dislike of sharing credit with others for his triumphs, he was basically considerate of his men.

Cortés knew that the first thing to do with the girls was to make Christians of them. Fray Bartolomé de Olmedo was called upon to baptize them. The young women were herded on deck, bewildered, now almost exhausted after all the strange sights and sounds, terrified of the future and with little in their brief pasts to console them. Their cheeks, covered with the pale yellow axin, were now streaked with bronze, showing the natural hue of their skin where tears had tunneled through make-up. Gathered around were the white gods, observing them with thumbs hooked in swordbelts, nostrils flaring with desire and eyes narrowing in appraisal of the bodies beneath the clothes, reacting very much like ordinary men deprived of women for a long time.

Before landing at Tabasco, Cortés had sailed into Cozumel where he found Jerónimo de Aguilar, who had been shipwrecked and living among the natives for eight years. A very devout man who had been a clerk in holy orders, he had never ceased to pray for rescue. As the only man among them who spoke the Mayan language fluently, he was called on deck to interpret the friar's commands during the baptism. When he said "kneel," the girls knelt. When he said "lower your head," they did so, but with great fear and trepidation, remembering the customs of their own religion where women dedicated to the goddesses of the earth had their heads struck off during the ritual. When the gentle sprinkling of holy water fell upon their brow, they must have shuddered, thinking that they might be thrown into the sea and left to drown as were the Aztec children offered to the rain god Tlaloc. When none of this happened, they were sure to be predisposed to submit gracefully and even gratefully to their new masters. After the christianizing they were given a Spanish name, the title of Doña, and bestowed upon the captains in a kind of pseudo-marital ceremony that implied some obligation on the part of the male, as well as the usual heavy load upon the female.

Cortés chose to give Doña Marina to one of his eleven captains who was a nobleman and relative of the count of Medellín. Alonso Hernando Puertocarrero was about Cortés' age and had gone on a previous expedition to the coast of Mexico with Juan de Grijalva. He was a trusted and seasoned soldier, a favorite of Cortés and a leader among the other officers. After the weddings the fleet continued on its way and at midday on Holy Thursday anchored at San Juan de Ulúa.

Within the hour several canoeloads of Aztecs were sighted rowing out from shore. Seeing standards flying on the biggest ship, they guessed that the chief was aboard and headed for that one. The deck was crowded with people watching their approach. Looking up, the men in the canoes hid their concern at the strange lack of color in the faces of the crew aboard the ship. They were as bleached as bird bones on the dunes at Ulúa. But the next moment they were somewhat reassured upon catching sight of women of their own race. The Aztecs were a dramatic looking group as they boarded. Barrel-chested from having been born in the heights of the *tierra fría*, the cold mountain country, they wore only a white loincloth beneath the ankle-length *tilmatli* (mantle) fastened at the throat. The cloak bore a red and white design representing the *ehecacoxtatl* (wind symbol) which indicated that they belonged to an order of priests representing the great god Quetzalcoatl. Their long black hair was drawn up and bound on top with a *copete* from which dangled vari-colored plumes worn only by warriors noted for their courage. Gold ornaments with feathers bedecked their ears and they each carried a large fan. The outfit was completed by sandals with red bindings that matched the cloak.

These men represented the other great player in the unfolding drama, Montezuma the Second. Montezuma was not called king, but by the title of *uei tlatoani* (first speaker). When the Spaniards landed he was fifty-two years old and had ruled for seventeen years. He was known to be a man of learning, an astrologer and philosopher as well as a high priest and distinguished general. Despite his erudition and the fact that his government was organized into councils, judiciary, army, civil service, treasury, etc., a system denoting an advanced civilization, First Speaker Montezuma was not the real monarch of the country. He was second in command to the terrible and bloodthirsty religion that ruled all Aztecs and held them in submission.

That the Aztecs practiced human sacrifice, the most sensational form of which was the excising of the heart from the living human body, cannot be denied. There were too many eyewitnesses. They also practiced cannibalism. That they did this because they were more cruel than other races is not so. They had believed for centuries that these barbarities were demanded by the gods for the salvation of not only their own people, but of all mankind. It was the only way to make more secure the perilous world in which all lived. When they ate human flesh they thought that they partook of the god himself and that this gave extra protection. The Spaniards were rightfully horrified at what they saw, but this in no way prevented them from slaughtering thousands upon thousands of innocent men, women and children in the name of their own god. They also seared the flesh of Indian slaves with a branding iron exactly as they did with their cattle. Wholesale butchery, plus the refinements of various forms of torture, were nothing new to Europeans.

As Montezuma's emissaries came on deck, the interpreter Aguilar stepped forward and greeted the men in the Mayan tongue. There was no response. The befeathered, bejeweled, bewildered delegation exchanged shrugs and helpless glances. Aguilar repeated the words. It was no different this time. Then one of the young native women detached herself from the group of onlookers and in an assured fashion spoke in Nahuatl, the Aztec tongue, to the men from the canoes. This time there was a vociferous response.

The scowl upon the brow of Cortés lifted and in a second he was all smiles as he watched the girl speak to Aguilar translating the Nahuatl into Mayan. Aguilar was now able to convert the conversation into Spanish and the problem was solved. Here was a find indeed, this bilingual maiden, and besides, she was the handsomest girl in the lot. Then Cortés realized that Doña Marina was the wife he had awarded to Puertocarrero who now beamed with husbandly pride.

Cortés, a master opportunist, must have thought "hands off" for now because Puertocarrero was a friend for whom he had true regard and he had proved it before the journey was undertaken. Out of pocket from an earlier expedition with Juan de Grijalva, Puertocarrero had no cash with which to by a horse.

An officer without a mount was unthinkable. Cortés, although short of money himself from the large advance outlay necessary for the venture, and having mortgaged his Cuban estates to the hilt, snipped the gold buttons off his jacket and with these was able to purchase a very good charger, a gray mare, for Puertocarrero. In these armies men often shared a woman when females were scarce but Puertocarrero had only possessed Doña Marina for a brief time. There would be plenty of others given as gifts as the campaign went on. Cortés could afford to wait, keep his friend and have his pick later. He would need allies badly in the days ahead because he planned to cross and doublecross the sponsor of the expedition, Diego Velásquez, the governor of Cuba, who was also planning on being governor of Mexico. Cortés had other ideas but a number of Velásquez' partisans were among the three hundred and fifty men that comprised the army. When Cortés found the time ripe to declare himself head man, he would need every supporter he could find.

The encounter with the Aztecs aboard ship having proceeded in friendly fashion, everyone disembarked the next day and went ashore to make camp and improvise an altar on the dunes. On Easter Sunday Fray Bartolomé de Olmedo conducted mass, then Cortés and some of his captains ate dinner with Montezuma's officers. When the meal was over, Aguilar and Doña Marina were sent for to interpret and Cortés had them explain to the guests that he and his men were Christians and that they represented a great emperor in their own country of Spain called Carlos the Fifth. Cortés expressed his desire to be friends with the famed Montezuma, to tell him many things about the Spanish ruler and to establish trade between his country and Mexico. Cortés also asked Tendile, chief representative of the Aztec king, to name the location and time for a meeting with Montezuma.

But Tendile made it clear that he thought this request premature and even presumptuous. Turning it aside he presented Cortés with a *petaca* (chest) filled with exquisitely wrought articles of gold sent by Montezuma. For these works of art fashioned of the precious metal the Aztecs called the excrement of the gods, the Spanish general sent the Mexican monarch a crimson cap decorated with a medal engraved with a figure of St. George slaying the dragon, some twisted green glass beads and a carved and inlaid armchair. Tendile also presented the conquistadors with quantities of food and ten loads of fine white cloth woven of cotton and feathers.

The glitter of the gold scarcely surpassed the gleam in the eyes of Cortés' officers and men as they feasted upon it.

Beneath the heavy steel helmets, their heads whirled with tropical heat and visions of the fortune that awaited them if they could claw their way to the place where this Croesus-king resided. The Aztec nobles took gold for granted and found feathers, precious and semi-precious stones far more desirable.

To turn the screw of fear in the breasts of Montezuma's emissaries, Cortés ordered his men to stage a drill accompanied by fife and drum. This was followed by an exhibition that included skilled horsemen, swordsmen and the firing of guns and cannon in simulated combat. After this fierce and frightening show Montezuma's representatives were convinced that Cortés was the god Quetzalcoatl returned and was able to smite them all dead, including Montezuma. Tendile made new excuses that their ruler was ill and would never be able to come to the coast and stated emphatically that Cortés and his men, because of high mountains and vast deserts where neither food nor water was available, could never reach Tenochtitlán (the city of Mexico) where Montezuma resided so that a meeting was impossible.

They did not reckon that the indomitable Cortés who had sniffed the heady aroma of gold mixed with glory would follow his nose until he reached the source of supply. He didn't argue, but with his special brand of deceptive amiability agreed that it was a knotty problem indeed, dismissed the subject and graciously gave permission to have sketches made of himself, his captains, ships, guns, horses, Doña Marina and even the two greyhound dogs whose speed and singular size amazed the Aztecs almost as much as the horses. Tendile had brought with him skilled painters who would depict all of these on white cotton cloth so that Montezuma would not have to rely upon words alone for information.

During the next few months Montezuma's envoys went back and forth bringing gifts of astonishing workmanship, among them a solid gold disk big as a cartwheel, representing the sun and valued at thousands of dollars. This was accompanied by another disk even larger and heavier depicting the moon and made of pure silver. Both were lavishly engraved. Each bestowal was terminated by the same statement brought from the emperor which, no matter how diplomatically phrased, boiled down to an appalling lack of desire to meet with Cortés, in fact a stubborn determination not to do so under any circumstances. The final bit of advice sent to the Spaniard was to pack up his ships and go home.

Doña Marina accompanied by Jerónimo de Aguilar was very much at the forefront during these negotiations, giving Cortés many opportunities to grow more and more aware of her as a woman as well as an aide. As she went along she began to learn Spanish although survival-wisdom may have cautioned her not to let her masters know how fast and how much. There is no evidence to show that her so-called husband Puertocarrero did not treat her well and that she did not think well of him in the brief time he acted as Marina's protector. The role of the Mexican-Aztec female was one of subordination and obedience to the male but no man could prevent a woman from grasping the opportunity to get ahead when she saw an opening. Wasn't she the only woman whose portrait had been taken to Montezuma? Having been catapulted into prominence, she was surely determined to remain there and had the intelligence to do so.

She must have extracted every nuance from the many sessions of interpreting and taken every opportunity of making Cortés notice her outstanding achievements and beauty. She knew that no position could be so exalted as consort to the chief and as yet Cortés had not taken a mistress. But even if his affections went in other directions, Doña Marina's future was much brighter than her past unless, or until, the Spaniards were defeated or taken captive; then high and low would fall. But Marina possessed much of the fatalism of the era. Lifespans were short, and from the time they were born humans were always just a shrug ahead of death.

At this time a very complicated plot-couterplot was fomented by Cortés among his followers. Cortés had declared the camp a settlement and had given it the name of Villa Rica de la Vera Cruz (the rich town of the true cross) because the land was fertile and the Spaniards had landed there on Good Friday. Grandiosely, he took possession of all of Mexico, conquered and unconquered, in the name of the King of Spain, then appointed two *alcaldes* (mayors) of the town of Vera Cruz. One was Francisco de Montejo, the other his dear and trusted friend, Hernando Alonso Puertocarrero, husband of Malinche.

Cortés had made friends with *caciques* of nearby towns and found that many of them hated Montezuma, though, out of fear, they paid taxes to him and obeyed his laws. Always scheming, always planning the next move, Cortés welcomed this information. He knew it would be virtually impossible with his small army to oust Montezuma. His troops were constantly being eroded from hunger and disease and his ships in no way had enough supplies to make a long march into *tierra fría*. If he could gather enough dissidents and persuade them to be allies, they would fatten the fighting force, provide bearers for heavy artillery and furnish the additional food and clothing necessary for the big push. In the meantime he must free himself from the dominion of another dear old friend, the governor of Cuba, Diego Velásquez, in whose name he had undertaken this expedition.

The original intent had been to make only a coastal trip gathering gold en route and returning in a short time. Now that he planned to penetrate the interior, a prolonged expedition, Cortés had to make himself chief, responsible only to his King, so that he could more or less legally announce that the orders of Velásquez to return to Cuba without further exploration were null and void. There were many henchmen of Velásquez' in Cortés' army and this group now proclaimed it time to depart with the healthy amount of gold, jewels and silver already acquired, considering the project a mission accomplished. Anticipating this, Cortés persuaded his followers to throw up a smokescreen by declaring they were infuriated, even betrayed because Cortés had deceived them in stating that he was sailing to Mexico to settle the territory in the name of king and country. With eel-like variations on this theme they twisted the whole thing around and elected Cortés General and Chief Justice, whereupon he solemnly swore to fulfill the promises made in Cuba and pay allegiance solely to his monarch Carlos, dumping Diego Velásquez and his orders as Velásquez would have dumped him under the same circumstances.

Although the women of the camp were not included in this jockeying for power they would certainly have been aware, if only by intuition, that big dealings were going on. Malinche, with her smattering of Spanish and mastery of Mayan and Nahuatl, would be the natural leader of the females and keep them apprised. These officer's ladies, their ranks swelled by further gifts of daughters and nieces by *caciques* in nearby provinces, would spend their days overseeing the work of servants and slaves. They would do their share of gossiping and speculating about things to come and console one another at loss of family and friends. Along with these activities would go their religious duties as Christian converts mixed with a bit of the old faith, just to be sure. Some would already be pregnant and trying to deduce the shade of white or brown the infant might turn out. If a boy, would it emerge with hair on its face like the Spaniards, or the way pure Indian babes were born, with a shock on their heads? If a girl, though less desirable, it would be interesting to see what she looked like because none of them had ever glimpsed a woman of the white race. And what of the blue eyes, so strange, so lifeless, like blind eyes or those of the dead. If the father's eyes were this ghostly color would the baby's be the same? Ugh! It was a chilling thought. And if the deities from the old religion were displeased because the girls had turned Christian, the vengeance they might wreak upon the child could be horrendous.

Having chattered in this way to each other at great length, the group took steps to allay the fears they had stirred up. Because of the Spaniards' dislike of the practice, the red teeth had been abandoned along with the axin ointment that had turned their skins yellow. Their tender, young, brown cheeks, thinner from duress and shorter rations in an army where hunger was almost always a reality, blanched with fright. Falling upon their knees with hands palmed together and lifted in supplication the way the Christian priests had taught them, they began by invoking the name of the Virgin Mary, a gentle goddess who exacted no sacrifices. Then singing a hymn to the Aztec mother of the gods, Tetoinnan, which concluded, "she feeds on the hearts of stags, our mother the goddess of the earth," the session ended with a long prayer to the greatest of Aztec female deities, Toci, the grandmother. *Copal* (incense) would be burned to all.

Feeling safer now, a voice in the crowd called out, "Did you see the statue of the Christian goddess Virgin Mary? The infant son Jesus she held in her arms had smooth cheeks like our babies but no hair upon his head." And another voice cried out, "What, not even a patch of the pale yellow kind that looks like the stains on the *maxlatl* (loincloth) of an old man?" Being young and exuberant, they had a good laugh at the expense of the pallid foreigners, crossing themselves to ward off evil as the Christian padres had taught them. Then it was time to go back to supervising the clothes-washing and maize-grinding that would make flour for the bread upon which the army existed.

Now that Cortés had seized command, he turned his attention to more important matters. Before he plotted his march to Montezuma in Tenochtitlán, he wrote to his King, told him what he'd done and planned to do for the greater glory of Spain, and sent enough gold, the pacifier of monarchs, to ensure royal approval. The letter explained that all the treasure so far amassed was nothing compared to that said to be guarded in Mexico City for Montezuma and which Cortés hoped to acquire for Carlos V. To send letter and treasure he needed a trusted cohort and who better than Alonso Puertocarrero who also happened to be, by some curious coincidence, the husband of that attractive young woman, Doña Marina. Francisco de Montejo was also sent with

Puertocarrero on one of the ships of the fleet. As a further sop to his conscience, Cortés gave them a bonus of several thousand dollars for making the journey.

By another curious coincidence, the two emissaries stopped in Cuba and, of course, word leaked out as to the high-handed manner in which Cortés had overridden the authority of Diego Velásquez and taken it upon himself to head an expedition to the interior of Mexico, making the governor swear revenge. Nothing more is known of Marina's mate except that he delivered loot and letter to the Spanish King. Shortly after Puertocarrero set sail for Spain, Doña Marina began the long, intimate relationship with Cortés that would make her one of the most notorious and controversial women in Latin American history. So inseparable would they become as a pair that the natives soon began calling Cortés "Malintzin," which came from Malinche's name with *tzin* (lord) tacked on.

It is not the purpose here to recount in detail the twists and turns of Cortés' campaign, but like him or not, the three hundred fifty-mile journey he made to Tenochtitlán, with somewhere near the same number of half-starved soldiers wearing improvised armor padded with cotton and marching the long distance in locally-made sandals for want of boots, is a feat surpassed by few generals in history. Some guides and porters were provided by *caciques* in nearby towns but these were not fighting force. In addition, Cortés had many malcontents in his army who favored Diego Velásquez. Fearing that the *velazquistas* would desert, flee to the coast and sail home, Cortés took the drastic step of literally burning his vessels behind him. On the pretext of freeing for his army the additional manpower that would be provided by the sailors left guarding the fleet, he ordered the ships burned, insuring that defectors would no longer be able to make their way back to Cuba, or anywhere else, by sea.

Doña Marina and a very few of the other women accompanied the men on the long march. They walked, as did the three priests. There were only fifteen horses left and Cortés and his officers rode these, the men wearing steel armor, the steeds protected by chain mail. A number of dogs accompanied the army including mastiffs, greyhounds and lurchers, a crossbreed animal trained to hunt silently and used by the hungry army for poaching. The starting date was August 16, 1519. For the next few months this army of conquistadors, depicted in fantasy as swashbuckling devils dueling for favors of fair maidens, would sweat through deserts where scarcely a trickle of brackish water could be found, freeze on mountaintops where frostbite chewed bare toes, and cope with dysentery, indiscriminate as to location.

Through all this, the indomitable Malinche, who was no more accustomed to desert heat and mountain cold than Cortés and his men, walked on and on, always able to dispatch her chores of translation. Did Cortés lift her onto his horse to ride now and then? Did he, from time to time, let her mount in his place while he walked or was that unthinkable for a commanding general? It is probable, if only from a practical point of view. Her health and happiness were more important than that of any man in his army except himself. Even if they had not been lovers and even if Doña Marina had been a hag instead of a handsome young woman, it would have been in Cortés' best interest to treat her with the utmost consideration. Undoubtedly, she was well aware that his concern was not solely from love. There was no greater realist than this woman who had to get along on her wits.

But the early part of the march to Tenochtitlán was not all bad. By this time the harried ruler of Mexico had unwillingly succumbed to Cortés' desire to meet him, although he continued to send messengers to try and persuade Cortés to turn back. After Montezuma had studied the drawings of the Spanish general and his entourage brought by his court painters, he became convinced that Cortés was, if not Quetzalcoatl himself, the forerunner of the god and closely connected. It was useless to resist the divine.

With this new attitude, the principalities along the way under Montezuma's dominion were instructed not to war upon Cortés and to assist him and his men with reasonable amounts of food, drink and water. The conquistadors did not meet with open hostility until they entered the territory of Tlaxcala. The Tlaxcalans were mortal enemies of Montezuma, but they did not trust the Spaniards either. For the next month Cortés' army battled back and forth with Tlaxcalan warriors. Many Spaniards were wounded and a number killed. A division of troops argued to quit and go back to the coast, especially when they found out that if they died in battle and their bodies were not recovered by their own men, the Tlaxcalans would eat them. Cortés broke up this rebellion and, though suffering from fever, continued to fight, giving daily pep talks to his troops to keep up their courage. The only soldier who never faltered and showed no fear was the doughty Doña Marina, who seemed to thrive on trouble as her horoscope had predicted. There are pictures of her drawn by Tlaxcalans where she is shown carrying a shield, so no doubt she accompanied Cortés into battle. Bernal Díaz del Castillo, a soldier with Cortés, said, "She had courage the likes of which no woman ever had."

Eventually the modern equipment, strange new tactics of the Europeans and Cortés' rumored divinity combined to make the Spaniards victorious. As usual, the *caciques* gave women to the conquerors and Chief Xicotenga presented his daughter to Cortés. The general, still so recently enamored of Malinche, singled out Captain Pedro de Alvarado as bridegroom for this native princess who was then baptized and given the name of Doña Luisa. The girl was reverenced by her people and received many valuable gifts. Alvarado is described as a handsome gentleman, frank, with a winning smile and sunny disposition. Cortés was particularly fond of him and thought him an excellent horseman and fighter. The general would shortly name Alvarado as an envoy to Montezuma. In the meantime his portrait was sent and the Aztecs were so impressed with his ruddy complexion and red hair that they gave him the name Tonatiuh, child of the sun.

But this child of the sun was not as wise as he was charming and would fall into temporary disgrace later on for ordering a dreadful and unnecessary massacre. The mock marriage with Doña Luisa would be as enduring as the rest, which was as long as was expedient for the soldier. In the future, Alvarado would become governor of Guatemala, order further unnecessary massacres and marry a Spanish lady, Beatriz de la Cueva, who achieved recognition by succeeding her husband in office after his death. Her tenure was brief, though, because she was drowned in a flood. Doña Luisa would quietly fade away, as old soldiers are erroneously reputed to do, along with hundreds of her sisters who, after servicing the Spaniards, were discarded for women from home.

The daughter of another great chief, Mase Escasi, was christened Doña Elvira on this occasion. She is described as a beauty given to Juan Velásquez de León from Castile. The two were fated to die shortly in Mexico City. Three others whose name we do not know were bestowed upon Gonzalo de Sandoval, Cristobal de Olid and Alonso de Avila. La Malinche represents the courage of all those known and unknown.

The conquerors moved on. The next territory reached was that of Cholula which paid tribute to Montezuma. Everything began in amiable fashion but most of the women and children had been cleared out of the city, which made Cortés suspicious. The mercurial Montezuma was rumored to have changed his mind again and instead of making ready to receive Cortés, was said to be sending twenty thousand troops to Cholula to engage the Spaniards in battle and capture their general. Whenever the army made camp, Doña Marina moved freely about and in the course of talking with people in the towns and cities brought back much valuable information to Cortés. In Cholula she became friendly with one of the *caciques* wives. This lady had noticed the elegant clothing and costly jewelry worn by Marina and, having an eligible son, decided, from greed, affection or both, to warn Marina that there was a secret plot to kill the Spaniards. For safety's sake, she suggested that La Malinche gather together all her possessions, bring them to her house and then marry her son whom she called a man of distinction.

Marina, whose trade was rapid articulation, said shrewdly, "Good mother, I appreciate all you have told me and will take your advice but my master is very noticing. I must wait until nightfall so I can do it under cover of darkness. Also, my possessions are many and I must procure an honest bearer who will not steal them from me." Then, trying to extract as much information as possible she asked, "One small question, noble lady, then I will be on my way. If this plan to murder the Spaniards is so secret, how did you hear it?"

And the woman replied that her husband was one of the ringleaders and had been sent gold and jewels by the great lord, Montezuma, to ensure that he would carry out his part in the affair. Marina gravely thanked her informer and, walking with measured tread so no one would think her disturbed, went back to the building where Cortés, his officers and their consorts were housed. The knowledge of this plot enabled the general to turn the tables so that instead of himself and his soldiers ending up in the boiling pots being prepared for them with salt, chili peppers and tomatoes, the Spanish army trapped and slaughtered thousands of hapless Cholulans.

It is interesting to note that Marina is spoken of in early chronicles as being rich and having many jewels only a short time after becoming Cortés' mistress. Either the general suffered a degree of infatuation he had never experienced before, or La Malinche had the wisdom to extract as much as she could while she was still invaluable to him. It was probably some of each, but all signs point to Doña Marina having had a healthy self-esteem and knowledge of her own worth. But this time, though, there would have been no way for her to extricate herself from Cortés even if she had wanted to. For better or worse, her fortunes were his until the campaign ended or he chose to discard her. The Christian faith might also have had a great deal to do with her loyalty to the Spaniards. She always interpreted the dissertations of Cortés and the priests in which they explained the ideals of their religion. No matter how bad the injustices of Christianity, a thinking person would prefer to see an end to sacrifices such as the Cholulans made on the eve of battle when three little girls and three little boys, age three, were routinely murdered. Wherever the Spaniards went, they witnessed the agony of victims ordered to death by soothsayer-priests and magicians who believed it was the will of the gods. It is easy to believe that La Malinche hoped the new faith would stop the cruelties of the old.

Cortés and his army left Cholula November 1 and entered Mexico City on November 8, 1519. During those eight days on the march, the Spaniards were approached again by envoys of Montezuma still trying to persuade them to turn back. The Aztec ruler, in his agony of indecision over Quetzalcoatl-Cortés, was forever beckoning him with one hand and pushing him away with the other. The signs, symbols and portents as read to the great monarch by his advisers augured ill, and his vacillation stemmed in large part from the priests and their dire astrological predictions. But despite all this, Montezuma and Cortés met on the outskirts of the city and the encounter was cordial.

Mention must be made of the beauties of the capital, a city which numbered about three hundred thousand people. It contained magnificent palaces, temples, towers, causeways, roads and much-needed bridges to cross the series of lakes on which Tenochtitlán was built. There was always heavy traffic of *acalli* (all-purpose, flat-bottomed canoes), used to transport civilians, soldiers, food and provisions. The extensive gardens were described as bowers of exquisite roses, lilies, rare and exotic trees, plants and herbs the likes of which the Spaniards had never seen before. The varieties of fruit, vegetables and game were endless and brought from all parts of the kingdom. Zoos and aviaries, complete with salt and fresh water pools, were maintained as part of the palace complex and each species was fed food imported from its natural habitat and given the utmost care. This was to make sure that the examples would continue to be the most healthy and outstanding of their kind, fit for royal eyes to rest upon.

Montezuma's permanent residence in Tenochtitlán was called Tecpan. He also had innumerable palaces in and around the city of Mexico. Tecpan's large courtyards featured intricately carved stonework, fountains, flowers and cages of exotic birds. It boasted more than one hundred rooms and one hundred baths and receptions halls of great size finished in marble and jaspar, a green ornamental stone. A thousand women (plus their slaves and servants) lived here and Montezuma selected the most attractive of them to be his mistresses. The system was Moorish in that the hundred or so females of the king's select harem were guarded by crones who would not permit another man to so much as glance their way. Aside from his concubines, Montezuma had two legitimate wives and hordes of children.

Aztec women wove fine fabrics embellished with intricate designs in featherwork. They also created elaborate and colorful embroideries. These seem to have been their special departments in crafts since they are not mentioned as gold or silversmiths, artists or architects. The symbols that appear in Aztec pictograph writing for the birth of a girl are a broom, workbasket and a spindle. Near the great temple of Huichilobos (god of war) was a convent. This differed from Christian nunneries because mothers placed their daughters there in religious retirement as tiny babies. When grown a girl could become a *ciuatlamacazqui* (woman-priest) but to retain that title she had to remain celibate. Later on, if she were asked in marriage and wanted to wed, she could be released from her vows and return home.

Midwives were a highly respected group, but women magicians were feared and considered outcasts. There were female poets and actresses who interpreted poetry in a dramatic combination of song, dance and pantomime. A separate class were the beautiful *auinime* whose primary function was to serve as companions to unmarried soldiers, accompanying them everywhere, even into battle. When brave warriors took part in the sacred dance called *uey tecuilhuitl*, the high feast of the dignitaries, they danced in pairs and each couple was joined by an exquisitely gowned and bejeweled *auinime*. These women were not to be confused with prostitutes, who were described by the Aztecs as "she who sells the lower part of her body" and "the badly smelling woman."

Widows could marry or not as they chose but their choices of a mate were limited. A wife might elevate a slave who had served her husband to the post of steward then wed him. She could also try persuading a brother-in-law, if she had any, to take her on as a secondary wife. The death of a woman at her first lying-in automatically raised her to the exalted status of a warrior killed in battle or one who had died on the sacrificial stone. The destiny of these *mociuaquetzque* (valiant women) was to go directly to the palace where the sun resided in the sky and become *ciuateteo* (divine women or goddesses). Polygamy was accepted practice and though the husband of a family held absolute authority, he was expected to treat all his wives equally. It comes as no surprise that this rarely happened. The only area where equal rights prevailed was in the slave class where women were beasts of burden along with men.

When Cortés and his men entered the stronghold of Montezuma, Tenochtitlán, they were housed in elegant quarters that had belonged to Montezuma's grandfather near the royal palace, Tecpan. At first they were showered with attention and treated with utmost courtesy, Cortés receiving the mask of Quetzalcoatl fashioned from gold and turquoise mosaic and other unique ornaments belonging to the great god, proof that Montezuma still thought the Spanish general to be the god himself or his messenger. But the conquistadors had scarcely been in the city five days when they received word from Villa Rica de la Vera Cruz, the town they had founded on the coast, that the Mexicans had killed Juan de Escalante, the *alguacil* (sheriff), his horse and six of his soldiers and that many surrounding villages that had previously been friendly were now in revolt and refused to supply food or serve in the fort. These were the first indications that the real struggle was about to begin.

Neither Cortés nor his men had been unaware that by accepting Montezuma's hospitality in the city they left themselves at the mercy of their hosts. The Aztecs were a warrior nation with a large standing army from which came their ruling class. At the snap of a finger from the emperor, they could wipe out the newcomers. Cortés and his officers, knowing they were overwhelmed in numbers and strength, had no choice but to use cunning. As the atmosphere chilled, they decided on one of those bold strokes so typical of Cortés. They would dupe Montezuma into becoming their prisoner and hold him hostage so that their own lives would be safe. Then, with such a treasure for bargaining, they could proceed to their real objective which was to take Mexico for Carlos V of Spain.

To bring off this coup, Cortés took with him to the palace of Tecpan five of his captains and, of course, Doña Marina and Aguilar. Cortés must have warned her in advance as to what this mission was about. She had already been in the presence of First Speaker Montezuma many times these past few days, having to look straight at him as she translated his words into Mayan for Aguilar who then phrased it in Spanish. Only a chosen few were ever permitted to gaze upon the ruler's face and only when he gave permission, yet this woman from the coast was entrusted with interpreting his very thoughts. Malinche had known for some time that Cortés and his men were mortal no matter how different their skins nor how strange the animals they rode. She now knew that the man to whom hundreds of thousands of her people paid reverence as to a god was mortal, too. With her facile mind she saw that the coming of the Spaniards signified the end of an era, although there was no guarantee that it would herald the beginning of a better one. But she could hope. By this time Cortés' child was stirring in her womb, a child who, if born, could be slaughtered like a jack rabbit if Cortés were defeated.

At the palace of Montezuma on this epochal occasion, there was no one more aware of the importance of the moment than Doña Marina. As she walked into the throne room at Cortés' side, Malinche and Malintzín, the inseparables, her heart beat faster knowing that upon her sagacity depended the lives of innumerable people including her own and that of her unborn child. Perhaps if she prayed hard to her new Christian god he would give her enough wisdom to prevent the slaughter of Spaniards and Mexicans alike. Montezuma, seated upon a chair embellished with jewels and golden designs, motioned to one just like it by his side. This was for Cortés. He smiled spontaneously at the Spanish general as did Cortés in return; despite the power struggle there was an almost mystical friendship between the two. Surrounding the emperor were relatives and trusted bodyguards. Outside the door Cortés had left thirty of his men.

As usual, Doña Marina was the only woman present. With head bowed and hands clasped loosely in front of her she waited for Aguilar, the male interpreter, to step forward first, then she followed, standing closer to the emperor than he. At a sign from the ruler she began by relaying Cortés' opening statements which protocol required to be the usual polite, flowery Spanish phrases inquiring after the health and welfare of the august ruler and every member of his family. Then she waited while Montezuma went through a series of compliments and greetings in the Aztec style which was equally flowery and long-winded. With the decks cleared for action she got down to business.

"My lord Montezuma, I have been much saddened and alarmed to hear that your soldiers have killed a number of my men on the coast and, the greatest shock of all, that they performed this odious task at your command. I am also informed that you are plotting further treachery and that your protestations of goodwill are not to be trusted. Now, because in my heart I am very fond of you, most noble lord, I do not believe these evil tidings and am asking that you show your good faith and innocence of these black deeds by coming with me and my officers to live for a while in our quarters. You will be treated like the great king that you are and receive all comforts and courtesies."

There was a long, shocked silence broken by an emphatic refusal from Montezuma to do any such foolish thing as surrender his sacred person to the Spaniards. Cortés retaliated with further accusations, and Montezuma, with further rejection until an impasse was reached. Fearing that more delay would bring the entire palace guard down upon them, one of Cortés' officers cried out, "Let us take him prisoner right now or stab him dead before he alarms the whole army and we are wiped out."

Montezuma caught the threatening tone and, turning to Doña Marina, asked what the man was shouting. Malinche having learned the value of double-talk in diplomacy replied:

"My Lord, if you will agree to go with them without struggle you will be treated with the utmost consideration, learn many interesting things concerning their way of life and be safer and happier than if you were in your own palace," softening the fighting words as she must often have done before in the past months with the Spaniards.

More refusal and persuasion went on with Marina forced to employ every ounce of her skill to placate both sides and keep negotiations open. All at once, Montezuma capitulated and we can only guess that the daring of Cortés' request had so unnerved the harassed ruler that he gave in from sheer inability to believe that any mortal would have the effrontery to take him prisoner. There was also the ever-present factor of the Cortés-Quetzalcoatl myth. Perhaps the monarch reasoned that only a god would dare confront him this way. The astrologers continued to claim that the second coming of Quetzalcoatl was due. Surprise tactics and superstition combined to create the monarch's downfall, but surely, as the party filed out and walked the short distance to Cortés' quarters with their royal hostage, there could have been no greater sigh of relief heaved than that from Doña Marina. She had avoided open conflict between two leaders.

Montezuma's confinement was very permissive and conducted with all proper respect. His own servants attended him and the rituals involving his separate meals and dishes were observed. Although watched day and night by Spanish guards, he conducted business of state as usual. His diversion was taken care of in part by Cortés who played Totoloque with him. This gambling game involved the tossing of small pellets with precious stones or gold for stakes, a game sure to interest Cortés. Doña Marina would be required to sit patiently through many a long session making sure that the famous gentlemen understood each other's bets and comments upon the plays. Montezuma went hunting and was also allowed to attend to his religious duties, although Cortés tried to extract promises from him not to make more human sacrifices. In short, the confinement was not very confining and could have been overthrown at any time by Montezuma's kinsmen had he indicated that he wanted it done. That he did not is still one of the great puzzles of history.

Cortés took Montezuma captive in November of 1519 and during the next six months, which were relatively tranquil, made good use of his time to learn more about Mexico. The Spanish general ferreted out many secrets of the country such as the size of the armed forces, location of gold and silver mines, and which nearby principalities were friends or enemies of the Aztec ruler. During this same period Montezuma formally gave himself and his country up to the King of Spain, all of which was properly recorded with witnesses and notaries accompanied by groans and tears from the Aztec nobles, warriors, merchants and long suffering peons. The prediction of the oracles that Montezuma's reign would end with the coming of white men from the east was proving true.

Cortés, master manipulator, had things tidily under control for the moment. In addition, he found himself a wealthy man. A few days after he relinquished the kingdom, the Mexican monarch answered the Spanish general's request for tribute by sending him to the aviary where several concealed rooms were opened, disclosing a treasure in plates, bars, jewels and carved ornaments in gold and silver such as the Spaniard had never seen before. Adding this to a secret cache the Spaniards had discovered in the walls of the palace where they were housed made a fortune. Cortés divided it among his men. At this point Mexico was surely close to paradise for these adventurers.

But, as with the serpent in the garden of Eden, Cortés' old friend and recent enemy Diego Velásquez, governor of Cuba, reared his ugly head. Infuriated at the news that Cortés had bypassed his authority, sent reports directly to the King of Spain, and had made himself virtually ruler of Mexico and its treasure, Velásquez put together a fleet. He sent nine hundred men under the command of Pánfilo de Narváez whom he appointed captain-general and governor to replace Cortés. When Cortés heard that Narváez had landed, he decided to march immediately to Cempoala on the coast where Narváez and his men were headquartered and there engage him in battle, if battle was necessary. Accused of many things but not of lacking courage and audacity, the general hoped to prevent Narváez from setting foot in Mexico City which he now considered his private kingdom.

No women or servants were taken on this emergency march to Cempoala, not even La Malinche. Cortés would be parleying in his own tongue of Castilian. He left Captain Pedro de Alvarado and two hundred men behind for the delicate task of guarding Montezuma and he knew that Doña Marina's services would be badly needed. For the first time in over a year, she could enjoy a few moments to herself between translating chores and have a few left over to spend with the other Indian wives of the Spanish captains. Late at night when her busy day had ended, she could sort out her thoughts, sitting quietly with hands clasped in her lap, feeling the child stir within her, wondering about its future. Cortés had decreed that, if a boy, it would be christened Martín after his father. He hadn't specified what a girl should be called, but Marina knew that his mother's name was Catalina and favored using that. Having been abandoned, Marina had no special affection for her own mother's name of Cimatl. *Tonalpouhqui* (soothsayers) and astrologers were traditionally consulted in the naming of a Mexican child and Marina felt a fleeting desire to send for a magic-man to help in the selection, but she quashed it. The Christian priests would frown upon such doings and if Cortés found out he might abandon her.

Relaxing for a moment to take a sip of the foaming chocolate left by her slave, her mind turned to other, more immediate problems. Since Cortés' departure for Cempoala there were rumblings to be heard in the palace and marketplace. Without his presence, she and the other wives feared an uprising against the Spanish garrison. A deep sigh escaped her. She had a retinue of servants now to do her bidding and there would be nurses and wet nurses for the babe if it were born under peaceful conditions; but if a war broke out soon, the child would still be within her womb and she would actually have to guard it with her own life.

How long would Malintzin continue to be her protector? As long as she was useful to him, no more. Since her pregnancy, he was not in bed with her so often. She shared him with one of Montezuma's daughters, Tecuichpochtzin, who was also rumored to be with child. Important men had many mistresses, it was the custom. *Caciques* along the way were always presenting Cortés with women. If they were attractive enough he tried them for awhile but so far had always come back to her. To keep him dependent, she never attempted to teach him Nahuatl but used every intimate moment between them to improve her Spanish. She was quite proficient now. Lately, Cortés' page, Orteguilla, a smart young boy who was learning the native tongue, sometimes accompanied her and Aguilar to interviews with the most high, Montezuma himself. It was only a matter of time until others would acquire enough proficiency in the language to displace her.

A slave girl slid out of the shadows and silently removed the empty cup of chocolate. These women liked her and served her willingly but La Malinche knew that others in Montezuma's court looked upon her askance. They considered it unseemly that a female should be present at conferences concerning affairs of state, boldly gazing upon the ruler, plucking sacred words from his mouth and profaning them with hers. Some murmured that she was a witch and in her constant contact with Montezuma had cast a spell on him, making him renounce his kingdom. But she had little time to worry over petty gossip. Doña Luisa's husband, Pedro de Alvarado, seemed very nervous since Cortés' departure for the coast. He had a fiery temper that went with his red hair and beard.

The uprising came sooner than expected. Alvarado seemed to have brought it upon himself by giving permission for the Aztecs to assemble in the temple yard for one of their big religious festivals. When he saw so large a group amassed, he panicked and ordered his troops to fire. Discharging cannon, they terrified the crowd, then Spanish soldiers rushed in and, laying about with pike and dagger, mercilessly slaughtered the dancers, wrenching from their throats and chests the jewels they wore in honor of the festival for their gods Huichilobos and Tezcatepuca. The Mexicans then turned upon Alvarado, killed some of his soldiers and burnt his quarters. They trapped him and his party, holding them prisoner without food or drink.

On the coast, Cortés' fight at Cempoala had been victorious over Pánfilo de Narváez. The general persuaded Narváez' men to join his army for the return to the capital. He told them, as inducement, that they would be received as kings in the provinces along the way and given gifts of great value. As soon as word reached Cortés that Alvarado was under siege in Tenochtitlán he gathered his army together, now numbering some thirteen hundred men and began a forced march to the capital. This was the moment when Montezuma should have retaken his kingdom but the strange ruler seemed to grow more depressed and impotent with each passing day and by now his lords and councils had turned against him and were seeking a successor to the throne.

Cortés' return to Mexico City was anything but triumphant. After all his boasting to the men of Pánfilo de Narváez, not a single *cacique* came out to do homage or offer help, food or gifts. Word had spread that the capital was once more in control of its rightful owners and none of the lesser lords wanted to be on the losing side. Cortés' temper grew shorter and shorter as he heard the grumbling of Narváez' men and was aware that they laughed scornfully at him and his premature predictions of gold and glory. What he feared most was that these new recruits would desert and return to the coast. He would need every hand for the coming strife ahead. He speeded up the march.

The first encounters took place on the roads outside Tenochtitlán and it was a battle every step of the way into the city. Squadrons of Aztec soldiers fell before the cannon, crossbows and muskets of the Spaniards, but more squadrons kept coming. Because the city was built upon lakes, there were drawbridges between residences so that house to house fighting, use of horses, or attempts to burn the defenders out were impossible. From the flat rooftops the Mexicans hurled rocks and stones, hitting their mark so often that the conquistadors were forced to retreat to their quarters. They barricaded themselves in and were kept busy trying to repair the breaches made in the walls by flaming torches. All the pent-up resentment of the natives boiled to the surface and they screamed epithets at the Spaniards, vowing to sacrifice their hearts to the gods, eat of their bodies until sated, then toss the entrails to the snakes and vipers. Threats can boomerang and who knows if the conquistadors might have performed less efficiently had they been less terrified of the consequences of capture.

In the next days the battles continued with hand to hand fighting up and down the steps of the great temple Teocalli, which housed the Aztecs' most important idols, until the stones grew slippery with blood. Unable to withstand a longer siege because of lack of food and water and not wanting to risk losing all of his men, Cortés asked Montezuma to speak to his people and order them to cease fighting. Sadly, the once great emperor replied that he feared his words would be of little weight because the council had already chosen his successor, a kinsman called Cuitlahuac, so that he was really not ruler anymore. Nevertheless, he agreed to try and with a contingent of Spanish soldiers guarding him, he was assisted to the roof.

He was richly dressed in full panoply as became a great king on such a solemn occasion. A thickly fringed cape covered with delicate feather embroidery hung from his shoulders. He wore golden-soled sandals upon his feet and a plumed headband for a crown. His face was elaborately painted and a nose ornament made of jade pierced both nostrils. Large turquoise gems decorated his ears and jewelry of exquisite Mexican craftsmanship encircled his neck and biceps. Holding out his arms as though to embrace the crowds below, he sorrowfully urged them to stop fighting so that Cortés and his men could depart the city and the shores of Mexico. At this request a volley of stones was let fly and three of them hit the ruler on the leg, arm and head. A cry of anguish went up from the crowd as Montezuma slumped.

Cortés' men carried him to his apartments but when they tried to dress his wounds he refused to let them touch him. At first no one believed his injuries were severe, but at the end of three days he was dead, caused they say, by a broken heart more than broken bones. Cortés ordered six high chieftains to carry out the body dressed in all its finery to show to his people and make sure they understood that their leader died by wounds inflicted by them, not the Spaniards. But though they wept at the sight, the Mexicans stubbornly continued fighting and Cortés' forces diminished daily. The conquistadors' supply of powder was going fast and food and water were now almost nonexistent. Calling a conference, Cortés and his officers decided to flee the city secretly that night. They made a rough portable bridge of beams and planks to span the water where the wily Mexicans had purposely broken down the usual exits, anticipating their foes' attempted escape. Cortés' army began evacuating before midnight. Using the improvised portable bridge many soldiers made it across the water but many others, unable to swim, fell into the moat on this foggy night and drowned. Suddenly, the Aztec troops converging by land and canoe fell upon them and soon they could no longer hold the portable bridge in place. Now began a slaughter of Spanish troops, horses, servants, women and slaves that would so fill the water that the remainder of Cortés' men used dead bodies as a bridge of flesh to cross upon. It would be known in the annals of history as *noche triste* (night of sorrow). Cannon, artillery and powder were abandoned along with a fortune in gold bullion and jewels.

A number of the Spaniards' Indian wives were killed that night but Doña Marina, Doña Luisa, wife of Pedro de Alvarado, and a Spanish woman, María de Estrada, who had come with the army of Narváez from Cuba, did escape. The travail was far from over, however, as the Mexicans pursued the fleeing army. The Spaniards escaped from Tenochtitlán on June 30, 1520 and on the 7th of July were engaged in the battle of Otumba from which they emerged with ranks so decimated that they were close to the four hundred men with which Cortés had originally started out. Weary, ill and with many wounded, they made their way to Tlaxcala, praying that Chief Xicotenga who had been such an enemy of Montezuma would still be a friend of theirs. They were not disappointed. Xicotenga embraced his daughter Doña Luisa while Chief Mase Escasi wept for the death of his daughter Doña Elvira, who had died with Juan Velásquez de León to whom she had been given.

From July until almost the end of December 1520, Cortés and his army remained in or around Tlaxcala. It is probable that Marina underwent her confinement at this time and that her son Martín was born. Cortés, as usual, was plotting his next move and was determined to storm the capital and retake it for himself and the Spanish King. But first he would have to subdue the peoples of the surrounding territories, which he did with the help of thousands of Tlaxcalans who joined forces with him. More reinforcements came from Spaniards arriving from Cuba. Then an even more formidable ally turned up unexpectedly. Smallpox had entered Mexico with Narváez' men. It had already killed Cuitlahuac, Montezuma's successor, and had swept through the common people, striking dead or weakening a good portion of the population. As part of the campaign, Cortés ordered thirteen brigantines built to sail upon the lakes. He knew he must overcome the fleet of Aztec canoes which carried warriors, food and military supplies and seize the waterways. The retaking of Tenochtitlán began at the end of December 1520 and terminated in August 1521.

Throughout these eight months of bloody struggle, La Malinche was constantly at the general's side, translating delicate negotiations while cannon roared and men fell all about her. She faced the same dangers Cortés did and is pictured wearing armor, but she was not the only brave woman recorded during the struggle. Near the end of the final month of siege, it was clear that the Aztec ranks were almost wiped out. But one morning the Spaniards were amazed to find the flat roofs of the city suddenly covered by Mexican warriors with swords agleam in the sun as far as the eye could see. This rooftop army set up a great hissing and yelling, hurling vile epithets along with rocks, ignoring the fact that they made excellent targets for the crossbowmen of the enemy below. A great confusion set in at the sight of this revitalized Aztec horde until the Spaniards realized that the roofgangs were composed solely of women. They had been sent as a diversionary measure while the last of the Aztec rulers, Cuauhtémoc, with singular courage, tried a surprise attack with the handful of warriors he had left.

The Spaniards, also greatly weakened from famine and losses, were equally indebted to their females. A small group of Spanish women who had entered Mexico with Pánfilo de Narváez' army and other newly arrived vessels, insisted upon accompanying their men to the final conflict. They became much-needed nurses for the numerous wounded, stood guard duty to provide relief for soldiers who needed rest and, at times, joined in combat. The names of five of them are known: María de Estrada, Beatriz Bermúdez, Beatriz de Palacios, Isabel Rodríguez and Juana Martín.

Calling upon every bit of his reserves and military genius, Cortés forced the city to succumb August 13. The saga was nearly at an end. Neither Cortés nor his men ever found the rumored treasure of Montezuma nor did they recover as much loot as they had been forced to leave behind on *noche triste*. The endless lists of pearls, opals, emeralds, turquoise, table services, pitchers, trays, bowls, animals, fruits, earrings, necklaces, crowns, all fashioned of precious metals, prove that the Spaniards emerged considerably richer when the experience ended than when it began. Cortés became a wealthy man overnight, taking much in fertile farm land as well as treasure.

The next few years were far from peaceful. Although the general had the capital under control, there were many outlying provinces that rebelled against the Spaniards, especially Zapoteca and Mixteca. Cortés was determined to dominate enough territory so that he would have access to the sea for trade and security. Once he had achieved this goal, he took time off to consolidate and start rebuilding Tenochtitlán which had been systematically destroyed, largely because of the pagan connotation of its temples, municipal buildings and palaces. The Spaniards cared nothing for the historic value of edifices unless they had built them themselves.

In the midst of all this, Cortés' long lost, long suffering and seldom-thought-of wife, Catalina Xuárez suddenly turned up from Cuba in June of 1522 and made her way to Mexico City and her mate. Cortés had plenty of time to hear of her arrival and remove Doña Marina and son Martín into quarters of their own. This may have been when La Malinche received her own house in the city. She was also said to have possessed a country place in Chapultepec and extensive gardens in Coyuacan which had belonged to emperor Montezuma. In addition to the prestige lent her by this property, it provided her with an income. She had earned every peso of it.

When Cortés' wife, Doña Catalina, arrived in Mexico City she was cordially greeted by her two-faced spouse. But the joy did not last nor did she. Three months later she was dead, passing on mysteriously. It was called a "delicate subject" but the delicate subject was bandied about indelicately until there were out and out accusations that Cortés had choked her to death. Doña Catalina was heard to exclaim, "I feel like letting myself die." Lo and behold, when Cortés summoned her maids, there he was holding her limp and lifeless body in his arms. Some witnesses said her necklace was broken and she had bruises on her neck. The matter was investigated but never brought to trial and Cortés was freed. His defenders claimed the lady had not been well since coming into the high altitude of Mexico City and that the change in climate killed her. Whether or not Cortés speeded the passage of the unfortunate Doña Catalina into the next world, it would not have been his love for La Malinche that forced his hand but ambition, as usual, as later events would prove.

In January of 1524 Cortés sent Cristóbal de Olid on an expedition to Honduras in search of a strait through which to sail to the Molucca Islands and also to investigate a report that the soil of Honduras was fertile and the area rich in gold. Olid was to sail first to Cuba to recruit men and purchase arms and horses. While in Havana he contacted Cortés' old enemy, Diego Velásquez, and a plot was devised to overturn Cortés authority. When Olid arrived in Honduras he abandoned the search for a strait. He founded the town Triunfo de la Cruz and, by killing off a number of Spaniards loyal to Cortés, took over the country with himself as head man.

When Cortés heard this, he was infuriated and sent two manned vessels in charge of Francisco de las Casas to arrest Olid. But Olid took Las Casas prisoner. In a power seesaw the prisoner, Las Casas, captured his captor and in a few days had Olid publicly beheaded. Cortés, not knowing Olid was dead, decided to organize a land expedition, head it himself and go to Honduras to punish Olid.

This was a far different journey made in the year 1524 than the one that started from Cuba in 1519. Though only five years had passed, the tough, spare warrior who took his chances alongside his men, eating the same slop and ignoring hardship, had all but disappeared. The entourage that set out for Honduras was worthy of an oriental potentate, including: musicians, acrobats, actors, falconers, butlers, stewards, pages, hairdressers, priests, courtesans and the luckless deposed king, Cuauhtémoc, who had been taken prisoner when Cortés took over Mexico. Treating himself as the most exalted of rulers, the general also took along gold and silver services from which to eat his meals which were prepared by a host of fine chefs. One of the few things that remained the same in this motley and unwieldy mass was his translator, La Malinche. By this time there must have been many others able to do the job but in a situation where treachery was afoot, and translators had been known to manipulate answers to suit themselves, Cortés trusted no one as he did Doña Marina.

The first leg of the journey was slated to end in Coatzacoalcos on the Coast so that Cortés could summon the *caciques* of the province to a meeting with him. Among these chiefs was the half-brother of Doña Marina accompanied by Marina's mother, Cimatl. The two were much afraid of what this great lady would do to them in revenge for the way she had been treated when a child, but La Malinche, in true Christian spirit, forgave them and presented them with gifts of jewels, gold and clothing. She persuaded them to adopt the new religion and they were christened Lázaro and Marta.

About this time an occurrence took place in the life of Marina that is hard to account for. Cortés married her off to Juan Jaramillo, a captain who had been in command of one of the brigantines so important in the capture of Mexico City. We know that Jaramillo performed his duties bravely because during a battle on the lake he went to the rescue of another brigantine captured by Aztec warriors who had killed the captain and three of the crew. Captain Jaramillo freed the ship from the Aztecs and retook it. One chronicle states that Cortés was much criticized for fostering this marriage because Jaramillo was drunk when it was performed. We do not know if this was a legal alliance sanctioned by the Church or another of the lordly little conferring rituals that passed as sanction until the conquistador could get hold of a proper Spanish dama. Malinche received a large estate in a village call Jilotopec fifty miles from Mexico City as a gift from Cortés. Despite the change of partner, Doña Marina continued her translating chores for Cortés during the long, difficult, dreary twenty-one months of the Honduran campaign through uncharted jungle fraught with more hardships and deprivations than she had ever endured before. She returned from it intact and presumably her new husband did also. This is the last record we have of the life of La Malinche.

Did Cortés unload her because he had grown tired of her as a mistress? Did he perhaps see that Juan Jaramillo was in love with her and, knowing he would have to discard her in time, pass her along out of consideration for her future? There were certainly others among both officers and men who had been smitten by this woman, not the least being Bernal Díaz del Castillo, one of the most famous historians of the discovery and conquest of Mexico. Díaz speaks of her again and again and in such glowing terms that he gives himself away.

We are told that La Malinche lived to a good age in wealth and comfort. No one tells us how she felt when Cortés became the Marqués del Valle and returned from Spain with his new wife, Doña Juana de Zuñiga, from the cream of Spanish nobility, to found his legitimate family. This realistic lady, Doña Marina, would probably not have been surprised nor even find it of much importance anymore. She was a famous person in her own right and became a goddess in the folklore of her people with a mountain near Tlaxcala named Malinche in her honor.

And what of the son she bore Cortés, the first Don Martín, some ten years older than the second Martín who became the Marqués del Valle, inheriting the title as the legitimate heir? Malinche's son had been wrested from her at an early age and taken to Spain by Cortés. The Pope legitimized him along with another bastard son, Luis. Don Martín was made a member of the knights of Santiago, a coveted military order and married a Spanish lady. He returned to Mexico, after Cortés' death, with his brother Martín, Marqués del Valle. The young Marqués, a dude and a featherweight for courage and brains, set up a court in Mexico City and tried to imitate his famous father whom he did not resemble in the least. The three brothers became involved in an uprising against the rule of Spain but the young Marqués, who was supposed to be the leader, withdrew from the group to save his skin. The conspiracy collapsed and many young men were beheaded, but the Marqués was sent to Spain. Don Martín was not so fortunate. Put to the rack and the water torture again and again, he bravely refused to divulge the names of his fellow plotters. He demonstrated an endurance and stoicism worthy of his parents. Although nothing could be proved against Don Martín, he was fined a thousand dollars and banished for life from Mexico City. Of Doña Marina's daughter by

Juan de Jaramillo, we know nothing.

La Malinche's achievements are recorded in many documents of the era and may also be found in a multitude of pictorial forms such as the *Codex Acatitlan* and the *lieazos de Tlaxcala* at the American Museum of Natural History. There are many other examples in the United States and Mexico. Cortés died December 2, 1547. The date of Doña Marina's death is unknown, but because of her involvement with the Spaniards the word *malinchista* means traitor. It should be changed to denote one possessed of outstanding intelligence and courage.

2
Of Tribulations and Trials

In pre-conquest Mexico the city-state of Texcoco lay across the lake from Tenochtitlán. An independent principality with its own dynasty, it was part of the federation that comprised the Mexico over which the Aztecs ruled supreme, but was considered the most beautiful of all cities with the greatest poets, philosophers and men of science. But despite its reputation for wisdom and culture, murder most foul committed in the name of love was an act well known to its most beneficent and famous ruler. In 1431 Nezahualcóyotl became king of Texcoco and though, in the style of the day, he had numerous concubines and endless children by them, he put off choosing a queen with whom to found his legitimate family. Finally he ordered girls from the highest nobility to be brought before him and he chose one. Since she was very young he gave her to his brother to care for until she was old enough to become his wife.

Shortly after, the brother died and his young son inherited the title, estates, palace and, he thought, everything in it including the tender, sweet, young thing meant to be the bride of King Nezahualcóyotl. He married her. The king, deciding that by now she should be ripe enough to wed, sent for her and was more than a little shocked when his nephew showed up instead and told him that he had known nothing of the arrangement between Nezahualcóyotl and his father and that she was already his bride. The nephew was brought to trial but the judges freed him, deciding he was innocent of malice--proof of the usually law-abiding reign of this king.

After this blow, Nezahualcóyotl fell into a state of depression, thinking himself doomed to be unlucky in love. Wandering about, trying to ease his aching heart he came upon a palace where he encountered a virginal maiden, Azcaxochitzin, with whom he immediately fell in love. The only stumbling block was that the girl was promised to the elderly lord of the palace. So smitten was Nezahualcóyotl that he decided then and there that his rival must be eliminated. He arranged for the lord to be slain in battle, ordering his officers to do it so skillfully that few, if any, would suspect that it was not an accident. The murder was done and the ruler married Azcaxochitzin. As time went by Nezahualcóyotl became famous for being a great and enlightened lawmaker, engineer, statesman, poet. He was said to have been a believer in one god and a non-believer in human sacrifice although, when his wife did not produce an heir, he resorted to human butchery as an offering to the gods on advice of his counselors. But he gave it up in disgust and instead fasted and prayed with excellent results. Azcaxochitzin bore a son of great intelligence called Prince Tetzauhpiltzintli (the wonderful child), but despite this blessing the trio did not live happily ever after.

Polygamy was widely practiced by those who could afford it, mostly nobles and kings, and routinely accepted by the concubines except that many of those who had sons were overly ambitious for their offspring, a common failing of mothers. They knew that if the legitimate heir died, then an illegitimate son could succeed to the throne under the law. One of the harem women concocted a plot involving the wonderful child and urged her own son to fabricate evidence that the prince planned a revolt against his father. These lies were so skillfully presented to King Nezahualcóyotl that he sent a messenger to spy upon his son. The ruler received a report that the walls of the prince's palace were covered with weapons. On this flimsy evidence the king called a conference with the two monarchs of nearby kingdoms, the rulers of Tlacopan and Mexico, and asked them to confront his son with the accusation that he was plotting to overthrow his father. These two monarchs were only too happy to have the opportunity to undermine the strength of the powerful kingdom of Texcoco. They hastened to the prince's palace accompanied by some of their officers who had been ordered to lovingly place a wreath of flowers around the neck of the wonderful child and tighten it until he strangled to death, which they did.

This was not the end of the tragedy involving women in this royal family. The successor to the throne of Texcoco after Nezahualcóyotl was King Nezahualpilli. For his queen he chose Chachiuhnenetzin, the very young daughter of the powerful Aztec king of Mexico. As seemed to have been the custom in those days, she was brought up in a splendid but separate palace of her own until such time as she was judged mature enough to wed. The girl was very precocious. As quick as lightning she shed her virginity and liked the change so much that whenever she saw a young blade who took her fancy she had him brought to her secretly. After sating her desire she had him put to death and in diabolical fashion ordered a lifelike statue of him to be made, which she adorned with clothing and jewels and placed in her bedchamber.

So great was her lust that in no time at all the room began to look like the streets of Texcoco on market day. One day King Nezahualpilli came to visit and asked her about the crowd. Artfully, she replied that they represented her gods. Knowing how numerous were the deities worshipped by the Mexicans and how rigid the religious duties, he believed her. But the truth leaked out eventually because Chachiuhnenetzin was not as thorough in exterminating her lovers as she should have been. Three handsome favorites of noble blood had been left alive and the king recognized on the garments of one of them an unusual jewel he had given his bride-to-be as a gift.

Suspicion aroused, he visited her palace and tried to see her, but was told she was asleep. He insisted upon entering her bedroom and found yet another statue, but this one was a dummy of herself in bed complete with a wig. Tracing her down, he discovered his beloved engaged in merry debauchery with the three young lords whose lives she had spared. From there on it was downhill all the way and the highly-sexed princess and her trio of lovers ended up being garroted; then, while the crowd roared, their bodies were burned along with the gallery of statues Chachiuhnenetzin had so blithely accumulated. No one thought it strange that she should be executed for playing a game in secret that was completely accepted when the king and his lords practiced it in public.

Nezahualpilli's troubles had not yet come to an end. His favorite concubine was a woman known as The Lady of Tula, who came from the capital city of the Toltecs in central Mexico. Though said to be the daughter of a humble trader who had not even been a member of the *pochteca*, the title used for those in charge of the powerful companies which controlled foreign commerce, her quick intelligence equalled her fabled beauty. She was housed in her own exquisite palace and held sway over a private court. The king was her slave and permitted only the most learned men in the kingdom to accompany him when he spent the evening with her because her knowledge was so great that she participated in discussions of warfare, science and mathematics. She excelled in reciting poetry and her interpretation of such beautiful lines as, "I sing my song, a scented song like a shining jewel, a shining turquoise and a blazing emerald, my flowering hymn to the spring," brought her renown in all of Mexico.

She was also an excellent poet in her own right and it was this ability that helped precipitate tragedy. King Nezahualpilli's eldest son, Huexotzincatzin, was a youth of charm and grace known as an outstanding philosopher and poet. He made The Lady of Tula the subject of a satire he composed. Not to be outdone, she parried with one of her own and so a battle of the poets began. It was only a matter of time before the handsome young prince was accused of trying to seduce his father's cherished mistress. This was interpreted by a court of law as a case of treason against the king, punishable by death. Although the king was said to have loved his son devotedly, the sentence was carried out. Had the beautiful Lady of Tula and Prince Huexotzincatzin actually enjoyed a few hours of stolen bliss, or had the prince been unjustly accused and never longed for her at all, or had he longed, but in vain? Romantics would favor the first, moralists the second, and realists, noting that the Lady of Tula had not been brought to trial as an adulteress, would favor the last. A royal mistress knew that if she was fool enough to lose her heart to anyone but her monarch she would literally have had it torn from her body.

In 1524 twelve friars of the Franciscan order arrived from Spain at Veracruz on the coast and walked barefoot, in their simple dusty habits, all the way to the valley of Mexico as proof of their humility and sincerity in bringing the Christian gospel to replace the old religion. The natives were amazed, being accustomed to seeing Indian lords bedecked with flowers, fringe and jewels, lolling in litters carried by slaves, or the new Spanish masters clad in shining armor, towering above them like gods. When the friars arrived in Tenochtitlán, Cortés knelt before the emaciated dozen, cap in hand, and the rest of the distinguished company of Spaniards and Indians immediately followed suit. Then a great series of ceremonies began in honor of these spirited spirituals including a mass for the feast of St. Anthony of Padua.

The festivities concluded with the baptism of the ruler of Texcoco, King Ixtlilxochitl, later known as a famous historian, plus a slew of descendants of former rulers. The king's name became Don Fernando de Alva Ixtlilxochitl and he embraced the Catholic faith willingly, but was highly embarrassed when his mother, Tlacochuatzin, refused to change. The testy lady went into a tirade, admonishing her son for being a turncoat and forsaking the gods worshipped by his ancestors, striking the only discordant note on this joyous occasion. To enforce her refusal she withdrew disdainfully to one of the Temples of Texcoco and refused to come out. Her son lost his temper and finally, at wit's end, sent word that he would set fire to her refuge and roast her alive unless she obeyed him. Only then did the old queen give in grudgingly to baptism and accept her new name of Doña María Tlacochuatzin. When this was accomplished, the king made good his promise and burned the temple to the ground.

The province of Tehuantepec, ruled by the Zapotecs in the valley of Oaxaca, was conquered by the Aztecs in a series of bloody wars that continued until the reign of the Zapotec king, Cosijoeza, who was crowned in 1487. He was a wise diplomat and a great general and when he heard that the Mexicans were preparing to attack him, he ordered a fortress city constructed on the mountain of Giengola, an amazing feat of engineering, some of which still stands today. Holed up within its mighty walls the Zapotecs withstood a seven month siege until finally the Aztec king Ahuizotl sued for peace and proposed that the two dynasties strengthen their ties through the marriage of Ahuizotl's daughter Princess Pelaxilla to Cosijoeza. Though this marriage was no myth, myths sprang up around it.

One legend goes that Cosijoeza refused to wed the girl at first because he was wary of the good faith of the Mexican ruler. Like all Aztec kings, Ahuizotl set great store by magic and to bring about the union ordered his sorcerers to create an illusion in which Princess Pelaxilla appeared to Cosijoeza as he was bathing in a limpid stream surrounded by tall trees. The beautiful princess took along a special soap used by her father (with magic properties perhaps) and with this she gently lathered the astonished king. Is it any wonder that he fell in love with her and proposed marriage on the spot?

Before the princess disappeared Cosijoeza promised to send an emissary to Tenochtitlán to make a formal declaration of marriage to her father. The emissary was instructed to look for a lady with a "graceful hairy mole on her hand" to make sure he got the right girl. Mole identified, Pelaxilla and Cosijoeza were betrothed and great festivities were held in both the Aztec and Zapotec capitals. The celebration concluded with a wedding of such luxury that there were no doubts as to the power and wealth of the Zapotec kingdom. But the wily Ahuizotl had no intentions of permitting the Zapotecs with all their assets to squirm out from under Aztec rule, so he instructed his daughter to find out secretly, once she was safely married, the best time and place for the Aztecs to renew their attacks upon the Zapotecs. Ahuizotl had not reckoned on human emotions though, because Pelaxilla had truly fallen in love with Cosijoeza. She told her husband all about the plot.

Cosijoeza now proved his statesmanship. He had to juggle the welfare of his kingdom, the pride of his father-in-law and the feelings of his wife. He sent all his military forces, armed to the teeth, to the border to meet the Aztec king under the pretext of graciously escorting Ahuizotl and his army across Zapotec territory and out. With this massive tongue-in-cheek guard-of-honor surrounding him, Ahuizotl was unable to carry out his plans. Queen Pelaxilla had saved the kingdom.

Doña María Bartola is spoken of as the first historian of Mexico. We do not know the Aztec name of this woman but only the Christian name given her after baptism. She wrote at length about important events during the conquest, going to battle sites and taking her chances in combat as an eye-witness to history. She was a patriot who loved her country dearly but she could report *noche triste* and its tremendous toll of Spanish lives with as much objectivity for its significance, and compassion for its dead and wounded, as she reported the massacre of the innocent ceremonial dancers in the Aztec temple captained by the butcher, Pedro de Alvarado, May 16, 1520. In his famous work entitled "Relaciones Históricas" the great Mexican historian Don Fernando de Alva Ixtlixóchitl extolls the ability of Doña María Bartola and the quality of the manuscripts she wrote in both Castilian and Nahuatl.

Doña María Bartola was the daughter of Cuitlahuac, brother of Montezuma and lord of Ixtapalapa and Texcoco. This prince was known for his erudite and inquiring mind, an inheritance he passed on to his daughter. Cuitlahuac succeeded Montezuma but died of smallpox shortly after becoming emperor. Doña Bartola became head of Ixtapalapa when Cuitlahuac took the throne of Mexico. Her father had assembled a great number of pictograph manuscripts, the books of Aztecs, and this library was probably an inspiration for Doña María Bartola's own historical work after she learned written language. Unfortunately, her manuscripts met the fate of so many others and were destroyed. All we know of them today is from historian Don Fernando de Alva Ixtlixóchitl.

Mexico City buzzed with gossip in 1566 concerning the daughter of the ill-starred Avila family. María, child of Gil Gonzalez de Avila and Doña Leonor de Alvarado, was born and raised like a princess in an enormous house in the capital. The aristocratic girls of those days were treated like rare flowers and imprisoned behind the thick walls of their homes where they were guarded by a retinue of maiden aunts. But somehow love will find a way to unlock a chastity belt. Right under her parent's noses the delicately nurtured young woman became wildly enamored of a plebian mestizo lad called Arrutia who humbly served as groom to her father, the haughty master of the house, Gil Gonzalez de Avila.

María was the apple of her father's eye and he planned to select a mate for her from among the wealthiest and noblest hidalgos that the new world had to offer. She and Arrutia the groom secretly pledged their troth and made plans to run away. The girl's brothers, Gil and Alonso, got wind of the affair and rid the house of Arrutia by sending him off to Spain. Even so, María's honor was sullied and she was no longer of value in the marriage market with her virginity in doubt. The men of the family ordered her to a convent. The girl obeyed because she had no choice but refused to become a nun because she hoped that her lover would return to claim her some day. Her nasty brothers forged letters saying that the mestizo Arrutia had died in Spain and with this blow, María sorrowfully took the veil.

Years later Arrutia came back and wrote to his old flame but by this time grief and frustration had unhinged the poor woman's mind. So mad had she become that she hung herself in the garden of the convent, knowing that her soul would be condemned to eternal damnation. The footnote to this story is that the two heartless brothers ended up just as badly. They were foremost in the plot to break with Spain and put Cortés' wishy-washy son, the Marqués del Valle, in power. The Marqués got off scot-free but both Avila brothers were beheaded in the public square of Mexico City on October 3, 1566--a grim form of poetic justice.

Women of more humble origins were making themselves memorable for reasons other than love in those days, too. It was not an easy life for a female, be she Criolla, Indian or Mestiza, but she had certain rights. Although the dowry was equally important for rich or poor in any marriage, a woman did not completely relinquish control over her property when she took her vows. The señoras seldom participated in the day to day affairs of the farms and *obrajes* (workshops) but they made a point of keeping themselves informed so that they would be capable of taking over should the need arise. Widowhood was the most common cause for a woman to be catapulted into the business world and a prime example of success is Mencia Pérez de Aragon. Born a mestiza and without education, this wise illiterate first married a Basque innkeeper. When he died in 1578, she inherited considerable real estate including a mill and grazing land. She married again and when her second husband Rodrigo Arias died in 1590 his carting and ranching enterprises were left to her. She added them to her holdings which now included a shingle business for which she employed a number of Indian workers in Huamantla where she lived. In a few short years she had become the richest woman in town and one of the wealthiest in the province.

Another business woman was Doña María Castilan Xochitl, a daughter of Indian nobility who lived in Tlaxcala. By the year 1616 she had set up an *obraje* for weaving cloth in her home, which she equipped with looms, spinning wheels, dyes and combs for carding. She made a point of only employing native labor and the shop produced sarapes, *huipiles*, yard goods and blankets. She bought wool from Indians or used that from her own sheep, operating a truly indigenous enterprise unlike foreign *obrajeros* who imported supplies from Europe. Doña María's enterprise supported herself and her children.

The woman who had just been shoved into the tiny windowless cell was as pale as death and trembling so hard she couldn't stand upright, but she was not permitted to sink to the floor. Rough hands jerked her to her feet and yanked a sleeveless yellow garment over her dress. Knee-length, it was made of a coarse fabric like burlap and was known as a sanbenito or holy sack which penitents were forced to wear. A rude cross was daubed on it along with leering red devils bearing pitchforks. When the lock clicked on the door of the prison cell, the woman fell to her knees and raised in supplication hands which no longer shook. Indignation at the coarse treatment and coarse garment seemed to have driven away her fear. She prayed soundlessly to the God of her ancestors, the God of Israel, although she had denied her allegiance to him when arrested for fear of involving her family. Isabel de Carvajal, widow, age thirty, comely and learned, had begun the last portion of her life. Little did she know that she would not be free of the ugly sanbenito for the next seven years, but forced to wear it no matter where she was.

Isabel was the first of the Carvajals to be arrested. The date was March 13, 1589. She was the oldest girl in a family of new Christians who were accused by the Inquisition of having reverted to their ancient and original faith of Judaism, a heresy forbidden by Spain. Her incarceration took place in the jail called fittingly, Flat House, maintained by the Inquisition in Mexico City for its victims. Those thrust into its forbidding gray walls knew well they might never be heard from again, except when they screamed under torture, and then their voices would be indistinguishable one from the other.

The Carvajals were raised Roman Catholics in Castile before their emigration to the new world. The children were not told of their part-Jewish ancestry until they were of an age to keep a secret. Starting with nine-year-old Anica, there were five girls and four boys one of whom, Gaspar, the oldest brother, was a Dominican priest teaching novitiates in the Mexico City monastery. Luis, the twenty-three-year-old, would be known in centuries to come for his memoirs which included poetry, a will and letters written under the most difficult circumstances in prison and constituting the only known documents of the era composed by an Iberian Jew in America.

New Christians were considered an inferior race by Spanish society and clergy alike, despite the edicts of the Church of Rome which did not hold with these concepts. Italy had long been a refuge for the persecuted fleeing from Spain since the laws of the Mother Church recognized full equality for those who embraced Catholicism without regard to race, ancestry or former religion. However, the doctrines of the Roman Church could not stem the massacres and persecutions of the Spanish inquisitors. Established in 1478 by Ferdinand V and Isabella, the purpose in the beginning had been to spy out converted Moors and Jews who had reverted to their original faiths. But after awhile no Spaniard could feel safe. Even St. Ignatius of Loyola and St. Theresa of Avila were investigated for heresy, and by the time the plague had spread to America, Protestants were included along with blasphemers, bigamists and people in categories that had nothing to do with religion.

Isabel, who had been intelligent and devout as a child, never neglecting her reading and praying, was also a spirited person who must have started planning her testimony and defense as soon as she got over the initial shock of imprisonment. She had proselytized avidly, teaching Hebrew prayers and songs to her younger brothers and sisters and, in her zeal, had even tried to convert her illustrious uncle, Luis de Carvajal y de La Cueva, former admiral and judicious governor of the province of Nuevo Leon in Mexico. Although he was very fond of his niece, he is said to have smacked her so hard for trying to sell her beliefs to him that he knocked her across the room. No one had ever suspected the governor of having Jewish ancestry and he wanted no doubts aroused as to the fervor of his Catholicism which he sincerely practiced. He was also afraid to hear more from Isabel because it was the duty of every subject of the King of Spain to report the names of any persons he suspected of being pseudo-Christians. Although the governor was very angry with his family for their secret practices he had no desire to denounce them to the authorities and implicate himself as well. His caution did not prevent him from being arrested by orders of the Viceroy.

It had been Isabel's fervor with Captain Felipe Nuñez, Governor Carvajal's aide, that had landed her in jail. When her attempts to convert him shocked Nuñez into a passionate declaration of his loyalty to Christianity, she had tried to make a joke of her proselytizing and thought she had convinced him that it was all in fun. But a few months later Captain Nuñez decided to tell all to Licentiate Santos García and with that the long tragedy began which would involve, in time, every member of this family and their descendants for generations to come.

The mailed fist of the Inquisition fell next upon Fray Gaspar Carvajal who was charged with knowing that his sister was a practicing Jewess and not denouncing her. Then Luis de Carvajal, the poet-brother, and his mother, Francisca, were hauled off to Flat House. In a short time sisters Leonor, Catalina and Mariana were incarcerated and finally even little Anica, age ten, was called in for questioning. At first all members of the family denied allegiance to the Jewish faith. They were urged to implicate others, which they resisted as best they could in the midst of the terrible confusion of being told lies and semi-truths about everyone they knew in an effort to trip them up and turn them against each other and their friends and relatives.

The cell that became Isabel's home was without heat or light, except for a candle that she was allowed to burn between the hours of 7:00 a.m. and 4:00 p.m. Total isolation was the rule, no visitors, no books, no mail, no writing materials were permitted. Later, Luis would enscribe his poems and letters upon the peel of oranges and other tough-skinned fruit and pits of avocados. This solitary confinement was psychologically sound. It broke the prisoner's morale and prevented him from discussing his defense or revealing to outsiders what occurred in his sessions with the inquisitors. The Council of the Holy Office in Spain had spent more than a century refining its ordinances and tortures. No Sephardic Jew was without knowledge of the physical and mental agony that was automatic when a heretic did not confess what was expected of him. Isabel de Carvajal could not have been under any illusions as to what lay ahead.

First came the verbal sessions with the tribunal. Isabel had a dramatic delivery and declared her loyalty to Christianity with such passion that she prostrated herself at Prosecutor Bonilla's feet and demanded a full pardon. When ordered to stand, she fainted dead away on the spot. Hoping to save her mother, Francisca, and brother Luis she implicated her uncle the governor and her brother Gaspar the Franciscan priest. Not the least of the tortures devised by the Inquisition was the anguish suffered by those who had to betray others in an attempt to save their nearest and dearest. It was bargaining with the devil and it seldom worked.

Months went by and, of course, no member of the family had any idea what the others had said. Isabel and her mother withheld as much information as they could in the endless meetings with their accusers. Finally on November 10, Doña Francisca was led to the torture chamber and stripped to the waist. When twisted cords drawn tighter and tighter around her arms failed to bring forth more information, her thighs and shins were bound and her body placed on the rack and stretched until her tongue loosened along with her aging bones. A few weeks later Isabel was given the same treatment and the testimony extracted from the ravings of the two tormented women was considered enough to implicate the rest of the members of their family. The delirium also elicited penitence for their Jewish allegiance and promises to return to Catholicism relinquishing all practices of their faith such as dietary laws forbidding pork and shellfish and keeping Saturday as the sabbath. The spirit was willing but the flesh had been weak. All members of the family who had been imprisoned were now penitents and would receive sentence at the auto-da-fé. Gaspar de Carvajal, the Dominican friar, would not be present but would receive sentence privately, no doubt to save the Church embarrassment that one of its members could be charged with concealing heretics in his own family.

Saturday, February 24, 1590 was the day chosen and the great cathedral in Mexico City was the site for the auto-da-fé, the public court which was the ultimate humiliation. There were half a dozen more Jews besides the Carvajals and a handful of other malefactors that ran the gamut from a cursing soldier to a learned Dominican Friar, Dr. Gregorio Calderon who was accused of favoring Protestants and practicing astrology, a strange combination of sins. The great cathedral was packed to the rafters with a crowd that looked upon the spectacle as a diversion created for them in much the same spirit as the Romans had enjoyed watching Christians pitted against lions centuries before.

When the penitents walked into the cathedral and took the places assigned to them they wore their crude yellow sanbenitos and carried lighted green candles. They were followed by the dignitaries of the Holy Office of the Inquisition whose gorgeous garments of red velvet, ermine, brocade and sparkling jewels pointed up the ugliness of the garb allotted to sinners. A stirring and a whispering ran through the crowd before they settled down for the show which took place traditionally in three acts. Act One was a lengthy sermon, given by a big-name, ranking member of the Church or a wealthy citizen, exalting the Holy Office and its work and heaping insults upon the prisoners until their egos were completely pulverized. Act Two was an oath wherein all assembled solemnly swore to tattle upon those they suspected of any of the innumerable sins punishable by the Inquisition, or suffer the consequences of eternal damnation. Act Three was the big thrill, the high point of the drama--the reading of the sentences.

The Inquisition gave no indication of what penalties would be imposed unless it were death. Then the condemned were informed of their fate the night before the auto-da-fé to give them time for confession and, hopefully, further statements implicating others. The dignitaries were long-winded and the sentencing took the form of a dissertation detailing the prisoner's birth, parents, childhood, home, thoughts, person, habits, in other words a complete biography that wound up with a smashing million or so words explaining the sentence while the poor creature before the judges shook from fright and exhaustion until the breeze from his flapping sanbenito threatened to extinguish the sputtering candle he was still required to hold. The Carvajals were not sentenced to death. This time. But their father, who had passed away long before they were imprisoned, was sentenced to be burned at the stake in effigy.

Various members of the family were imprisoned for various periods of time, but eventually all were released with many restrictions including the continued wearing of the loathsome sanbenito. Once more they had been rounded up and herded back into the corral of Christianity. It was certainly a safer place to be in a Spain-ruled country than galloping free on the prairies riding the wild horse of Judaism. But the Carvajals did not seem to realize how lucky they were because, once more, in secret, they began backsliding. Doña Francisca and her daughters had been assigned by the Inquisition a chaplain and confessor by the name of Fray Pedro de Oroz, a monk of the Franciscan order known for his scholarship and brilliance. He was most considerate of the Carvajals and had Luis transferred to the Colegio de Santa Cruz (Academy of the Holy Cross) where he was rector. Here Luis had access to a library that contained many documents and books that he had never known existed before. The Old Testament was forbidden to all Spaniards of the era, let alone volumes like the Talmud, a compilation of Jewish law. Actually the Carvajal's small knowledge of the tenets of their faith was mouth-to-mouth, meager and often erroneous. Fray Pedro de Oroz must have been aware that the family was not wholeheartedly embracing Christianity, but for some reason, perhaps because he too had faced the Inquisition in his early years, he turned a blind eye upon their subterranean activities. He was a cultured man who enjoyed and seemed fond of the people he was assigned.

Soon the Carvajal women were as active as before in bringing as many secret Jews as possible into their group. When they held services did they speak Ladino to keep any informers among them from understanding too much? Ladino, a colorful combination of Hebrew, Spanish, other European languages and Arabic, although not as widespread as Yiddish, was, and still is, spoken by Sephardic Jews. We know that the Carvajals observed fast days and would not work or sew on Saturdays even though, as camouflage in their home, they kept pork and cooked with lard for visitors. Doña Francisca and daughters Isabel, Leonor and Catalina were careful to keep their practices hidden, but they had a problem with Mariana. Her mind had been affected by the prison stay and her madness took the form of flamboyantly declaring her Judaism by tossing into the street religious statues filched from the Christian chapel that the family maintained in their house. She also decided to become a martyr by going to the Inquisition and denouncing herself. but was persuaded not to by the other women who pointed out that it would result in their martyrdom as well.

Many Jewish women took their chances attending secret religious services at the home of the Carvajals. Among them was Justa Méndez who was said to have converted solely because of conviction not because of Jewish ancestry. Luis was much taken with this brilliant and attractive woman and taught her a great deal he had recently learned about the ceremonies and history of Judaism. They were soon in love. It was a peaceful period too good to last.

One of the family friends, Manuel de Lucena, who had attended the Carvajal's secret religious rituals in their home was arrested by the Inquisition. Under the pressure which his tormentors know so well how to apply, he brought up Luis de Carvajal's name. In February of 1595 Luis was rearrested. Doña Francisca, Catalina and Leonor followed in the spring. On June 7 Isabel was incarcerated again. Catalina's little daughter was taken to the home of a friend where she was retaught her Christian prayers by a devoted black female servant named Ana de Los Reyes, who hoped to spare the child a sentence of death by bringing her back into the fold.

The terrible sessions with the Inquisitors in Flat House began for the members of the family. Their knowledge of the agonies of torture and the betrayal of their dear ones that could be extracted by it was no longer hearsay. They had gone through it before. This time, so brutal was the torture applied to Luis, and so despairing was he after having testimony wrung from him against his mother, brothers and sisters, other relatives and friends, that he attempted suicide by breaking from his guards and throwing himself into the courtyard below. After that he was handcuffed and two other prisoners were placed in his cell to report on his smallest activity.

Isabel held out for a year, even refusing for a while to inform under torture. Finally, so weak she was unable to walk to the chambers, she asked for an audience in her cell. Half-delirious from the pain of the rack she revealed the activities of herself, her friends and family. These sessions went on from July

14, 1596 until August 30 when she was reported as too ill to sign her completed confession. An occasional stalwart was able to withstand the torture without breaking. Such had been Martín Del Valle, son of Cortés and La Malinche. Another was the Carvajals' brother-in-law, Antonio Díaz de Cáceres, but, as the Inquisition knew and counted on, stoics were few and far between.

It was the biggest and most exciting auto-da-fé the city had ever witnessed. Held outdoors in the great square, it drew crowds which clambered up on the stands constructed especially for the occasion, jostling each other good naturedly and licking their lips in anticipation of the day-long spectacle with its climax of crackling death. It was December 8, 1596. For several days in advance of the holiday, bonfires burned and people walked the streets until late at night buying *dulces* (sweets) from the vendors and watching the procession of the Inquisitors as they solemnly marched to Flat House, keeping time to the slow beat of the kettledrums.

At 3:00 a.m. the prisoners who were to participate in the auto-da-fé were ordered to dress and make ready for the final march to the great square. The Carvajals wore their sanbenitos plus *corozas*, a tall hat shaped like a bishop's bejeweled miter but painted instead for heretics with serpents, flames and devils. The traditional green candle was thrust into unwilling hands and lit for the procession of the damned. What if the careless jailers scorched the prisoner's fingers with their tapers? There would be more skin than that singed in the big burn that was to take place later. Each prisoner wore a placard with his name, place of birth and crime written on it. Today the place of greatest dishonor was given to Luis de Carvajal whose mouth was gagged to prevent him shouting words of encouragement to his mothers and sisters in maintaining their faith. He was the last in line.

Dignitaries marched after the prisoners: the Senior Inquisitor, the Junior Inquisitor, the Prosecutor. Crimson banners of the Holy Office, fastened to a silver pole with golden tassels and topped with a cross, added color. Churchmen and important citizens followed the ensign. The seating for the criminals had been built in a tiered triangle. At the point at the very top Luis de Carvajal was placed and below him his sisters and mother. Lesser offenders sat on the bottom tiers. The dignitaries had special seats and the Viceroy rated a three-room apartment built for his use near the scaffold with all luxuries and conveniences, should he grow hungry, weary or bored during the long day.

The crowd settled down resignedly to listen to the usual

lengthy opening sermon given by the Archbishop of the Philippines. Then that crowd-pleaser, the oath, was administered and it was the people's turn to vocalize with great roars and shouts filled with promises to defend the faith by informing on all heretics. This was followed by the thrill of cursing, en masse, in demonstration of what would happen to them should they ever hide and not deride malefactors. It was a highly satisfactory beginning to the holiday for everyone except the prisoners.

Minor offenders were sentenced first. Among them were black slaves who had been starved and beaten to the point where they had dared utter the sentiments that it was better to be criminals than Christians. To change their opinions they were sentenced to be beaten again more fiercely. Sorcerers, adulterers and bigamists followed, then came the fifty-three Jews, forty-five of whom were present and eight of whom were represented in effigy because, lucky for them they were either far from the clutches of the Inquisition or dead.

Luis, Isabel, Doña Francisca, Leonor and Catalina were sentenced to die that day. Their hands were tied and they were placed on mules led by guards to the *quemadero* (burning grounds). The Inquisition, always looking for a fitting twist at the end, gave them a last-minute opportunity to embrace the Church and as a reward be mercifully garroted before being burned at the stake. Was it less dreadful to choke to death before burning? They decided, as most of us would, that anything was better than feeling your flesh fry. The validity of such a reconversion is hardly to be considered. Luis was said by some to refuse to give up Judaism, but others said he was dead by garroting by the time they tied his body to the stake and set off the pyre.

Mariana Núnez de Carvajal, the mad sister, was garroted and burned four and a half years later despite the fact that when her sanity returned she became a model of piety, a sincere and practicing Catholic. Luis de Carvajal's brothers survived. Baltasar and Miguel escaped to Europe and Fray Gaspar continued in the Church. It took many years before the youngest sister Ana, or Anica as they fondly called her, was caught in the jaws of the Inquisition but on April 11, 1649, with over a hundred prisoners involved in this most enormous of all Mexican auto-da-fé, Anica was burned. Almost seventy years old at the time she died, she had been imprisoned for six years before and adhered to Judaism during this time. She suffered so from advanced cancer of the breast that it was said that her entrails could be seen through the decaying flesh. Perhaps the tortures of the Inquisition were unable to compete. Justa Méndez survived, thrived and married but was burned in effigy posthumously in the same gruesome farce that took what was left of Anica.

In regard to numbers of arrests, trials, tortures and burnings, the tribunal of New Spain was by far the most active of the four areas of North and South America in which the Inquisition held forth. Many Lutherans were tried, especially from 1536 to the early 1600s, and there were also Calvinists. The first woman accused, listed in *Mexico Viejo* by Luis Gonzalez Obregón, was María Ocampo, born in Guatemala and accused of trafficking with the devil. At that time Guatemala came within the territory controlled by New Spain. Without making an actual count of those persecuted in Mexico, it appears that approximately one quarter were women. Since women of races other than Indian and origins other than Mexican were greatly outnumbered by men in the early centuries after the conquest, the actual percentage in relation to their numbers is probably much higher.

Although many persecuted women were from Spain or Portugal, many were born in Mexico. The age range was vast. At one end we have Ana Núñez, age thirteen, criolla, accused of observing Mosaic Laws; at the other end, Catalina de Campos, age eighty-five, who died in her cell of an unnamed disease. The old one had been left unattended so long that rats had eaten part of her body. There must not have been enough left to make a proper blaze since she was burned in effigy in the 1649 auto-da-fé.

Among Jewish women the charges ranged from being a *Judía* (Jewess) or *Judaizante* (one who observes the teachings) to being the daughter or sister of penitents, proselytizing, witchcraft and wearing silks, a strange infraction of which male Jews were accused as well as females. These common offenses were used singly or in combination. María Felipa de Alcázar from Oaxaca was accused in 1739 of "acts of Judaism, idolatry, witchcraft and pacts with the devil."

The sentences for women of any race or faith could include an indefinite number of penalties. Clara Antuñez, age nineteen, had her property confiscated, was jailed for a year, forced to wear the sanbenito, and exiled from the Indies, Seville and Madrid. She renounced her faith (Judaism) but was still burned at the stake in 1646. Other penalties were beatings that ranged from one hundred to two hundred lashes, and re-imprisonment for not wearing the sanbenito or returning to forbidden practices. For blasphemy one could be led through the streets by a rope tied around the neck with a large clamp fastened to the tongue.

Exile was also common.

Mention was seldom made of working women in the lists, but Blanca de Rivera, a widow with six children, was described as a maker of hoopskirts. Accused of practicing Judaism, she received, among other punishments, life imprisonment in Spain. All of her five daughters were apprehended by the Holy Office. Catalina, age twenty-seven, died in her cell. Clara, at age twenty-six, did the same. Isabel, twenty-five years old, was beaten, exiled and imprisoned for life. Margarita, no age given, received life imprisonment in Seville. María, the oldest at age thirty-eight, died in the cells. This group is reminiscent of the Carvajal women who were also wiped out by the Inquisition.

A curious hope ran through some of the Jews of Mexico during these trying times and perhaps because of them. It was believed that Inés Pereira of Ixmiquilpan would give birth to the Messiah, but instead she had her property confiscated by the Inquisition, was ordered to wear the sanbenito and sentenced to jail for ten years. After this disappointment the family Jerónima named their daughter Esperanza (Hope) because they hoped she would birth the Messiah. When it became apparent that the dream would not be fulfilled, the honor was transferred to Esperanza's niece, Juana Enríquez. The Holy Office had other ideas. Esperanza was burned in effigy in 1649 and Juana received life imprisonment. Persecution continued unrelieved by men or miracles.

For a summary of ridiculous accusations we have María Marín from Cholula, who, along with her brothers and sisters, was accused of using silk, bearing arms, riding horses and being the granddaughter of penitents who had been burned in effigy. And for sheer courage and audacity, there is Christina Tsipaqua, a Tarascan Indian woman who complained that Juan Duran, an Augustine friar from the pueblo of San Felipe, had made amorous advances to her after confession. The affair was investigated by the Inquisition who heard the testimony of Cristina in June of 1608, but no witnesses were summoned until October 22 of 1612, a four year lapse. In addition, Cristina had conveniently died the year before. The records of this trial found in the Harkness collection are incomplete so that the fate of the accused cleric is unknown.

For comedic relief after the horrors just described, we come to a kind of Doña Quixote whose exploits may be almost as legendary. This woman who became known as the nun-ensign, Doña Catalina de Erazu, starts off in Spain where her devout family persuaded her to enter a convent. After taking the veil, the young girl realized the life was not for her and somehow acquired male clothing and made good her escape. Continuing to wear masculine attire, she fought her way to Peru and Chile, sometimes serving as an *arriero* (muledriver), sometimes as a soldier gaining fame for her swordsmanship. Sought by officials in many countries because of the deaths resulting from her duels, she was captured in Peru and escaped the chopping block by declaring herself a nun and a virgin and proving it.

Not knowing how to handle the scandal of this wild male-female who claimed the Church as sanctuary, the Peruvian courts freed her but sent her back to Spain. Her case ultimately reached the ears of the Pope who is said to have given her special dispensation to wear male clothing for the rest of her life. In 1640 she set sail for Mexico. Despite having been given a pension of 500 pesos a year by the Spanish king, Philip, Catalina decided she must work to make ends meet or perhaps just for the excitement of it. She went back to her old profession of *arriero* and tore so madly up and down the Veracruz road that she terrorized travelers. The final scene in the farce was played when our heroine in her rollicking fashion threw caution to the winds and allowed herself to fall head over heels in love with the wife of a nobleman. She challenged the astonished husband to a duel but the contest never came off. Her niche assured in Mexican folklore for centuries to come, Catalina, the nun-ensign, died in 1650 and was buried on a hillside near the village of Cuitlaxtla. A few years after her death a play about her was published called *La Monja Alférez* by Juan Pérez Montalbán, a Spanish playwright.

The Catholic clergy were not safe from the long arm of the Inquisition either and it was under Archbishop Alonso de Montúfar that the first *procesos* (trials) of nuns were held. It started on December 5, 1562 with the investigation of Sister Francisca de La Anunción from the convent of the Immaculate Conception in Mexico City. Fray Bartolomé de Ledesma was the inquisitor and he began questioning the mother superior and five of her nuns about the views held by Francisca on the subject of suicide and the dogma of the Church. The investigation had started because one of the sisters had hanged herself and Francisca had stated that in her eyes the unhappy woman should not be judged by others and that God would not condemn her to hell. To add to this unorthodox view, Francisca staunchly declared that when found, the body still seemed possessed of a soul and the features were peaceful and not distorted.

Francisca was able to clear one of the biggest hurdles by

stating that her family had neither Jews nor Moors in its background and that her father, Francisco Chávez, had never previously been questioned by the Holy Office of the Inquisition. But as the investigation went on, the testimony of the mother superior and her convent sisters made Francisca appear a highly excitable person constantly on the verge of emotional breakdown. This was thought by many to be a deliberate cover-up by the other women to substantiate that it was only Francisca's daft state of mind that caused her to make such questionable and heretical statements concerning a suicide. Since the temper of the times was such that one poor sinner was declared guilty of heresy for drying chilies on a crucifix, it is no wonder that Francisca's compassion and tolerance for the nun who hanged herself was highly suspicious.

Fray Ledesma reported back to his chief, Archbishop Montúfar, and after warning the sisters to be on watch for any other suspicious acts among the members of the convent, they let Francisca de La Anunción off with only a reproof.

Six years later on July 16, 1568 from the same convent of the Immaculate Conception, which seems to have harbored a nest of free-thinkers, the investigation of Sister Elena de la Cruz began. This erudite, forty-three-year-old nun was the daughter of an attorney, Licenciado Juan Gutiérrez Altamirano, who had worked for Hernán Cortés and been governor of the Cortés estate. Elena was said to be related to the Marqués del Valle, Cortés legitimate son, who had instigated the conspiracy in which the Avila brothers lost their lives. At this time the young Marqués was being tried for the crime in Spain and it is believed that Montúfar's decision to go after Elena was largely political. He wanted to make an example of her questioning the God-given authority of the Church because another member of her family had plotted the overthrow of the God-given authority of the crown.

The charges against Elena were that, before witnesses, she had held forth on the dubious rights of Archbishop Montúfar and even the Pope himself to exact obedience to Church mandates aside from the seven mortal sins. She declared that after much study salvation would be assured if an individual obeyed the Ten Commandments and committed no mortal sin.

Her inquisitors Ledesma and Montúfar did not like free-thinking that simplified sin and made humans less subject to intricate, artificial and entrapping rules and regulations. It turned out under questioning that Elena had read such revolutionary documents as a treatise by a Carthusian monk claiming that perfection is attainable by observing the Ten Commandments, and works along the same lines by Fray Luis de Granada which were forbidden. Although her trial had not been completed, she was ordered to be imprisoned on August 14, 1568. No one was allowed to visit her except the mother superior of the convent.

By this time the public was well aware of the trial and Elena's family, the Altamiranos, came to her rescue. They hired a pair of clever lawyers to defend her, Juan Vellerino and Licenciado Fulgencio de Vigue. These two devised a defense which leaned heavily on foolish, fluttery, so-called feminine qualities which the defendant did not possess and completely disposed of the strong intellect and inquiring mind which many feel made Elena de La Cruz the forerunner of the brilliant nun, and partial namesake, Sor Juana Inés de La Cruz of the seventeenth century.

Sadly, as was the custom in almost all these cases, to save her life Elena was forced to destroy it, blaming her downfall upon the philosophers she had read before entering the convent, denying that she believed these liberal ideas anymore, doing penance by going "on her knees with tears streaming down her cheeks" before her convent sisters to plead forgiveness. Her lawyers also leaned heavily upon the good name of her family and status as an hidalgo's daughter.

Money, power and prestige, the unholy three that often influenced the Holy See, resulted in a light sentence after a lengthy trial. Elena was ordered to stand holding a green penitential candle when mass was being heard while the other nuns were properly on their knees. She was required to recite penitential psalms, publicly declare her sins and, repeating the psalms again, to fast on three successive Fridays. She was never again to think or speak of any philosophy or teachings contrary to the official doctrine of the Holy Mother Church and, should she break any of these rules, Montúfar promised to prosecute her with the full force of the law, which implied burning at the stake.

An interesting group of women that started coming from Spain in the 1520s were the Beatas, affiliated with the Franciscans as a teaching unit. Their basic function was to instruct the daughters of Indian royalty in household management and Christianity. Warmly welcomed by the early friars, they were well housed and clothed and put in charge of the education of the aristocratic Indian maidens. Much to the dismay of the good fathers, gossip concerning the unorthodox views of some of the Beatas was soon bandied about. One Beata in particular, Catalina

Hernández, a dear friend (possibly a relative) of Francisca Hernández, who had been accused of being a Lutheran in Seville in 1529, was especially suspect. Guilt by association was taken for granted until proved otherwise, and often even then. Catalina had come to Mexico with a group of Beatas accompanied by a male retainer-protector, Calisto de Sá, whom she had known in Spain. Calisto had been a friend of Ignatius Loyola, the outspoken founder of the Jesuit order, and shared with Catalina an interest in illuminism, a type of visionary Christianity forbidden by the Inquisition. Archbishop Zumárraga ordered an investigation of Calisto and was much taken aback and then infuriated at the feisty maestra, Catalina Hernández, when she lectured the *oidores* (judges) on the injustice of their decision to exile Calisto de Sá.

Disgusted with such a forceful woman and other beatas like her Zumárraga wrote to Prince Philip that he wanted no more of these creatures who raised Indias uninterested in serving their husbands. He now declared that he would not accept teachers for the convents unless they "would not flaunt their lack of obedience or go about in the world or refuse to go to Church with the girls...."

During this era the cult of the Virgin of Guadalupe was founded. In pre-Columbian days the area that would later be called Guadalupe Hidalgo was a great religious center. On one of the hills there had been a temple where the Aztecs sacrificed to the rain gods. These gods were dwarfs and so it was thought that only the tiny hearts of babies and children would propitiate them. On the nearby hill of Tepeyac had stood a great temple to Tonantzín, the virgin goddess of corn and earth, who carried a cradle on her back in which her divine son lay sleeping.

After the conquest, on December 9, 1531, an Indian named Quauhtatohua, who had been baptized Juan Diego, passed this hill which had been stripped of its ancient temple with the advent of Christianity and was now barren of anything but a few rocks. Suddenly he heard heavenly music and saw a vision of a beautiful, olive-skinned woman surrounded by an aura of light. When he approached the apparition, she told him she was the Virgin Mary and wanted a shrine built in her name on this very spot. Juan had been on his way to mass at Tlatelolco, but instead he obeyed the instructions given him by the Virgin to proceed to the palace of Archbishop Zumárraga and tell him of her demand. The Archbishop was not impressed and dismissed Juan and his tale of miracles. Juan returned to the hill and there was a repeat of the same happening. As ordered by the stubborn, olive-skinned Virgin he went back to the Archbishop with the story of the re-occurrence and although Zumárraga listened, the stern Basque prelate did not say he believed it. He demanded that the Indian bring him some proof of the divine happening. Meanwhile the Archbishop secretly assigned two spies to follow Juan and report on his actions.

Several days later Juan again had to make a trip to Tlatelolco to obtain a priest to give last rites to his uncle Bernardino who was dying. As he passed the hill he scurried along, wanting to avoid seeing more visions because of the problems and embarrassment they had caused him, but, as before, the apparition appeared. The Virgin assured Juan that he needn't worry about his uncle because she had already cured him, then she directed Juan to climb the hill, pick the roses he would find there and bring them back to her. Juan was reluctant because he knew that the hill was barren, but he obeyed. To his astonishment, when he reached the top he found a garden of roses and he picked a bouquet to bring back to the Virgin. After she had held the blooms in her arms for a short time she placed them in Juan's mantle. Juan felt that this time the roses would be proof enough for the archbishop of the truth of the miracle so he sped off to Zumárraga clutching the mantle full of flowers.

When the humble Indian finally gained admission to the austere presence of the archbishop, he knelt upon the floor at the feet of his highness and opened the ragged mantle. He and the archbishop were amazed to see painted on it, in all her tender beauty, the figure of the Virgin just as she had appeared to the Indian. The spies assigned to Juan verified his story of the roses, uncle Bernardino recovered as promised, and word of the miracle spread throughout the countryside. The archbishop was compelled to show the picture on the altar of the cathedral until a year later when a little shrine was built to the Christian Virgin on the hill of Tepeyac where once the Aztec goddess Tonantzín had reigned.

History has claimed that from that moment on the importance of the Virgin of Guadalupe was established, but later research shows that the cult was minor and scarcely sanctioned by the Church in the sixteenth and the early part of the seventeenth century. Most Franciscans claimed it to be idolatry trying to mask itself as Christianity. Thirty-eight years after the miracle, in 1570, the township had only a few people and the shrine only one priest. At that time the Spanish Catholic faith in Mexico had drifted into two factions. Indians were under the authority of friars and monks, with Creoles and Gachupines followers of the parish priests. This segregation made for much dissension and weakened the impact of the faith. In the 1620s Archbishop Pérez de La Serna was astute enough to see the olive-skinned Virgin of Guadalupe as an instrument that might help unify Spaniards and Indians. She could present a dramatic Mexican version of Catholicism that would be emotionally satisfying to all. The secular clergy grasped the opportunity to further the cult and Archbishop Pérez de La Serna systematically and forcefully pushed it as well. It was an uphill job until 1648 when a priest named Miguel Sánchez published *Imagen de La Virgen María de Dios de Guadalupe Milagrosamente Aparecida en La Ciudad of México* and started the cult rolling. This publication was the first of an avalanche of materials on the subject that included carvings, talismans and paintings that continue to the present day and which firmly established Nuestra Señora de Guadalupe as the first lady of Mexico and its most unique symbol of the faith.

3
Practical Nuns and Other Sisters

In the early 1600s the new city of Mexico built on the ruins of old Tenochtitlán became a boomtown, complete with color and crudity. As in the pre-conquest era, it teemed with Indians who worked for and supported the ruling class, which instead of their own Aztec nobility, had become a few thousand whites who composed government, clergy and high-level business. As the century wore on many of the charming waterways which had made the city so distinctive became filled with trash, although a pair of large reservoirs still embraced the metropolis. But there were enough canals so that canoe-commerce survived and the *chinampas* (floating islands) continued being sources of firewood, vegetables, cattle fodder and other produce. Here and there, sagging but picturesque bridges spanned pools that flooded in the rainy season and became stagnant pestholes in summer. Official buildings sprang up around the Zócalo, the central plaza; the archbishop's and viceroy's palaces stood side by side, competing with each other in opulence. The city boasted a prison and a half dozen hospitals; one for blacks and mestizos, another for Indians and, for the relative handful of *peninsulares* (Spaniards) and criollos, (Spaniards born in Mexico), there were four.

By mid-century there were many monasteries and convents in the city. The nunneries, whose basic function was to provide refuge for women who wanted to serve the Lord, were also havens for impoverished widows, unwanted maidens without dowries and females of fine family forced out of the marriage market by vanished virtue. Although the good sisters gave part of each day to the arts of embroidery and cooking, the greatest number of hours were spent on their knees, for Mexico was a city that needed much prayer. Prostitutes abounded and drunkards flourished; even the poor imbibed when they were lucky enough to find pesos for the pulque (a fermented drink made from the juice of the maguey cactus) that softened the rough edges of their dreary lives. Hovels and huge villas grew up side by side, displayed indiscriminately by the brilliant mountain sunlight. It enhanced the glitter of silver and jewels that encrusted the sedan chairs and carriages of the ruling class and highlighted the gold braid on the elegant livery of their black slaves. It clearly defined the pinched brown faces of the non-decorative conquered who acted as beasts of burden and performed stoop labor of all kinds.

Before 1640, when Spain still dominated Portugal, the importation of Africans into New Spain was facilitated by Portuguese slave traders. The estimate of the number of blacks, mulattoes, and Zambangos (Negro-Indians) has been as high as one hundred forty thousand with mulattoes outnumbering the rest three to one. Many mulattoes were descendants of the conquistadors and were proud of their ancestry. Pedro de Escobar, a soldier with Cortés during the conquest, married a mulatta, Beatriz de Palacios. She is written of as having performed the duties of a soldier, tending horses as well as wounded, standing watch, cleaning weapons and dispatching whatever other chores would have fallen to a male in her stead. The children of these alliances were high-spirited and tended to dominate the newly arrived Africans known as Bozals. The ratio of male imports to female was three to one so there was much mixing of black men and Indian women. Mexican residents of European blood were allowed to import *esclavas blancas* (white slaves). These were usually women destined for prostitution and included Moors, Berbers and Jewesses.

There were blacks who agitated their enslaved brethren, urging them to become runaways, and the countryside abounded with these Maroons as they were called. A leader sprang up among them by the name of Yanga, himself a runaway, an older man and former African chief. Yanga had many followers both male and female. In 1610 rumors of blacks' plots to kill the whites and take over the government abounded. The Viceroy, the Marqués de Salinas, ordered a force of six hundred soldiers to go in search of Yanga and his followers, but the expedition was unable to pry the chief and his group loose from their mountain stronghold and had to accept a compromise with the African leader. After this, blacks and mulattoes were seized and tortured in Mexico City but the inquisitors were unable to wring from them the elements of a sinister plot and peace was restored.

It was a temporary lull. The following year, 1611, there

were a number of incidents on the coast involving Maroons and in Mexico City the rumor spread that a black woman slave had been beaten to death, triggering a riot. It culminated in demonstrations by a Negro mob outside the viceroy's palace and an assault upon the house of the dead woman's owner. Thoroughly aroused now, the blacks decided to select a king and queen to lead them and they chose Pablo and María from the Portuguese West African colony of Angola. Having been unjustly accused of treachery in the past, this time they planned a genuine uprising to take place on Holy Thursday.

The plot was discovered and the leaders of all known black groups in Mexico were seized. The Inquisition tortured hundreds including mulattoes. The Spanish officials were so terrified of the black menace that they ordered all shops and public buildings closed tight including churches, a measure previously unheard of especially since Holy Week was coming up. Severe restrictions enacted against Negroes in the past and allowed to lapse were reimposed. These included curfews and prohibition of firearms, meetings of more than three persons, and attendance at fraternal organizations. Black women and mulattas were prohibited from wearing jewels, seductive clothing or fine fabrics. In the central plaza on May 2, 1612, crowds gathered for one of the spectacles put on by the Inquisition: Seven black women and twenty-nine black men were hanged with the usual display of severed heads exhibited on pikes afterwards. Soon crows picked out the bulging eyeballs and the scorching rays of the sun fried the skin until it was crisped and shredded.

It is an interesting comment upon the then status of people of color throughout the world that the Spanish colonies were considered much more humane in their treatment of Negroes than the Dutch, French or English. The children of black slave women or mulattas, if sired by white Spaniards, could purchase their liberty if they could drum up the going price. If married, male Negroes could buy their own freedom and do the same for their wives and children, if they could afford it. That so many Mexican Creole blacks did find the money was the result of being favored over the Indians by their masters. Negroes were seldom used for heavy labor, but were given choice jobs as foremen, overseers and armed bodyguards. Their greater height and assurance gave them a natural advantage, but the Spaniards, accustomed to blacks from Moorish times, were disposed by tradition to award them the pick of the jobs in their households as well as in the fields.

In the big cities of Puebla and Mexico, handsome black

women were first choice as mistresses for the rich. Forbidden by law to wear Indian or Spanish dress, these courtesans developed a flamboyant style of their own. Their costume was described at great length by an English traveler, Thomas Gage, who was also a Dominican friar with an eye for pulchritude and detail. He mentions silver petticoats trimmed with bands of gold or silver lace, gaily colored ribbons, sleeveless bodices that scarcely covered the breasts and a girdle of precious stones fastened round the waist. A mantilla of cobweb lace thrown casually over the head or bare shoulders plus jewels, especially pearls, encircling throat and wrist and dangling from ear lobes completed the costume. If the courtesans were clever and far-sighted, they could acquire money and property as well as jewels from their lovers.

Back in 1536, before the formal beginning of the Inquisition, Fray Juan de Zumárraga had tried five black women on charges of sorcery and occult practices in Mexico City. These were the first Negroes, male or female, to fall into the clutches of what would become the Holy Office. Some of the magic listed included chicken claws, chants that cast spells, rabbit's ears and signs, symbols and love potions concocted of mysterious ingredients. These were usually to aid in snaring a husband, ensuring his potency and guaranteeing his faithfulness, but were also valid to induce a master to give a slave her freedom. In an attempt to curb the excesses committed in the name of sorcery and magic, the royal government forbade the sale of certain chemicals used to make some of the more exotic formulas.

The only reform brought about by the edict was to cause practitioners to resort to everyday, easily obtainable items. One black woman was seized because she told fortunes with a handful of lowly beans, while a freedwoman, a mulatta, was charged with the use of the weed peyote to determine whether or not she was pregnant. The accurate prediction of ship arrivals, by what means we do not know, was enough to cause one black female to be called before the Inquisitors. Fortunately, the punishments for the crimes were not burning at the stake, although public beatings had to be painful and humiliating.

There were female slaves and mulattas who practiced the Hebrew faith. María de La Cruz, a slave, was tried for being a Jew and blasphemer. Juana del Bosque, a mulatta seamstress, although converted to Christianity in the auto-da-fé of 1646 was sent into exile. María Magdalena, another mulatta, had been previously tried by the Inquisition in Córdoba, Spain but was accused of having relapsed back into her old heretical ways.

Since she was dead and buried, the Holy Office in its wisdom and logic had to be satisfied with disinterring her bones and burning what was left of them. Mulatta seamstress Esperanza Rodríguez, widow of German-Jewish sculptor and carpenter Juan Baptista del Bosque of Guadalajara, Mexico, was jailed for six months then exiled. A mulatta who was not Jewish but was an unusually freethinker for the times was Juana Magdalena, born in Topatalcingo. Accused of heresy because she said she ate bread and wine at the mass and did not believe in hell, she was ordered, after repenting, to spend several years in a convent correcting her misconceptions of Christianity.

Nothing is all bad. Even the Inquisition had its milder moments. There is a recorded case of a Spanish master being denounced in 1574 for his inhumane treatment of a black woman. The court heard her testimony against her master as well as the testimony of other blacks who had witnessed the cruel deeds. The outcome of the trial is unknown. In a more conclusive case of clemency, a young mulatta woman was released from a charge of blasphemy after investigation revealed that she took the name of the Lord in vain because she was in great pain from a jar of hot oil spilled on her. The renunciation of God was the reason for the trial of a black slave woman in which the Inquisition shows up best of all. In the course of the *proceso* the slave's master and mistress were shown to be sadists. The master was accused of beating one of his slaves mercilessly before forcing a band of iron around her throat and dragging her off to church. The mistress was accused of having beaten another slave girl to death and of being unceasingly cruel. Although the woman slave was found guilty of the original charge of renunciation, the Inquisitors decided that her life was in danger if she remained with her owners. To ease her hard lot, she was given a change of Spanish masters. Let us hope that the new ones were better than the old.

To be fair to all concerned, there were a number of cases on record of Spaniard bringing Spaniard to justice for inhumane treatment of slaves. In one instance a gachupín was reported to the Inquisition for allowing boys to assault a Negress with sticks after she had been staked to the ground. Another was denounced for the sexual abuse of a mulatta girl and, in Pachuca, a Spanish wife denounced her husband because he had spoken against blacks having the right to marry.

In the closing years of the seventeenth century, Spaniards not only defended their slaves but, according to the records of the city of Puebla, were marrying them. Over twenty couples are listed in *La población negra* by Aguirre Beltrán, for the year 1690, of gachupín men and their intended wives. For example we have "Bartolomé Gómez (español) con Manuela de Medina (mulatta libre)." "Diego de Lizago (español) con Inés María (mulatta esclava)." "Bernardo de Torres Sarmiento (español) con Gertrudis Ramírez (mulatta)." And on and on. Almost all the alliances appear to have been between master and slave or ex-slave. The unions were being legalized because of pressure from the Catholic Church in Mexico in its fight against polygamy and a sincere desire to improve the lot of the disadvantaged. Also, the threat was held over the heads of the gentlemen that they would roast in eternal hell unless their mistresses became spouses sanctioned by law.

Black women were also immortalized in the legends of Mexico. Perhaps the most famous is that of the mulatta of Córdoba who accomplished what all prisoners of the Inquisition, no matter their color or sex, wished, hoped and prayed that they could do, too. There are no exact dates in connection with this lady of legend but it all took place more or less in the mid-seventeenth century. In the city of Córdoba in the state of Veracruz, Mexico there lived a mulatta of great fame and beauty who never seemed to age with the passage of time. Nobody knew who her parents were or anything about her past but the people of the town thought she was an *hechicera* (spell caster) and that her house was visited nightly by the devil. Many citizens claimed that when they passed by at midnight they saw a weird light seeping through doors and windows like a tremendous fire was burning inside, and yet smoke never billowed forth nor did the house burn down. Others claimed they had seen her flying over rooftops; black eyes snapping with satanic delight, ripe red lips curved in a devilish smile.

When she appeared in the city her beauty was such that all the young blades fell over each other in their haste to catch her attention. Not only did she ignore them but openly showed her disdain for the whole lot which gave rise to the gossip that her lover was none other than the prince of darkness and this was why she could not tolerate ordinary men. But this woman who stayed forever young also attended mass regularly and celebrated the holy days faithfully. She never turned away anyone who sought her help, caring for rich and poor alike and keeping watch at the bedside of the dying.

As the years went on the wonders attributed to her grew. She was often seen at different places at the same time. Some claimed to have seen her in Mexico City and Córdoba simultaneously, others in a cave, a hovel, or a modest home of hardworking unpretentious people. Young girls without sweethearts consulted her, and old girls without hopes of finding a sweetheart consulted her, as did doctors without patients, lawyers without cases, youths without fortunes and rich old men without youth. All came away happy and with their desires fulfilled. So great was the success of La Mulata de Córdoba with the seemingly impossible that to this day when one asks help with a very difficult project in Mexico it is the custom to say, "No soy La Mulata de Córdoba."

No one knows how long she lived and practiced her arts, but suddenly one day Córdoba was stunned by the news that La Mulata had been seized by the Inquisition and thrust into jail in Mexico City. All kinds of speculation ran rife starting with rumors that she had been denounced by a scorned lover, to witchcraft, to declarations that the Inquisitors had taken her because she refused to tell the location of an immense fortune in gold dust that she had hidden away in huge clay pots. It was the talk of the town for months; wherever people clustered on the streets or in drawing rooms the topic was sure to come up. But gradually, as with every wonder, gossip died down and the tale was almost forgotten with the years. Then something happened to bring it to life again.

The first news relayed from Mexico City was that La Mulata had been slated to appear in the next auto-da-fé complete with sanbenito, crown and green candle, but that when the jailer came to get her she flew past him and headed for Manila. The whole town was talking again and the subject was La Mulata. Eventually the "true" story filtered down from the capital. It was different from the original and much, much better. It seemed that when the jailer entered the miserable cell of La Mulata to take her before the tribunal he was amazed to see on one of the walls the outline of a ship drawn in charcoal. It was so lifelike he could almost imagine that its sails were billowing.

La Mulata, who stood there watching him, hand on hip, young and beautiful as ever, a tiny smile flicking over her red lips, said, "Jailer, can you tell me what this ship lacks?"

The jailer replied, "Unfortunately woman, perfect as it is, it can't move."

Turning her dark, mysterious glance in his direction, La Mulata then switched it to the ship saying, "But dear sir, if you really want to see it go, it will and very fast."

"How? Show me," said the jailer.

"Like this." With a snap of her fingers, La Mulata leaped into the ship and though it started slowly it rapidly picked up speed and disappeared through a corner of the jail carrying to freedom the beautiful lady who still hadn't aged a bit and, thanks to the story tellers of Mexico, never will.

Not only men, but also women of the wicked capital city, whether maids or mistresses, enjoyed gambling. Our roving reporter of the eighteenth century, Thomas Gage, recounts an incident when he was out strolling with a fellow friar. They were hailed from an open window by a lady of good birth, a perfect stranger, and invited inside to join her in a game of cards.

Gage also extols the skills of nuns in Oaxaca in preparing two native drinks, *atole* and foaming chocolate. The *atole* was made from young corn cooked with sugar. The chocolate was spiced with anise, hot chili peppers, sugar, cinnamon, cloves, almonds, orange blossoms, vanilla and *achiote*, a seed that yields red coloring. All were boiled together in water and to this elixir chocolate tablets were added. The tablets were made from cocoa beans ground into powder, heated until it formed a paste then poured into molds to harden. The good sisters were not only practical but practitioners of culinary art. The conclusion of the preparation was to beat the mixture with a *molinete* (little stick) and drink it while it still foamed. The tablets also provided excellent nourishment and were ideal for long journeys because a large number could be carried with little weight or space. They had been prepared for centuries by the native women of Mexico who thereby invented the first instant cocoa. Many nuns of the colonial period were of Indian ancestry and took their invention with them to the convents.

The order of the Discalced Carmelites was founded in 1616 by two intelligent, determined and no-nonsense nuns, Mariana de la Encarnación and Sister Inés de La Cruz. The latter was a forerunner of, and not to be confused with, the famous poet-nun Sor Juana Inés de La Cruz. Sisters Mariana and Inés started out as members of the Royal Convent of Jesus and Mary. Both musically gifted, they played the organ and strummed *rabeles* (ancient stringed instruments) in accompaniment to the plaintive and sometimes piquant little songs they sang for gentlemen of the clergy who dropped in for refreshment and entertainment. This kind of socializing was a common practice of Catholic clerics, as pointed out by Thomas Gage who said, "It is ordinary for the friars to visit their devoted nuns and to spend whole days with them hearing their musick, feeding on their sweetmeats." Some prelates were more likely than others to crave diversion, and when a new archbishop came to town, Fray García Guerra, an amiable and self-indulgent sort, the sisters found that he loved bullfights best but also ballads, food and drink. He visited them often.

Neither sister Mariana nor Inés was by nature frivolous. It had long been a dream of theirs to found a convent of the most severe, austere variety. Pegging the new archbishop as a man they could enlist in their cause if they plied him with enough of the good things in life, they lured him into thinking they were devoted to him and were waiting breathlessly for afternoon visits. It was partial truth because while they urged delicacies upon him and sang charming love songs, they tried to extract a promise from him to approve the new convent they wanted to found, and to grant them additional money to supplement funds they had already been given by working their charms upon a rich patron.

The worldly Fray García promised them nothing as he enjoyed their goodies but he did confide that he had hopes of becoming viceroy of Mexico and that, when he realized his ambition, he would approve the grant.

The two sisters did not let up on him. The dreams of the trio became a sort of chess game with the wily women on one side of the board and the equally wily archbishop on the other. The offerings of canapes and cookies were interspersed with constant pleas for help in getting the new convent underway, but no matter how much García oh'ed and ah'ed at the quality of the sweetmeats and drummed his pudgy fingers on the table in time to the tunes, his answer remained the same: "... when I become viceroy."

In the spring of 1611 it came to pass. Fray García Guerra was named viceroy as successor to don Luis de Velasco. The sisters prepared to start building but the funds he had set aside for the new convent were diverted instead to bullfighting, his favorite diversion. The deceitful archbishop-viceroy decreed that the spectacle should take place every Friday afternoon in a ring specially constructed within the palace grounds so that he could enjoy the sport in private.

Ominously, the first *corrida* was set to take place on Good Friday. No one dared voice disapproval except Sister Inés, who, seeing her chance to reprimand the promise-breaking Fray García, sent him a letter expressing shock that he wold permit such a vulgar spectacle to take place on the holy day commemorating the passion of Jesus. She was ignored. The show went on as scheduled. The next Friday though, just as the *corrida* was about to begin, the earth shook violently enough to postpone the event. The following Friday a severe quake was visited upon the city of Mexico during the bullfight and the grandstand and houses near the bullring collapsed. The archbishop-viceroy narrowly missed being killed by a piece of falling stone, but so confirmed an aficionado was he that he refused to cancel the weekly event.

García's term of office was marked by pomp, glitter and a number of close shaves. An acrobat swinging from a tall pole just missed the archbishop before falling dead at his feet. Seismic disturbances were followed by a total eclipse of the sun, showers of ashes and floods. The people spent a great deal of time on their knees in church. It seemed that sisters Inés and Mariana were not the only ones displeased with García, but heavenly powers as well. As though to confirm the opinion the official became very ill. In January of 1612 the archbishop-viceroy was so sick that he begged Sister Inés to pray for him and promised that if he recovered, he would at last fulfill his promise to give funds for the new convent.

He was disappointed. Being of a practical turn of mind and noting García's dreadful appearance, Sister Inés decided not to waste her time in prayer. She didn't go so far as to tell the foolish fellow that it served him right for putting *corridas* before convents, but she calmly and coolly advised her old friend to prepare to meet his maker and offer thanks to the Lord for the good life he had enjoyed. Having no choice but to take her advice he breathed his last on February 22, 1612. The unsentimental pair of nuns then turned their attention to more reliable sources of fund-raising and within four years opened the doors of the new convent.

The territory of new Spain was rapidly becoming a very mixed society. It included Portuguese (of whom many were Jews), a few French and Germans, Italians, Filipinos who along with blacks had been brought in as slaves, and free Chinese who became peddlers, barbers and bakers and who shared with all the other races involvement in crime. The power of Spain the mother country had declined. European scientists and philosophers such as the Jesuit-educated Frenchman, René Descartes, were substituting mathematics for magic and astronomy for astrology. The new thinkers were often in conflict with older church doctrine and the Inquisition tightened its hold by burning books and men alike, and forcing Mexican women to retreat three steps for every step forward.

In the year 1692 the country of Mexico began undergoing a series of dire events. The crops failed because of heavy rains and flooding and blight, called *chiahuitztli*, spread through wheat and barley fields as rapidly as plague spreads through people. Meat became almost nonexistent and the little that was available was as lean as Jack Spratt since the cattle had no place to pasture nor fodder to eat. Corn, the backbone of the Indian diet, was also in very scarce supply because of weather conditions and the rains were so heavy that many adobe houses dissolved back into the mud from which they were made. To add to the misery, there was an eclipse of the sun in August which brought on unnaturally cool weather and sent the populace to their knees in dread that the end of the world was in the offing. People were hungry and frightened and all of this laid the groundwork for the riot of 1692.

The disturbance is of particular note because the engineering of it was attributed to women. It was the custom for Indian women to make and sell tortillas in the main plaza of Mexico City. Because the wheat crop had failed there was a lack of bread so that the unleavened corn cakes were more in demand than ever. The female tortilla-makers, en masse, purchased their corn at night at the public granary and on Saturday evening of June 7, 1692, for the first time, there was not enough to go around. When the women heard this, they pressed closer to the officials, protesting the shortage vociferously. Knowing that officials often created false scarcities to drive up prices, they were also well aware that the wheat crop had failed but knew that there was still some of the resistant, enduring native corn. These were tough, seasoned street *vendedoras* (saleswomen), hard workers whose very existence and that of their families depended on their day to day struggle to make the only product that gave them sustenance and a few pesos with which to buy other necessities of life.

Since the angry crowd of women greatly outnumbered the handful of officials, the males began to panic as the viragos pressed in, shouting and screaming that they wanted corn. Losing his control completely, one of the attendants grabbed a whip and lashed out indiscriminately causing the infuriated females to draw back. But one *vendedora* refused to be intimidated and, shaking her fist belligerently insisted on being served. This so enraged the whipmaster that he struck her again and again about the head and shoulders, hitting a number of other women nearby.

The rest of the women cried out in protest as they bandaged the bleeding scalp of their sobbing cohort. Someone suggested that they march to the palace of the archbishop, Francisco de Aguiar y Seijas, the woman-hater, and demand to have their complaints heard that corn was being withheld and that they, the women, were being mistreated. Hoisting the injured *vendedora* onto their backs, they marched the length of the public square to the archbishop's palace. There, as was to be expected from this quaint gentleman who so detested the sight of women, they were turned away without seeing his excellency or being able to air their grievances. Determined to reach someone in authority the mob, now numbering several hundred, turned and started for the viceroy's palace unaccompanied by a single male Indian. They stormed the first floor of the royal palace but were prevented by guards from getting upstairs into the chambers occupied by the Conde de Galve and his wife.

Still seeking justice, the redoubtables turned around once more and headed back to the archbishop's. By screaming at the guards that the injured woman they carried was suffering a miscarriage from the beating she'd sustained and was about to die, a messenger was sent to the frightened prelate hiding out on the second floor of his palace, all a-quiver at the thought that he might be forced to see, not one woman but two hundred of them. The guards returned with the less than satisfactory word from Archbishop Seijas that he was advising the men in the public granary to be more compassionate toward the Indian women. This weak-as-water action did not please our heroines. By now they had gathered even more irate females, many of whom expressed their noisy disdain in colorful language and unladylike gestures from the gutters. Still hoping they could force an authority to deal justly with them, they returned for a final try at the viceroy's palace.

They did not succeed that night in seeing any head of church or state, but the next day Viceroy Galve, fearing the continuance of the commotion, sent Don Juan de Escalante y Mendoza, a public prosecutor of the criminal court, to oversee the officials who distributed the corn to make sure they used proper restraint when dealing with the *vendedoras* who came to purchase. This worked until the rations ran out, when once more the women began protesting and once more violence erupted. One of them was trampled upon until dead. Now with a greater uproar than ever before, the women poured out of the granary carrying the body of their fallen comrade. This time they were joined by Indian, Chinese, black and mulatto males and a ragtag, bobtail group of *léperos*, teen-age beggars of European descent who were disease-ridden. It had become a truly dangerous mob that streamed back to the plaza and the palaces of the archbishop and viceroy.

There is one small footnote to this chapter in the history of Mexican women which is bound to give satisfaction to the entire sex. In a moment of bravado our woman-hating Archbishop Aguiar y Seijas decided to show his face in the plaza in hopes that his venerable presence might soothe the crowd and stop the riot. Sending his coach ahead to clear the way, he walked behind it with the cross held high in his hands for all to see, accompanied by a number of supporters from the high nobility. The archbishop did not get far. When he saw that one of his coachmen had been knocked off his perch and was sprawled senseless in the street from a rock thrown by the irreverent crowd, the archbishop turned tail and ran back to his safe and celibate palace without regard for his dignity.

In this way the riots and lootings of 1695 began which resulted in the burning of the viceroy's palace, the *cabildo*, (town hall) where bound books and judicial records were kept, the public jail and granary. The shouts of "Down with the viceroy and the *corregidor*, down with bad government and gachupines" were a preview of things to come in the next century when the Mexicans struggled to free themselves from Spain.

When a *mexicana* appears in an outfit consisting of a white, puffed-sleeve blouse with a square neck banded by embroidery, a *rebozo* (long, narrow scarf) tossed over her shoulders, a full skirt whose upper section is girdled with a band of green or yellow flannel followed by red flannel reaching to the ankles, and silk stockings with pink slippers, she is wearing one of the national costumes known as the *china poblana*. There are variations which depend upon age, wealth and custom. Some wear a large bow atop the head, others make two long braids of hair interwoven with bright-colored ribbon then fastened across the head in a sort of crown. Many wear high-heeled red or green shoes. Gold and silver spangles, glass beads and fake pearls are sometimes worked into the embroidery. *Charras* (cowgirls) and folk singers add a felt sombrero with a wide brim and an actress may employ a variety of colors other than red and green. Those most likely to wear the traditional outfit are dancers who perform the Jarabe Tapatío known in English as the Mexican hat dance. Literally translated, the term *china poblana* means a Chinese girl from the city of Puebla where the costume originated. The odd title goes back to a legend concerning a princess. The legend has some basis in fact; how much is anybody's guess.

One version states that in the latter part of the seventeenth century there was a Hindu princess named Mirrha whose father was ruler of the kingdom of Indra Prastha. When the Turks attacked the country, Mirrha was sent along with other members of the household to a seaport town where her father thought she would be safe. Unfortunately, pirates frequently put in at this port and one day when the princess went out walking with her brother and their servants she was kidnapped by the captain of a Portuguese ship. He confiscated her fancy clothes and valuable jewels and gave her a gunny sack to wear just like the rest of his prisoners. Later on he put in at Cochin China, the area known to us in the present day as Vietnam. Here, some Jesuit priests came aboard and baptized all the captives, as was the custom, and changed Princess Mirrha's name to Catarina de San Juan.

When the ship stopped in Manila, the princess was sold as a domestic servant to a Filipino family. Mexicans of means frequently bought household slaves and a merchant who arrived in Manila had been given an order by a Captain Miguel Sosa and his wife to purchase a healthy, attractive girl for domestic service in Puebla. Able to strike a good bargain with Mirrha's Filipino masters, the merchant acquired her and took her back to Mexico in his boat.

Catarina's new owners were pleased with the exotic creature who was virtuous as well as beautiful. Here the tale becomes garbled with our Hindu maiden being described by a Father Aguila as having a "graceful elegance of body" along with light skin and blond hair, which sounds more like a misplaced Anglo-Saxon than a captive Hindu. But some of these old tales require stretches of the imagination carried almost to the breaking point.

Catarina's masters betrothed her to a Chinese slave named Domingo Súarez who was called El Chino by his owners. After the marriage, Mirrha-Catarina, because of her husband's race, became known as Catarina, La China Poblana. Missing the grandeur of her former life, it is said that she tried to create a costume as elegant as those she wore as a girl. Having only Mexican fabrics to work with, she designed the dress worn by the *chinas* of Puebla. The state museum exhibits an outfit which they claim to have been Catarina's; but it was found in an old wardrobe trunk filled with clothes worn by actors of the nineteenth century, so its origin is doubtful.

Very pious and given to much church-going, Catarina became a visionary who talked with saints and helped the poor with their illnesses and problems. Her marriage to El Chino was not the happiest because Princess Mirrha Catarina San Juan de Suárez, the original *china poblana*, felt herself superior to her mate and refused to consummate the union with a man she now considered a commoner.

During the conquest and for a time thereafter, females had been frequently pressed into service and given roles traditionally assigned only to males. Fighting side by side with soldiers during the Spanish-Aztec wars, they often got their chance to show what they could do. Later, when conditions were still unsettled we know that they started businesses and successfully managed haciendas when lovers or husbands died or were disabled. Although women could not hold office, they could hold sway over decision-making men and their influence, when they cared, or dared, to exert it, was great. At the same time the female had to bear and tend children, run households, do stoop labor and nurse aged and ailing relatives and field hands.

By mid-seventeenth century, New Spain was settling back into the old pattern of "get thee behind walls and bury yourself solely in your duties as wife, mother or nun." The crisis had passed. There were enough men to take over worldly affairs which were often considered basic reading and writing, let alone politics, and women were completely excluded from science, literature, or any other upper level studies. Into this retrogressive, anti-female intellect atmosphere, a woman of genius had the bad luck to be born--a woman destined for tragedy because of the era, but a woman who would inspire as many others in her way as the Virgin of Guadalupe had in hers. Her name was Sor Juana Inés de La Cruz.

Moctezuma Xocoyotzin II, last of the Great Lords of the Aztecs. Described by Bernal Díaz as "well proportioned, slender ... showed ... tenderness and gravity."

Hernán Cortés, the greedy conquistador who Moctezuma mistook for the Aztec's revered, white-skinned Quetzalcoatl (the fair god).

La Malinche (Doña Marina), whose beauty, brains and bedfellow, Hernán Cortés, continue to make her a controversial figure in Mexican history.

La Malinche acting as interpreter with Cortés and an Aztec messenger. (Detail from a drawing in the "Atlas," a sketchbook of the era.)

Pedro de Alvarado, whose lack of wisdom caused "noche triste" (night of sorrow) in which thousands of Aztecs and Spaniards were slaughtered.

Codex Mendoza

New Spain's first viceroy after the conquest, Don Antonio de Mendoza, ordered the Codex done by a *tlacuilo,* a painted book artist. So that the Spanish monarch could understand the Codex, a Catholic priest-translator who spoke Nahuatl wrote copious notes of explanation in Spanish on the pictographs.

In the Codex women appear with two tufts of hair above their foreheads except for little girls and brides. The rectangular pin on the *huipil* (tunic) also always appears on the female. As in other societies of the era, Aztec daughters were primarily taught household chores.

The mother is showing her three-year-old the spindle. In the center is the single tortilla that the girl receives as a daily ration. The *comalli* (baking stone) for Aztec corn bread measured close to a foot in diameter. Accompanied by beans, wild game or fish, the diet was nourishing. The symbol near the mother's mouth indicates that she is talking--possibly explaining what the strange object is for. She holds a handful of cotton or wool fibers.

The girl has grown and the mother is demonstrating manipulation of the spindle.

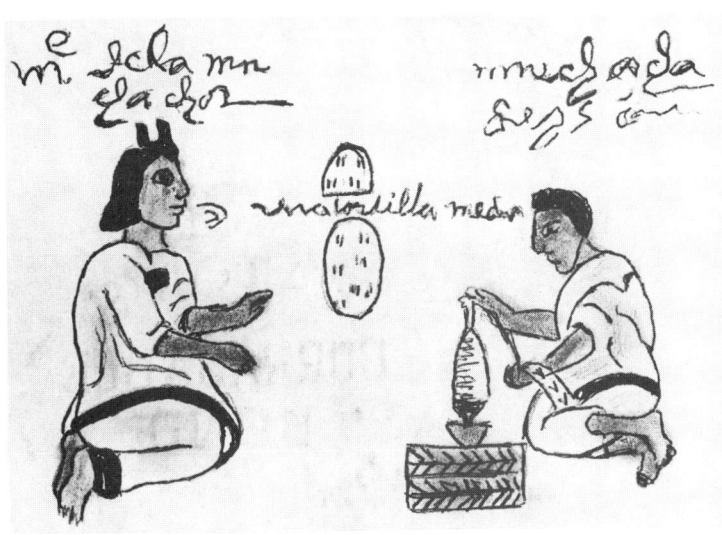

The spindle is in use by the daughter although, because of the speech symbol, the mother is still presumably giving instructions. The girl now seems deft enough and old enough to merit a tortilla and a half.

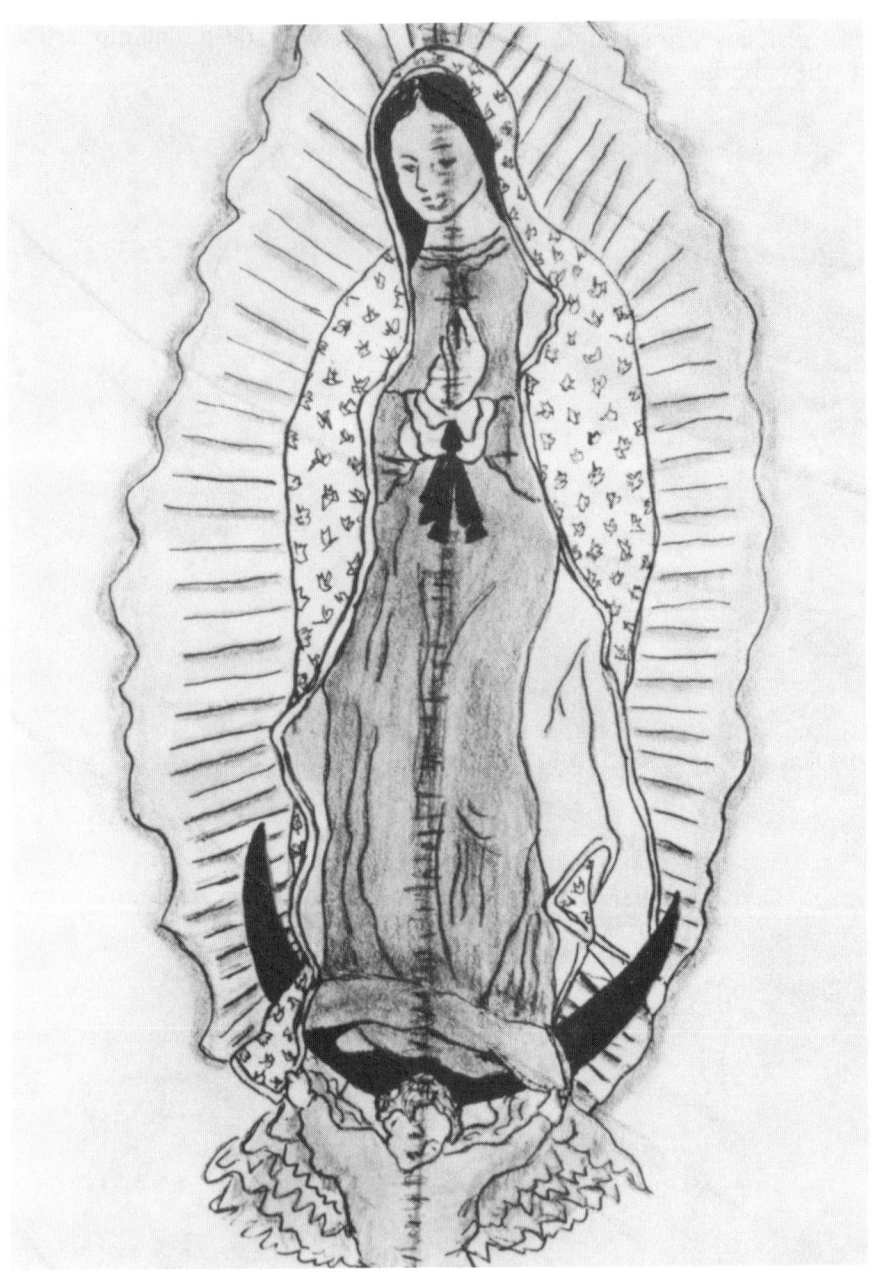

Our Lady of Guadalupe, who performed a miracle for humble Juan Diego in thanks for the bouquet of roses he placed in her arms.

Carlos Sigüenza y Góngora, the brilliant scholar and man of the cloth who befriended Sor Juana Inés de la Cruz.

Sor Juana Inés de la Cruz (La Decima Musa) painstakingly accumulated a large library. These books became her children, her lovers, her passion.

Agustín de Iturbide, handsome emperor of Mexico. He was a lover of the seductive "La Güerra Rodgriguez," who ignored rules and lived as she pleased.

Josefa Ortiz, beloved heroine. She would not renounce her liberal views to gain freedom from prison, but did renounce her son when he joined Iturbide's royalists.

José María Morelos, priest-general, who fought for freedom from Spain. He was executed December 22, 1815, a sacrifice to the bloody war of independence.

Margarita Maza de Juárez, whose courage, determination and faith brought her and her children through hardship and sorrow that finally ended in triumph.

Benito Juárez. The Mexican congress awarded him the title "El Benemérito" (honored patriot) and declared his birthday, March 21, a national holiday.

Austrian Archduke Maximilian and Belgian Princess Carlota, foreigners who became rulers of Mexico, landing at Veracruz. The crowds were an artist's dream.

Francisca Escandón y Landa, lady in waiting. Her husband, Antonio Escandón, was among those appointed to investigate Maximilian's qualifications for emperor.

Concepción Lizardi del Valle, lady in waiting. Count del Valle, her husband, was Grand Chamberlain of the staff that accompanied Empress Carlota to Paris.

Princess Agnes zu Salm Salm. Among this American woman's astounding activities was an attempt to rescue Emperor Maximilian from execution.

4
La Decima Musa

The teacher stared in disbelief at the child confronting her and surreptitiously crossed herself. One could never tell what weird or wicked spirit might possess the body of the precocious three-year-old. It could be an ancient savant or, and she hated to so much as think it because the girl's mother was a friend, one of the imps of Lucifer himself. It was otherworldly, the manner in which this angelic looking youngster, with the big melting brown eyes and thick, bronze hair that hung almost to her waist, had risen without hesitation or timidity and read off the lesson of the day far better than any of the older pupils including her sister. Now she was demonstrating her skill at handwriting, the tiny fist, soft as a folded rose petal, clasped the quill with authority and delineated large, well-formed letters.

For a while the little girl had come to school with her sister, sitting quietly on the bench alongside María Josefa, not saying a word. Then, one day, she tugged at the teacher's skirt and said, "My mother wants me to have lessons in reading and writing, too, just like my sister."

The teacher, herself a young person, empathized and knew that children like to pretend they are part of the grown-up world, so she said, "Very well," with a smile and promptly forgot the incident.

Now, only a short time later, this little girl was demonstrating what she'd absorbed from an instructor who had never been aware that she was giving lessons. Twenty-six years later, this same teacher would recall her first awesome contact with the genius of the child who would be known to history as *La Decima Musa* (the tenth muse). Later, when the girl had become the learned nun, Sor Juana Inés de La Cruz, she would write of the incident.

"Seeing that lessons were being given fired me with such a desire to learn to read that it seemed like a good idea to tell the teacher that my mother had ordered that I be given lessons."

This extraordinary being who was destined to be consumed all her short life with a passion for learning was born Juana Inés de Asabaje Ramírez de Santillana on November 12, 1651. The location was the hacienda San Miguel Nepantla not far from the town of Amecameca in the province of Chalco. The natural beauty of the two magnificent volcanoes, Popocatepetl and Ixtaccihuatl with their glittering peaks, dominated the verdant countryside. Beside the deep arroyos and crystalline streams *tamemes* (Indian porters) ran, bent double under the weight of hundred-pound loads. Frightening legends abounded and there were picaresque tales of wayfarers and adventurers who braved the rutted country roads en route to the fabled city of Mexico which lay some forty miles distant.

Juana was christened December 2, 1651 in the town of Chimalhuacan-Chalco, called Chimal by the local people. The ceremony took place in the simple, austere Dominican convent of Santo Domingo. The records of the church show that she was baptized "hija de la iglesia; fueron sus padrinos Miguel Ramírez y Beatriz Ramírez" (daughter of the church; Miguel and Beatriz Ramírez godparents). The Ramírez's were her mother's cousins.
For Juana to have been designated "a daughter of the church" without her parents being named indicates, according to the customs of the times, that she was illegitimate. How it came about that her parents did not marry is unknown. Her father was Don Pedro Manuel de Asbaje y Vargas, a member of the lesser and poorer nobility of Guipúzcoa in the Basque region of Spain. He went to the new world seeking adventure and fortune as had so many before him. In Mexico he met the criolla Isabel Ramírez whose parents were of the hidalgo class and had also emigrated from Spain. Isabel was one of the eleven daughters of Don Pedro Ramírez de Santillana. In those days no man, especially a Spanish gentleman would marry a girl without a dowry. It is said that it was not unusual in good families for liaisons to be formed that were considered honorable even without legal ties. Perhaps Juana's parents had one of these arrangements. Certainly Isabel's father would have found it difficult to provide adequate marriage portions for all eleven of his daughters.

For the first three years of her life, Juana's family lived at her grandfather's hacienda at Nepantla. History tells us that Don Pedro Ramírez was not well off. Perhaps he was not, considering the fortunes amassed from silver mines and huge *estancias* (ranches); but he must have been a man of culture and have had some means because Juana tells us that the sight of her grandfather's library inspired her with the desire to learn how to read. Although the first printing press in the new world was established in Mexico City in 1536 it was still not easy nor inexpensive in the 1600s to amass enough books to form a library. Books imported from Europe cost three times as much as one printed in Mexico. The only volume that remains from the shelves of Don Pedro Ramírez is entitled "Illustrium Poetarum Flora" signed with the initials J.H.S. published in Latin and written by Octavio Mirandola in 1590. Juana kept it with her all her life. There are indications that Juana Inés' father managed for a time Hacienda San Miguel Nepantla where the *casita* (little house) still stands in which the famous nun was born. When the family moved to Hacienda Panoayan, not far from the town of Amecameca and also owned by her grandfather Don Pedro Ramírez de Santillana, the other Don Pedro (Manuel de Asbaje), her father, seems to pass out of her life.

Poems like the following intimate that the young woman was hurt by illegitimacy.

El no ser de padre honrado
fuera defecto a mi ver
si, como recibí el ser
de él, yo se lo hubiera dado

Not being from an honorable father
should be my defect.
As I see it, I received his being
So I have given him that dishonor.*

(* Translation by Mexican American poet-artist José Antonio Burciaga)

These were bitter lines pouring from her heart through her pen; but records uncovered from the two convents in which she later served indicate that she either was legitimate or else deliberately lied. This hardly seems in character nor would it have been of benefit to her since such information was kept in confidence. But Juana Inés could also have been unaware of her illegitimacy until someone, like her Aunt María, with whom she did not get along, told her the truth out of spite, or envy of her beauty and brains. Then later, fearing that illegitimacy might cause problems with her highly desired admittance to the convent, she could have justified the evasion in her own mind because it was for a good cause.

The following excerpts are from convent documents quoted in *Mexico Viejo*, by Luis González Obregon.

Sunday, August 14, 1667 Convent Santa Teresa.

> "*Recibiose para Religiosa a Juana Inés de La Cruz, hija legitima de Don Pedro Desauaje y de Isabel Ramires su muger, es, natural desta nueva Espana...*"

And from the archives of San Jerónimo, the second convent that Juana entered, dated February 24, 1669:

> "*Yo soror Juana Inés de la Chruz higa legitima de don Pedro de Asabaje y bargas machuca y de Isabel rramires...*"

Both documents state that Juana is the legitimate daughter of her parents and the second is confirmed by Juana's signature. At first glance it may seem that the documents refer to fathers with two different names. In those days spelling was not standardized and each writer gave his own interpretation of what his ear had heard. If the two names are read aloud it is clear that they are one and the same. If these records are true and the church records misleading concerning her baptism, perhaps her father's early disappearance from her life was enough to embitter the sensitive child. Documents still to be found may also shed more light in the future.

Much that we know about the childhood of this prodigy comes from her autobiographical sketch. She tells us that when she was six or seven years old she heard that there was a university in the city of Mexico where science could be studied. She bothered her mother constantly with requests to be sent to this school. When Doña Isabel explained that women did not attend the university, the spirited child declared she would wear men's clothes and go anyway. Even at this tender age she displayed her variety of interests. She felt an avid curiosity for all knowledge and, like Leonardo da Vinci, to whom she has been compared, wanted to study astronomy, biology, ancient and living languages, mathematics, music, drawing and painting. That she succeeded is testimony to her iron will and tremendous intellect. Finding that women were not allowed within the sacred precincts of the institution of higher learning, she studied on her own.

Of her remarkable self-discipline she tells us that when she set herself the task of learning a particular subject within a certain period, she cut off a number of inches of her hair and declared to herself that she must master the lessons by the time it grew back or forfeit more of her crowning glory. This was a terrible sacrifice for a beautiful young girl to make because abundant hair worn long, loose and flowing was the height of fashion for the times. She also tells us that when she was a little girl, one of the superstitions of the countryfolk was that eating cheese made people stupid. She gave it up at once.

Among the house servants at her grandfather's hacienda in Panoayan were seven Negro slaves. The oldest, forty-year-old Catalina, was probably nursemaid to Juana and her sister. There was also a mulatta named Francisca who had four children: María, eight years; Beatriz, six; Matías, four; and one-year-old José. The two oldest girls would have been right in age as playmates for Juana Inés and her sister María Josefa. A brilliant, impressionable child like Juana would absorb much from those around her. Most blacks in the new world were recently enough arrived not to have lost their musical heritage. African influence in rhythm and beat could have enhanced the development of Juana's poetic ear.

When she was seven she wrote her first poem, a *loa* (dramatic verse in praise of a special event) for a Corpus Christi festival, for which she won a book as a prize. Her career was launched. No doubt she was becoming aware of her abilities and the awe with which grown-ups regarded her. She must have been an attractive child because the portraits of her that remain, although all were painted after she became a nun, show a slender woman with a sensitive, heart-shaped face, large dark eyes framed in curving brows and hands with long tapering fingers. She was spoken of as a "radiant beauty" and her classic features aglow with the keenness of her mind prove it to be an appropriate description.

When Juana was eight years old she was sent to Mexico City to live with her Aunt María, her mother's sister, who was married to Juan de Mata, known as a man of property. It was in this house that Juana Inés realized one of her greatest ambitions. She was allowed to receive instruction in Latin from Martín de Olivas. Her professor did not make much money because in twenty lessons his pupil had mastered the subject. The little girl brought her whole intellect to bear upon the language because, until she was fluent in it, many texts of the day were closed to her since the greatest number were written in Latin. Aside from this we know very little about the next four years of her life.

We can deduce from a comedy-drama that she wrote later called, *Los empeños de una casa* (the obligations of a home) that she did not get along too well with her aunt, for in the play she complains of mothers-in-law, relatives and aunts. It would not be hard to imagine that Tía María may have resented the brains and beauty of this prodigy-niece and the prodigy, gaining fame daily, was not so easy to live with either. It might have been thrown up to Juana Inés more than once that she was illegitimate and living on the bounty of her relatives. Some of the memories must have been painful or at least unpleasant because the adult Sor Juana leaves these years blank when she writes of her childhood.

The rulers of Mexico after the conquest were nobles sent from Spain and given the title of Viceroy. In the summer of 1664 when Juana Inés was not yet thirteen years old, the new Viceroy, Don Antonio Sebastián de Toledo, and his wife the marquesa, Doña Leonor Carreto, arrived in Mexico City. These two people were to become very important in the life of the young woman. When the marquesa died in Tepeaca in 1674, the poet-nun immortalized her in three sonnets written after death called *Amorous of Laura's Loveliness*, Laura being the familiar name by which Juana called her friend Leonor. The Viceroy was an able administrator but had the reputation of being a gentleman who was generous to a fault, dipping into the treasury often and pulling out a fistful of money to lavish upon his brilliant court. Accused of being profligate, nevertheless, it was he and his wife who opened the portals of recognition for Juana. Also, the Marquesa was an educated woman who had a great interest in literature and poetry.

The regulations in those days as laid down by Spain permitted the viceroy of a Spanish-owned country to invite outstanding children and grandchildren of Creoles of good family to live at court so that they might learn proper etiquette and have the advantage of a fine education. With a limited number of openings, the competition was heavy. Brought to the attention of the Viceroy by her family, the thirteen-year-old genius and beauty was immediately invited to make her residence at the royal palace. The Mexican rulers fell in love with her and made her a lady-in-waiting with the special title created exclusively for her by the marquesa: *muy querida de la virreina* (dearly beloved of the señora viceroy).

The royal palace where Juana Inés went to live had been originally constructed by Hernán Cortés who built it on the sites of houses that had been owned by Montezuma. Bought by the crown in 1562, it was enlarged and improved then designated the royal residence but it also serviced the crown's business and legal affairs. The building faced the *plaza mayor* (the main square) and was a huge edifice complete with royal audience chambers, courts of law and endless salons. The salon of the judges, most lavish of all, boasted portraits of the twenty-four rulers of Mexico and a copy of a portrait of Charles V by Titian.

Juana's eyes must have opened in wonder when she first saw the living quarters of the viceroy and his court. The *salon de comedias* where plays were given was the first theatre in the Americas. Its walls were painted with landscapes of mountains and other pastoral scenes typical of Mexican terrain, an unusual thing in colonial art which almost always depicted religious subjects. The spacious balcony that went with the quarters of the marquesa was elaborately carved with cherubs, semi-draped female torsos and coats of arms. The marquesa and her ladies-in-waiting escaped to it as often as they could, away from the incessant ceremony and chitchat of the court, stealing a few breaths of fresh air and watching the passing scene down below.

Shortly after coming to live at the palace, young Juana found herself a sensation. Forty professors deemed the top authorities in their respective fields of mathematics, science, literature, history, theology, etc. were invited to query her on all subjects. Imagine the excitement of the thirteen-year-old upon hearing this news. Her dear friend and mentor, the Marquesa de Mancera, along with her husband the viceroy would be present at the scholastic inquisition. We can imagine Juana Inés coming for a last inspection to the chambers of the marquesa before proceeding to the great salon. The court ladies in Mexico City eagerly awaited the arrival of each ship bearing the beautiful fabrics they had ordered from Spain accompanied by drawings of the newest modes in Madrid. Today Juana was decked out in her most recently completed outfit, one she had never worn before which was selected for her by the marquesa, who had impeccable taste. The outfit had a v-shaped black velvet bodice drawn tight over the bosom, enormous puffed blue satin sleeves bound here and there with ribbon, bare shoulders and a full-flaring skirt of rich, peach-colored brocade. The garment was based upon a copy of a popular painting in Madrid called the *Maids of Honor* by the famous painter Velásquez. Juana's abundant hair was arranged in soft waves that fell to her shoulders and was pinned back off her forehead on one side by a gold hair ornament decorated with pearls and turquoise which matched her long dangling earrings.

"How handsome you look, *hijita* (little daughter). You are even prettier than the Velásquez painting," the marquesa said as she stepped forward and stroked a loose tendril of shining brown hair off the forehead of her protégé. "Are you frightened, *mi amor*?"

"A little," the young woman replied, but there was no tremor in her voice and no tremble in the firm fingers that clasped the hand of the marquesa as they turned toward the door. Walking down the corridor with its high stone arches and thick columns, Juana wondered how well she would acquit herself. She was aware that the judges would not be likely to go easy on her, but quite the contrary because precocious females were always suspect. She realized as well that there were those at court who would like to see her fail, or at least do poorly. The paint on the faces of many of the court ladies was not nearly thick enough to hide the lines of jealousy when they observed the favorite. Juana Inés fared better with the gentlemen because most of them ignored her brains while delighting in her beauty.

Entering the star chamber she said a quick prayer when she saw the forty solemn and learned professors staring at her. She had experienced very little formal instruction in her brief life, her only school attendance had been at the "Amiga" elementary school in the pueblo of Amecameca for a few years. The greatest part of what she knew had been acquired by devouring book after book, then sorting and storing the knowledge in her prodigious memory. Every subject interested her and she retained details because she loved learning for its own sake. Her elders always emphasized her poetic ability because that seemed to be the most acceptable thing for a woman to excel in, but science and mathematics were equally dear to her heart.

She glanced across the room where the Viceroy Mancera and his wife sat side by side upon their thrones. The viceroy with a slight nod of his head for the judges and a brief smile for her indicated that the questioning should begin. Taking a deep breath, Juana Inés gave her first answer. How well she did with the savants is a matter of record. Thirty years later Viceroy Mancera said of the occasion that the downy-cheeked young woman had handled herself, "a la manera de un galeón real que se defiende de unas pocas chalupas que lo embisten" (in the way a royal galleon might defend itself against a horde of attacking canoes).

Spanish poetry of the era was often stilted and flowery with endless play upon words to the point where meaning was missing and contrived cleverness all important. The poets of colonial Mexico were greatly influenced by it and Juana Inés shows traces of this Baroque style but uses it more sparingly and therefore more effectively. Here are some examples of her work.

En perseguirme mundo, que interesas?
En que te ofendo, cuando sólo intento
poner bellezas en mi intendimiento
y no mi entendimiento en las bellezas

Yo no estimo tesoros ni riquezas;
y así, siempre me causa mas contento
poner riquezas en mi pensamiento
que no mi pensamiento en las riquezas.

Yo no estima hermosura que, vencida,
es despojo civil de las edades,
ni riqueza me agrada fementida,
teniendo por mejor en mis verdades,
consumir vanidades de la vida
que consumir la vida en vanidades.

You pester me world, why do I interest you?
How do I offend you when I only intend
To bring beauty into my thought
And not put all my thought upon beauty

I don't value treasure nor money
And so it always makes me happier
To put riches into my mind
Than to have my thoughts dwell upon riches.

I don't value good looks that waste away,
politely despoiled by time,
nor does the treachery of wealth appeal to me,
I think it much better in all truth,
To burn the vanity out of life
Than to have life consumed by vanity.

It was during the next two years at court that the young woman wrote many of her impassioned love lyrics. Although she speaks the names of a host of men in these poems--Fabio, Celio, Silvio, Febo, Feliciano, Lisardo--no one knows who they were, if she actually fell in love with one or more of them, or if, indeed, they even existed. Some interpreters favor the unrequited love theory; others feel that this poetry stemmed from the same awakening that has provoked lyrics from adolescents throughout the centuries because they are in love with the very idea of love. The theme of having the wrong man in love with her and she in love with someone else runs through many of these court poems. These verses are typical.

> *Feliciano me adora y le aborrezco;*
> *Lisardo me aborece y yo le adoro;*
> *por quien no me apetece ingrato,lloro*
> *y al que me llora tierno, no apetezco.*
>
> *A quien más me desdora, el alma ofrezco,*
> *a quien me ofrece víctimas, desdoro;*
> *desprecio al que enriquece mi decoro,*
> *y al que le hace desprecios, enriquezco.*
>
> *Si con mi ofensa al uno reconvengo,*
> *me reconviene el otro a mí, ofendido*
> *y a padecer de todos modos vengo.*
>
> *pues ambos atormentan mi sentido;*
> *aquéste, con pedir lo que no tengo;*
> *y aquel, con no tener lo que le pido.*

> Feliciano adores me and I detest him;
> Lisardo detests me and I adore him;
> Whatever ungrateful man doesn't yearn for me I cry for
> And whoever yearns for me tenderly I have no use for.
>
> Whoever dishonors me the most I offer my soul to,
> Whoever offers himself to me as victim I dishonor;
> I disdain the man who respects my reputation,
> And whoever sullies my reputation I respect.
>
> If I offend one with reprimands,
> the other, offended, reprimands me
> so that in the end I'm the one who suffers in every way.

Thus both of them wound my sensibilities
One by asking for what I lack
and the other by lacking what I ask for.

Many more of the poems of the budding young poet are in this vein: *Al que ingrata me deja* (He Who Ungratefully Leaves Me); *Silvio, yo te aborrezco* (Silvio, I Hate You); *Hombres necios* (Foolish Men). The love-hate relationship with the opposite sex is very pronounced.

There is one man of whom we know a great deal who exerted tremendous influence upon Juana throughout her short life. His name was Don Carlos de Sigüenza y Góngora. After she became a nun, he collaborated with her on one of her plays, was her friend and confidant, helped direct her studies and delivered the *elogio fúnebre* (funeral oration) when she died. They were both renaissance people, although born a century later than the full flowering of the period in Europe. Versatility, enlightenment, the inquiring mind, a desire to investigate a variety of subjects, even good looks were shared by them.

Sigüenza y Góngora was born in 1645 in Mexico City. He came from an illustrious family and was the nephew of Luis de Góngora y Argote, the famous and controversial Spanish poet (1561-1627) whose involved Baroque style bordered on the unintelligible and was imitated disastrously by so many Spanish and Latin American poets.

At age fifteen, Sigüenza y Góngora joined the Society of Jesus and took his first vows in the school at Tepozotlán in 1662. In August of 1667 he either left the Jesuits or was expelled and a few years later became chaplain in the Hospital de Amor de Dios. Mathematics, astronomy and physics were his forte although he was also learned in language, philosophy and Mexican-Indian history, collecting many antiquities and manuscripts that contributed to the knowledge of pre-Hispanic tribes. His poetry was mediocre but his prose was excellent. Only a dozen or so volumes of his total output were published because of financial difficulties and many of his historical works unfortunately have been lost.

Juana and Carlos Sigüenza y Góngora may have first met at court where Viceroy Mancera and his wife gathered talented youth. She would have been thirteen or fourteen, he, nineteen or twenty. Although they were close friends throughout Sor Juana's life, there is no evidence to show that they were ever lovers. Yet it is not beyond the realm of reason that the beautiful adolescent could have been strongly attracted to this intellectual young man of the cloth whose mental and physical attributes measured up to hers. To fall in love with a cleric in seventeenth century Mexico was not only unwise but unthinkable. We can be sure that if Juana felt this kind of attraction to the youth her first instinct would have been to suppress it. Subconsciously, her second instinct might have been to take the veil for harboring such unseemly emotions. She could not have known at the time that Sigüenza y Góngora would remain in Mexico City and that eventually she would see more of him by becoming a nun.

The two years that Juana Inés spent at court were productive ones. Whatever the occasion, she wrote poetry in honor of it be it the birthday of her patron, the marquesa, or a religious festival. She composed many sonnets and lyrics and continued her studies in other fields. Surrounded by love and attention from her sponsors, petted and made much of by a slew of courtiers, able to satisfy her thirst for learning, what made her, in the midst of glory and comfort, suddenly decide to become a nun? Speculation is endless and the reasons were probably many, including the thought of the walls of matrimony closing down around her, possibly with a man she didn't care for, and the tasks of a wife and mother which would curb, if not eliminate, her beloved writing and research. There is some evidence to show that her illegitimacy and penniless state figured in the decision. If she had felt a special desire for any man of good standing, despite her looks and tremendous abilities, a lack of dowry and a father who had possibly not bothered with a marriage ceremony were tremendous handicaps in the society to which she had become accustomed. A convent would be a refuge where her studies could continue and money would be relatively unimportant.

She consulted her confessor about becoming a nun and Father Antonio Nuñez de Miranda, who was also confessor to the viceroy and his wife, advised that the young woman, not yet sixteen, should proceed with her plans. In *Respuesta a Sor Filotea* (Reply to Sister Filotea), which is an autobiography in the guise of a letter, she says:

"I became a nun because although I knew there were many things (I speak of the trappings, not the basics) at odds with my temperament, and with my complete denial of marriage, it was the least unlikely and most satisfactory choice I could make ..."

Santa Teresa La Antigua was the convent Juana Inés chose to enter on August 14, 1667. Founded by the unsentimental nuns, Mariana de La Encarnación and Sister Inés de La Cruz, it was run by the *Carmelitas Descalzas* (the barefoot Carmelites) and known for severity and austerity. The young woman, still three months distant from celebrating her sixteenth birthday, must have had only a dim and romanticized idea of what her life inside would be like. The occasion was enjoyed by the court as a social event. The pretty ceremony attended by the viceroy and his wife and other exalted gentry in no way helped the imaginative and sensitive adolescent to realize what she was getting into. Despite the fact that she was now officially called Sor Juana Inés de La Cruz, she didn't last long. She got sick almost immediately and doctors advised that she leave. Her mentors, the Marqués and Marquesa de Mancera, always sympathetic, took her to the royal palace to recuperate and she was well enough by December 22 of the same year, 1667, to accompany them to the long and elaborate ceremonies in honor of the great new cathedral of Mexico.

Still determined to live the cloistered life, her next choice of refuge was much better. She entered the convent of San Jerónimo February 24, 1669 at age seventeen. The history of this convent was a happy one. It was founded in the year 1585 by Doña Isabel de Barrios, daughter of Andrés de Barrios, a conquistador whose nickname had been *el danzador* (the dancer) because he loved to dance. After his death his widow, and four daughters who were nuns, decided to start a new convent. The order they chose was La Jerónimo and upon receiving papal approval, they officially opened the doors on September 26. The improvised quarters started out in the home of its founders, Doña Isabel and daughters: Isabel de San Jerónimo, María de La Concepción, Antonia de Los Reyes and Juana Bautista. To enlarge the limited facilities of their little home Doña Isabel bought the house next door which had belonged to a man named Ortiz who was called *El Músico* (the musician). So it came to pass that Sor Juana Inés de La Cruz, who would be called La Decima Musa, fittingly passed the rest of her years on ground once owned by a dancer and a musician.

Now Sor Juana began in earnest the life of learning she had longed for. But, as she found out in time, criticism could be leveled at one even in the cloister. To say that the young nun withdrew from worldly contact would be entirely wrong. Actually she was able to enjoy the intellectual friends she had always preferred without having to bother, except in rare instances, with the kind of socially frivolous people who bored her. She now had control of whom she would see and what she would do in a way she had never been able to attain at court.

Of course, nothing is perfect. There were interruptions. She speaks of trying to study and often being distracted by nuns in neighboring cells practicing music or singing religious songs. Afraid of losing time in idle conversation, she asked her sisters not to interrupt her work unless the topic was of a religious or charitable nature. As the years went by she accumulated a library of four thousand volumes, the largest in Mexico at that time, and also collected musical and scientific instruments and maps, creating in her cell a mini-university to compensate for the experience denied her at the University of Mexico because of her sex. In some of the more liberal convents of the era, it was not unusual for nuns to have as many as two or three servants of their own. So Juana would probably have had at least one personal maid, making it relatively easy for her to guard her study time and pursue her own interests. Even so, she kept the archives for the convent and was also the accountant, not neglecting her duties, although she twice refused the post of mother superior.

Sor Juana became the most important figure in San Jerónimo, what with visits from her dear friends the viceroy and his wife who frequently brought honored guests visiting them at the palace from Europe. Carlos Sigüenza y Góngora often consulted her as did other Mexican scholars. She was certainly made much of, one might even say spoiled, and when Viceroy Mancera was replaced, the wife of the new viceroy, La Condesa de Paredes, took Juana to her bosom with as much enthusiasm as her friend "Laura," visiting her almost daily. This pattern continued with the wife of the third viceroy, La Condesa de Galve, a very pious lady who also became Sor Juana's close friend and admirer.

The convent was frequently enlivened with evenings of poetry, plays or music organized by its famous sister, and it is said that no festival was complete without obtaining from the pen of Sor Juana *un soneto* (a sonnet), *villancico* (a poem in praise of a person or event), or *un endecasílibo* (a verse whose lines were composed of eleven syllables). José Loaysa de Agurto, another friend, composed music for many of Sor Juana's *villancicos*. Although she lived among women, her intellectual companions were men, a sad commentary on the educational level of most females of her time.

The brilliant nun's first volume of poetry was collected and published in Madrid by Juan de Camacho Gayna. Nothing could more pointedly illustrate the ridiculous excesses of the Baroque influence than the title bestowed upon the book, not by Sor

Juana,· but by the editors:

"Castalid Flood of the Only Poetess, tenth muse, Sor Juana Inés de La Cruz, Nun in The Monastery of San Jerónimo of the Imperial City of Mexico; where in various meters, idioms and styles, she fertilizes several matters with elegant subtle clear, ingenious, useful verses for teaching, recreation and Admiration."

Only in modern times has government bureaucracy stretched jargon as far. Her second volume of verse appeared in Sevilla in 1692 and the third and final one was published posthumously in Madrid. Other male friends who were part of her inner circle were Juan de Guevara, remembered because of his collaboration with Juana on her play, *Love is a Labyrinth*, and Mexican poet Ramírez de Vargas. But none could approach in quality the work of the woman that critics have called the finest poet of her era.

In the year 1680 she began her most productive period, writing more than a hundred poems. Should this not seem so prodigious an output, keep in mind that the work considered by many critics to be Sor Juana's finest, the last written in 1690 before her death, called *Primero Sueño* (First Dream) is composed of more than 950 verses and was not considered unusually long. Also she kept up her other interests. Her friend and adviser Don Carlos Sigüenza y Góngora had outlined a course of study for her in the sciences, in which he was so able, while she helped him with poetry in which he was not so able. They were a close pair and expressed their mutual esteem for each other. Here is an example of Sigüenza extolling the abilities of Sor Juana.

"I should like to omit the esteem with which I regard her, the veneration which she has won by her works, in order to make manifest to the world how much, in the encyclopedic nature and universality of her letters, is contained in her genius so that it may be known that in one single person Mexico enjoys what, in past centuries, the graces have imparted to all the learned women who are the great wonders of history."

And from Sor Juana came an equally laudatory poem written for and dedicated to Don Carlos Sigüenza y Góngora.

It is good to know that she enjoyed the satisfaction of having the most outstanding male mind of seventeenth century Mexico appreciate her outstanding female mind, because Sor Juana's intellectual achievements got her in trouble with other men of the period and eventually killed her. Her knowledge of philosophers, such as the French mathematician René Descartes and the Englishman Francis Bacon and his scientific theories, turned the reptilian eyes of the Inquisition upon her briefly. The churchmen in power in Mexico at the time were traditionalists who mistrusted the inquiring mind. No wonder that Juana was suspect, what with her sense of humor and often playful touch in poetry. Besides, she was a nun who, instead of spending her life in self-abnegation, seemed to be devoting it to self-glorification; a woman who studied the same subjects men did, ignoring needlework and cookery. It was her play *The Divine Narcissus* that caught the attention of the Inquisition. In it, she states that Christian and pagan symbolism have much in common--thin ice to skate on at a time when freethinkers were burned at the stake.

We have seen before that the man who became Archbishop of Mexico in 1682, Francisco de Aguiar y Seijas, was a notorious woman-hater. His fanatic sermons were almost exclusively directed against the deceptions practiced by females, their grave lack of conscience, sense of duty and general intelligence. His phobia extended to refusing to pay an official call upon the viceroy because he would have to encounter his wife; nor would the archbishop allow female servants in his household. He also threatened to excommunicate any woman who dared set foot in his palace. He was said, though, to have been highly compassionate in his dealings with the poor and sinners. We assume that no women were among them. We can imagine that when this gentleman was told of the popularity of the wise and witty nun, the pet of royalty and scholars alike, that his dislike was instant. Archbishop Seijas misogyny probably spread to other high clergy too, who, in order to please the boss, would imitate him even though they might not agree with him. Whether a net was woven deliberately in which to catch Sor Juana is uncertain but with the advent of Archbishop Seijas, the future was not auspicious for any woman, let alone one with a mind like hers.

At this time there was a well known Jesuit theologian born in Portugal, Antonio Vieira. Juana, in one of her quick studies, taught herself the Portuguese language in order to read his works. Disagreeing with his theories as expressed in "El Sermón del Mandato" (Maundy Thursday sermon) given in the Royal Chapel of the College of Lisbon in 1650, she set herself to writing a refutation. The contents of the sermon were largely devoted to the manifestation of the intensity of the sorrow shown at the death of Jesus and other fine points of doctrine with which Sor Juana took issue. None of it seems very vital to us now, neither the sermon nor the essay refuting it. It is thought that Sor Juana may have toned down her pen because the dark shadow of the Inquisition fell across the pages as she was writing.

When this essay, called the *Carta Atenagórica* (Athenian letter), was read by Juana's friend the Bishop of Puebla, Manuel Fernández de Santa Cruz, to whom she sent it, he published it without her permission and set himself the task of writing a reply to her. He hid behind a pseudonym, pretending he was another nun, entitling his answer *Carta de Sor Filotea de la Cruz* (letter from Sister Filotea of the Cross), an imaginary person. In this epistle he systematically cut down everything Sor Juana held dear, criticizing her life of intellectual achievement as not being sufficiently godly and self-sacrificing and advising her to give up her selfish ways and devote herself to the humdrum duties of ordinary nuns which would earn her a place in heaven. He carps at her writings as being much more of worldly and human matters than sacred and warns that her audacity in writing on forbidden themes has brought her under the scrutiny of the Inquisition. One reason that this letter hurt so much was that Sor Juana had thought the Bishop of Puebla a wise and sympathetic friend.

It took Sor Juana three months to compose her famous reply to the phony Filotea. Perhaps she took so long because she knew that when she completed it, she would be writing *finis* to her creative life, giving up her greatest joy by never setting pen to paper again nor opening a book. We can see her in her cell, the big dark eyes honed hollow from sleepless nights filled with self-accusation, the classic beauty of her features emphasized by the thinness of her face. Her hand flew over the pages but she paused often to think out her next sentences even though she knew, fine artist that she was, that she would revise the reply many times until she considered it as near perfect as she could make it.

It was an autobiographical sketch that she wrote, thirty-six pages that started with her birth and childhood, went on to Mexico City and the royal court, and then to the convent. There were important omissions. She revealed nothing of her true feelings about her parents, loves or lovers if there were any, but she gave us something much more valuable. It was a manifesto ahead of its time, presenting the rights of women to be thinking human beings, intellectuals if they chose, to bury themselves in books and studies if that was the way they enjoyed living their lives. Here she expressed her desire for knowledge:

"I returned to (that's badly said because I never stopped) I went on with, the studious tasks (that for me were a rest, in every moment that could be spared from my obligation) of reading and more reading, study and more study without any other instructor than these same books. I know how hard it is to study these soulless characters, lacking the live voice and explanations of a teacher; but I suffered through all this work very joyfully from the love of letters."

Sor Juana continued defending herself study by study, using biblical references to show how logic, physics, arithmetic, architecture, painting, etc. enabled her to better understand theology and sacred scripture. She did not forget that she was parrying criticism leveled at her by an official of the church. She mentioned Soloman, Jeremiah and St. Isadore as scriptural poets who brought honor to religion. She talked of her habit of going from one subject to another, brought about by having no time limits or need to complete a particular course for grades or credits in a university, as an aid to understanding all because wisdom is a universal chain with one link dependent upon the other. With false but becoming modesty, she added that if she was deficient in any of the subjects she studied it was not because of too great a variety but because of too little intelligence. She spoke of the many interruptions and tells us that though her work was received with acclaim, inevitably there was much envy and she was stabbed by thorns of persecution from those who were aghast at a woman who wanted nothing more than to be a scholar.

In 1690 at the age of forty-two, she wrote her longest and most ambitious poem *Primero Sueño* (First Dream). Reams have been written about this work; even the title immediately provokes modern-day psychological interpretations, the very word "dream" conjuring up Freud. The poem depicts the battle between illusion and reality, the battle constantly taking place within Sor Juana between her religion and its duties, her life of illusion, and her scientific and literary studies, her real life. It is filled with difficult references, both mythological and symbolical. The work is enigmatic; each reads into it his own desires and fantasies, his own frustrations and deprivations. It wanders formlessly in the way of dreams, giving it a strong ring of truth. Sor Juana claimed that it was the only piece of her work that she had truly enjoyed writing, perhaps because so much of the previous work had been command performance, poetry in honor of this or that occasion or plays produced for royal enjoyment. In *Primero Sueño* the preciosity of some of her earlier poetry has been replaced. This great work coupled with her lucid prose in *Respuesta a Sor Filotea* mark the climax of her career.

There is not a great deal left to say about the brief life of this brilliant comet that streaked across the seventeenth century Mexican sky, causing as much controversy as did the actual great comet seen in Mexico City in 1680. After sending her *Respuesta a Sor Filotea* to the bishop of Puebla, Sor Juana sold her extensive library, donating the proceeds to beggars, got rid of her scientific and musical instruments, paints and palettes, and vowed never to write again. She willed her own death by strangling her intellect, the oxygen of her body and soul. The last sad years of her life are shrouded in darkness as she went about her routine duties at San Jerónimo. She was even denied the consolation of a visit or message from her friend Sigüenza y Góngora because he had gone on a long expedition to Florida.

When an epidemic of plague broke out in 1695 in Mexico City, Sor Juana immediately took to the streets to nurse the poor, working day and night. With her scientific knowledge she must have been aware that direct contact almost inevitably resulted in infection. In her exhausted condition the inevitable took place and she fell ill and died April 17, 1695. The myriad bells of the city churches tolled mournfully for their gifted daughter and there was an impressive funeral attended by the most famous and titled personages of the capitol. Her grieving friend, home now from the journey to Florida, spoke of her accomplishments in his funeral oration. Although the text has unfortunately been lost to posterity we can use an appropriate quote from him when he speaks of her another time, "There is no pen that can rise to the eminence which hers e'ertops."

Her last written words express the terrible oppression she suffered at the end from the burden of guilt laid upon her for her intelligence. Having vowed never again to set pen to paper she scratched a sentence on parchment by dipping her fingernail in her own blood. "I have been the worst woman in the world." It is dreadful to think that no one assured Sor Juana that humanity cries out for women like her, but rarely is it blessed with even so much as a reasonable facsimile.

5
Freedom Fighters

    The seventeenth century slid into the eighteenth without great change until the second half was well underway. Overextended throughout the world and fearful of losing her possessions to foreign invaders, Spain in 1765 started increasing the Mexican army, composed of less than three thousand native soldiers, by sending in several thousand troops most of which were Swiss and Walloon (French-speaking Belgians). The forces were increased until by 1790 they numbered over 31,000 men. Large numbers of Portuguese, Italian, German, French, Chinese and even Malayan immigrants were putting a strain on the economy and also straining the facilities of the Inquisition which was trying to keep track of anything suspicious concerning these foreigners-- their mail, connections in the old country, religion etc. On August 10, 1785 a royal decree was received ordering the viceroy to confiscate and burn all copies he could find of the works of Machiavelli, Montesquieu and other freethinkers. Much subversive literature from the French revolution with its philosophy of liberty and equality was finding its way into Mexico. These new ideas foretold that the Inquisition and the Spanish government were on their way out.

    Probably the most traumatic event for the common people was the expulsion of the Jesuits. The official announcement came June 25, 1767 in Mexico City in the form of a mandate read by the viceroy, Carlos Francisco de Croix, from his monarch Carlos III:

    "... So that you may immediately direct yourself with force against the houses of the Jesuits. Seize all of their persons and send them as prisoners within twenty-four hours to the port of Veracruz .... No individual shall be permitted to take anything besides his prayer books and such clothing as is absolutely indispensable for the journey."

With this arbitrary command, two hundred years of work in New Spain, thirty colleges with their libraries and churches, plus the Indian missions were to be wiped out. But it was more easily said than done. There were approximately seven hundred Jesuits scattered throughout the large country and it was almost three years before all were rounded up, herded vast distances by an escort of soldiers and sent on their way. The sluggishness of the exodus was due in large part to the violent reaction against the expulsion by Indians at the missions founded by the Jesuit fathers. In Sonora at Mission San Luis de La Paz the Indians used force to prevent the departure of their revered clergy. The protest was suppressed rapidly with brutal measures taken by the viceroy's soldiers and a number of Indian and Mestizo men and women were imprisoned. In less than a month sentence was pronounced by the *visitador* (visiting judge): "... I find that I must condemn and do condemn to death Ana María Guatemala, an Indian widow, Julián Martínez Serrano, Vicente Ferral Rángel and Marcos Perez de León ... to be shot by a firing squad as traitors; and on the place of execution their heads will be separated from their bodies and placed on pikes where they shall remain until time consumes them."

Ana María Guatemala was the first woman to die protesting this unpopular decree that came from a tyrannical and unpopular king. The violent reaction against the crown brought about by the expulsion is thought to be the first explosion that ultimately blew the monarchy to bits.

In 1730 the widow of Miguel de Rivera, Doña María de Rivera, was operating her husband's printing shop. There were only two printers at this time who published regularly and produced a sizeable output of volumes. The other, Joseph Bernardo de Hogal also had his press taken over by his wife when he died. Mexico seems to have had an enormous appetite for religious works, especially those concerned with the miraculous. It is interesting to note some of the titles produced by the two female proprietors of the printing establishments.

Doña María de Rivera put out a sermon by J. Fernández de Palos, rector of the University of Mexico City, entitled, "Obsidional Triumph ... By Means of the Virgin Mary, Our Lady, In Her Prodigious Image of Guadalupe," which was such a best seller that her rival, Doña de Hogal, reprinted 900 copies of it in 1746. Most book purchases were made by convent libraries and rich patrons who owned land, silver mines or were aristocrats with inherited wealth.

In 1749 Doña María de Rivera's establishment issued "The Marvel of Prodigies and the Flower of Miracles Which Appeared at Guadalupe, Giving a Clear Witness of the Conception in Grace and of the Glory of Mary Our Lady," by Father Juan José M. Montúfar. Not to be outdone, Doña de Hogal produced the following year, "The History of the Very Miraculous Image of Our Lady of Ocotlán Which is Venerated Outside the Walls of Tlaxcala."

So the rivalry went back and forth, sharpened by the addition of more printing houses until by 1761 there was a total of six in the capital city as well as others in Puebla, Guadalajara and Veracruz. Considering the high cost of publications at the time, and the red tape imposed by Church and state, making almost impossible the birth of any volume whatsoever, these two women deserve credit for successfully running difficult businesses.

In the mid 1700s both Church and crown became concerned over the worldliness of some of the convents and decided that all nunneries must switch to what was called a *vida común*, meaning that the sisters lived a life of uniform simplicity. The viceroy who bore the brunt of the ire manifested by many convents at this interference with their customs was Antonio María Bucareli who had been a bachelor all his life and had no idea of the wrath he would engender by trying to enforce the decree.

In the beginning, with the early establishment of convents after the conquest, their constitutions and sets of regulations had prescribed that nuns live in common dormitories, keep a minimum of servants and have as little to do with secular women as possible. Gradually the picture changed. When young women of wealthy families began entering, they brought large dowries, servants, luxurious personal possessions, books, pictures, and musical instruments. Secular women also began to be admitted and these ladies often had cells which were actually good-sized rooms with their own private entrance onto the street, so they could come and go as they pleased and have visitors of any quantity or quality. Female children were adopted by the sisters, educated and made much of, satisfying the maternal instincts instead of sublimating it. Women who functioned as nursemaids, not merely servants, were hired to care for these little girls who were petted and loved. The cuisine, furniture and objets d'art in some of the convents rivaled that of the viceroy's palace.

It was the nuns themselves who started the controversy when several of them in the city of Puebla asked their bishop to institute reforms. When the *vida común* was ordered reinstated, other nuns in other convents in Puebla immediately protested this change to the Spanish king, Charles III and the battle was on. The most vocal group against the simple life was at Santa Inés convent and the ringleader was Sor María Ana de San Joaquín.

In January of 1772 the Santa Inés dissidents composed a list of grievances, accusing the bishop of having used threats to make them accept the *vida común*, enticing nuns to the new system by illegal promises, ordering all the expensive cells torn out and on and on. They wanted the case to be heard in court with a lawyer appointed on behalf of the protestors and, most audacious of all, asked that the bishop be suspended until the case was decided. The bishop appealed to Bucareli for help, claiming that a number of the nuns at Santa Inés had accepted the reforms and that only a small group was resisting. Bucareli handed the hot potato right back with the observation that the bishop was in charge of the matter, but advising tact in handling these women whose militant character was the result of having abused their religious vows for two centuries.

On February 11 the peace and quiet of convent Santa Inés was exchanged for a scene out of Dante's inferno. Several more of the sisters had accepted the *vida común* and had moved into a part of the convent set aside temporarily for those who wanted to practice the austere life. This seemed to tip the balance of pros versus cons and also the sanity of several nuns who, in demented fashion, ran to the convent gate screaming that they wanted out. A few others came charging out and joined the uproar while a passel of servants assaulted the tower and clanged the bells. The turmoil grew and the governor of Puebla was sent for to quell the riot. He managed to achieve a measure of tranquility which continued until February 15 when Bucareli received the communique telling him of the incident and stating that the number of nuns who remained unrepentant for their part in stirring up the affair had been whittled down to five. The agitating Sor María Ana de San Joaquín was not among them. Bucareli had written early in the struggle to José de Gálvez, "the ire of women is more fearful than that of men, because once they make it known, they have little place for reflexion and are less concerned over consequences than that their caprice be fulfilled."

Of course, Sor María Ana de San Joaquín had to give in after a few weeks. She wrote a letter to the bishop in which she blamed her rebellious actions on her own stupidity, renouncing any claims she had made. The Church held all the cards. If the women had been accustomed to being responsible for their own decisions they might have had a democratic organization in which, within the same walls of any given convent if they chose to have it so, a part could be set aside permanently for the *vida común* and a part for those who wanted less austerity.

This did not by any means end the struggle. It spread to convents in Mexico City and forced a royal cedula from King Charles in May, 1774 ordering the *vida común* reinstated in all nunneries not yet practicing it. It was a justly composed edict that did not precipitately phase out the secular ways and gradually phased in most of the reforms that were lumped under the heading *vida común*. But again the nuns in half a dozen different convents in Puebla caused agitation by refusing to accept the cedula and accusing the bishop of unreasonable conduct. Another sister, Sor Phelipa Francesca de San José of the Santa Catalina convent, stuck her neck out, demanding that Bucareli relieve the sisters from the bishop's harsh rule. It was a twenty-year fight. The controversy did not abate until 1780.

Looking at the upheaval from one point of view Bernard E. Bobb says in *The Viceregency of Antonio Bucareli*:

"There is more to be derived from a study of the *vida común* controversy than the lesson that one should never underestimate the power of a woman. The conflict also represents one of the hazards of attempting a program of reform, much as the reform may be needed, justified as it may be in terms of its objective."

What is not taken into consideration here is that the more relaxed and opulent convents that included not only wealthy nuns and seculars but needy female children, servants and nurses provided shelter for many classes of women. It also provided a haven for women who wanted to study, meditate or please themselves as to the routine of the day instead of being at the beck and call of domestic duties which many, even in those days, found not to their taste. It was not only unwanted old maids and impoverished aunties who sought sanctuary. Perhaps this kind of refuge did not need reforming.

María Ignacia Rodríguez de Velasco y Osorio Barba, known to history as La Güera Rodríguez (the fair Rodríguez) was born November 1778 in Mexico City. La Güera was notable for her direct and daring approach to life, an attitude frequently found among the peasant women, occasionally in the middle class but seldom in the upper class of that time. She and her sister,

María Josefa, were a pair of exceptionally beautiful and intelligent girls, part of a Mexican aristocracy whose females were surrounded from birth by a battery of artificial rules and regulations so that to strike up a conversation with men to whom they had not been properly introduced, and without a dueña standing guard, constituted an act of great courage or foolhardiness, depending upon the point of view.

Every afternoon the lovely sisters promenaded past the barracks of a regiment whose officers were composed of the scions of Mexico's blue-blooded families. Although at first the girls flirted with all, they soon settled down to intimate conversations with a couple of the young men stationed there that they singled out from the others. The daily rendezvous did not escape the curious eyes of onlookers and it happened that the viceroy of New Spain, Count Juan Vicente Revilla Gigedo, was passing by one day and noticed the scandalous goings on. This man was a vigorous administrator who did much for Mexico but was also known for his interest and frequent interference in matters that were none of his affair. Sure enough, the busy-body immediately contacted the father of the bold sisters, Don Antonio Rodríguez de Velasco, and asked for an interview.

When the gentlemen got together the stern viceroy queried Don Antonio as to how he passed his time and received the reply that the pious father went each afternoon to pray at the *sagrario* (sanctuary). Revilla Gigedo advised the unwitting Don Antonio to perform his heavenly chores in the morning and keep an eye out for his daughter's activities after lunch. Not satisfied with just giving advice, upon second thought the imperious meddler decided that the girls must marry the two officers and ordered poor Don Antonio to commence the endless formalities and legalities that preceded marriages in the high society of eighteenth century Mexico.

La Güera's wedding to José Jerónimo Lopez de Peralta de Villar Villamil took place September 7, 1794, just before her sixteenth birthday. Her sister, María Josefa, married the son of the Marqués de Uluapa in 1796. María Josefa would not be as famous a beauty nor have as spectacular a career as her sister, but her marriage would be a happy one and her looks and intelligence impressed many famous people including fifteen-year-old Simón Bolívar when he stayed with her and her husband in 1799 on his way to Spain. Unfortunately, the alliance forced upon La Güera was notable mostly for its unhappiness. But the resilient La Güera, though often down, was never out. At age twenty-four, her looks undiminished by the birth of four children, she met the eminent German naturalist, explorer and author Baron Alexander Von Humboldt who, many years later after traveling the world, still declared her to be the most fascinating woman he had seen in all his journeys. Von Humboldt spent every free hour possible while in Mexico in the company of the lady, never tiring of her wit and handsome looks.

In 1803 when architect-sculptor Manuel Tolsá, director of the San Carlos Academy of Art, completed his bronze equestrian statue of the unpopular Spanish king Charles IV, Baron Von Humboldt was asked to give one of the dedication speeches. The statue still stands at the center of a *glorieta* (traffic circle) off of the Avenida Reforma in Mexico City and has an inscription which reads: "Mexico preserves this as an art relic." Should anyone think that the monument is maintained out of respect for the monarch they should note that the name given it is "El Caballito" (the little horse). But in spite of the dislike that the Mexicans felt for the king the occasion was very gala with all the officials and important families present and the ladies decked out in their best finery. At the side of the good baron was his boon companion, the blond, bold and beautiful Señora María Ignacia Rodríguez de Villamil, the unconventional La Güera whose name was on every tongue--sometimes salaciously since her friendship with Von Humboldt.

You can be sure she was dressed in the latest fashion, a silk or velvet empire dress of white or pastel shade with a long, straight skirt, high bodice and puffed sleeves. The neckline, so low cut as to display an ample bosom, would be set off by a ruff of delicate lace across the back that stopped in front just past the shoulders. A fringed cashmere shawl, whose graceful manipulation was a practiced art, along with the silent language of parasol and fan would replace cape or coat. Her hands would be covered with white gloves of softest kidskin ending just above the elbow. Completing the outfit would be a bonnet, trimmed with feathers or flowers. The eyes of La Güera sparkling within its depths were enhanced by the fashionable hairstyle of the period, ringlets on forehead and cheeks.

La Güera's husband, Villamil, died in 1805 in Querétaro where he had been sent with his regiment. She was left with a son, Jerónimo, and three daughters, María Josefa, María de La Paz and María Antonia, who were also so beautiful that, when with their mother, the four were called Venus and the three graces. So great was their fame that the king of Spain ordered a portrait painted of mother and daughters to be sent to him. If

La Güera had been a widow during Von Humboldt's visit he would probably never have remained a bachelor all his ninety years.

Most of the innumerable anecdotes told of this woman are amusing but frivolous tales highly embroidered and resting upon her undoubted attraction for men. Not nearly so much is made of her sympathy for and secret activities on behalf of the revolution. They became well enough known in her era to the point that she was summoned before a tribunal of the Inquisition to answer charges that she had conspired against the royal government. Unfortunately for the judges, they were well known to La Güera and the trial bordered on farce as the beautiful and witty lady twisted them around her little finger. No doubt her judges would have preferred to try her on charges of being a scarlet woman. The punishment frequently decreed for street walkers and adulterers was *mujer emplumada*, where a woman was stripped of her clothes, slathered with honey and daubed all over with feathers before being forced to walk through the streets. It was the female version of tarring and feathering and some of La Güera's frustrated admirers, including many from the tribunal, would have fought for the honor of being honey-daubers while others would have preferred thumbing feathers. The sentence given her by Archbishop Francisco Javier de Lizana y Beaumont was a brief exile to the city of Querétaro which she undertook in great style and enjoyment. It did not stop her connections with the revolution.

Another of her lover-admirers was Agustín de Iturbide, the daring and brilliant army officer who later became liberator-emperor. His infatuation for her was so great that it resulted in a scene right out of an old operetta. When it came time for Iturbide to enter Mexico City at the head of the Army of the Three Guaranties, he rerouted the whole shebang so that La Güera could watch his triumphant parade in comfort from her house on the Avenida La Profesa. As he rode in front of her domicile and caught sight of his beautiful *querida* waving at him, the dashing general stopped his horse and with a flourish plucked a tri-color feather from his hat and sent one of his lieutenants to present it to La Güera. During the years he was so enamored of her, La Güera took part in some of the political decisions made by Iturbide, including a plot devised by liberal Mexican clerics who were dissatisfied with Spain's policy concerning matters of religion. La Güera suggested modifications which were accepted by Iturbide. It was during this period in 1820 that the Inquisition at long last ended, helped along by people of good will in all classes.

There was gossip to the effect that the handsome Iturbide not only fell in love with La Güera, but also with her youngest daughter, María Antonia, and had mother and daughter as amors which, even for Iturbide, required a lot of nerve. The story hardly seems likely since María Antonia had wed, at age fifteen in 1812, the Marqués de San Miguel de Aguayo, but the tale was mentioned in the diary kept by a Mexican of the era named Beruete. More gossip claimed that the emperor had spent so much money on La Güera that he accused his not overly-attractive wife Ana María of his own failing, infidelity, and had the astonished woman locked up in a convent. Ana María was able to survive in the cloistered atmosphere on very few pesos, which left Iturbide with more to spend on his friend La Güera. That Ana María did indeed do a stint in a convent is a matter of record.

La Güera's second marriage was to Don Mariano de Briones who held an important government post and came from a wealthy family. Briones died shortly after the wedding, leaving La Güera pregnant. She gave birth to a daughter, Victoria, whose authenticity was questioned by the Briones family. They claimed there were no witnesses present at the birth, but being a resourceful woman as well as a fighter, La Güera triumphed. She had her servant call in persons passing by in the street to witness the child's entry in the world, thereby insuring its right to inherit. Unfortunately, Victoria died at an early age.

In mid life La Güera was declared by a French admirer to be as indestructible as Ninon de Lenclos, a seventeenth century Parisienne of wit and charm who continued to fascinate into her later years. Another comparison might be the mother of Winston Churchill, the incomparable Jenny from New York, who never seemed to age and whose brain equalled her beauty. La Güera's appeal seemed to have been composed of great vitality, a quick mind that grasped the essentials, plus a remarkable memory for anecdotes and the ability to tell them amusingly.

A bout with cholera in her late fifties was supposed to have affected her looks but she continued to be much in demand in society and never lacked for friends and invitations. Fanny Calderón de La Barca, the English school teacher who married an Argentine diplomat and spent several years in Mexico, writes of the lady frequently in her book *Life in Mexico*. Here she describes her first meeting with La Güera, then aged sixty-two:

"... In spite of years and of the furrows which it pleases time to plough in the loveliest faces, La Güera retains a profusion of fair curls without one gray hair, a set of beautiful white teeth, very fine eyes--but plenty of rouge and wrinkles.... I found La Güera very agreeable, a great talker and perfect living chronicle. She must have been more pretty than beautiful--lovely hair, complexion and figure and very gay and witty. She is lately married to her third husband, and had three daughters, all celebrated beauties ..."

Her third and final marriage was proof of her continuing charm into later life because Juan Manuel de Elizalde was twelve years younger than she, a most unusual occurrence for those times when the order of the day was for a male to be at least ten years older than his spouse and often twenty or thirty years. Elizalde was a Chilean by birth who later became consul in Mexico representing his native country. In La Güera's final years she switched to the pious life, becoming a member of the Brothers and Sisters of Penance, Third Order of St. Francis of Assisi. This Franciscan organization had very severe rules although La Güera was not cloistered. When she died on the eve of her 73rd birthday in November 1851, her husband Elizalde entered the Oratory of San Felipe Neri. Before his death in 1870 at eighty years of age he gave La Güera's magnificent collection of jewels to adorn one of the images in the church of La Profesa.

And so the fame of La Güera Rodriguez lives on, not for great accomplishments but for natural endowments and a zest for living. In addition, she broke the rules of a rigid society so gracefully that she continued to be accepted and admired not only by men but by women, no small feat for the times in which she lived.

The long series of bloody wars that constituted the struggle for independence by the Mexican people started early in the nineteenth century. The opening shot was fired by Father Miguel Hidalgo y Costilla, a liberal priest who had been a brilliant scholar at the college of San Nicolás in Morelia where he later taught philosophy and theology and became rector. Eventually he moved on and assumed leadership of the congregation of Dolores, a pueblo located eleven miles from the capitol of Guanajuato. This sleepy town was destined to become famous for the *grito de Dolores* (freedom cry) which roused the people of Mexico to throw off the yoke of the mother country Spain.

The most famous heroine of the independence movement of 1810 was María Josefa Ortiz, born in Morelia in 1769 and orphaned when she was very young. Her mother died shortly after her birth and her father, Don José María Ortiz, passed away a few years later. The portraits that we have of this courageous woman show a stern face with eyes that look straight ahead and mouth and chin set in lines of determination. To survive her rugged childhood and youth Josefa needed a will of iron.

After the death of her parents she was placed in an orphanage-school called La Viscaínas and was probably accepted there because her father had been born in Vizcaya, Spain. Having no money, she had to pay for her board, room and instruction by washing dishes and scrubbing floors. She also made and mended clothing for the well-to-do students. She worked as hard as most servants throughout her early years and, thinking there were no other opportunities open to her, prepared to become a nun. Fate had other ideas.

A young lawyer by the name of Miguel Domínguez, an official in the viceroy's office, came to the orphanage on business and, encountering Josefa Ortiz in the hallways, fell instantly in love with her. He asked for and received permission to visit the orphanage regularly and in the year 1791 Josefa wore a veil, not for the purpose of entering a convent but as the bride of Don Miguel.

She had married an important man in an important position and in 1802 Don Miguel stepped up another notch in his career by being named *corregidor* (magistrate) of Querétaro by Viceroy Félix Berenguer de Marquina. The post of magistrate of a province carried much prestige, not only for the title and money that went with it, but because the most difficult persons to contact, the viceroy, archbishop and generals of the army, automatically became available. Equally important to a woman was becoming La Corregidora, the name by which Doña Josefa would be known to history. The orphan who had scrubbed floors was now a great lady about to give birth to her seventh child when her husband took office, a great lady who never forgot for a moment her years of hard labor when her hands were as red and tender as her raw and scabby knees.

The house of El Corregidor became a center for cultural activities. Many gatherings were held in the evenings to which not only literary and musical people came but many military figures as well, among them Mariano Abasolo, Juan Aldama and Miguel Allende. The handsome Captain Allende, a wealthy creole, was attracted to the Domínguez home for several reasons, one of the most important being a daughter of the house with whom he was in love. Through Allende, Doña Josefa was introduced to the soft-spoken priest who had read a great deal about the French revolution, Miguel Hidalgo y Costilla. Hidalgo's ideas of equality and opportunity for all struck a sympathetic note in the breast of La Corregidora. The first step along the road was to free Mexico from Spanish rule, and the *tertulias* (evening gatherings) at the home of Don Miguel Domínguez in Querétaro rapidly became more political than literary. Doña Josefa and her husband were aware that Miguel Allende was hatching a plot to seize rich Spaniards and Spanish authorities and their property as a preliminary to proclaiming Mexican independence. Father Hidalgo and other confederates agreed to the plan but the government got wind of it and sent agents to Dolores to keep an eye on Hidalgo and developments there and to arrest Allende and Aldama. Suspecting that the Corregidor and his wife were involved too, the viceroy's messengers ordered the Corregidor to search various houses in the area and commandeer the arms hidden there. Corregidor Domínguez had no choice but to obey or admit the guilt of himself and his wife by refusal. The weapons were discovered and the plot foiled. Fearing that Josefa would try to warn Hidalgo and get more involved, Domínguez locked her in the bedroom and put Ignacio Pérez in the room below to act as her jailer. When her husband left the house Josefa managed to attract the attention of her jailer by stamping on the floor. When he came upstairs and put his ear to the keyhole she whispered to him to jump on his horse and ride first to Allende to tell him the conspiracy was discovered and then get the word to Father Hidalgo in Dolores. Hidalgo was able to seize the town and, ordering the church bells rung earlier than usual, proclaimed to the people the famous cry, "Hail our Lady of Guadalupe! Long live independence!"

On September 15, 1810 papers implicating Hidalgo, Allende, Corregidor Domínguez and La Corregidora were brought to the attention of Ochoa, Mayor of Querétaro, who arrested the Domínguez and others who had participated in the secret revolutionary meetings. Don Miguel and Doña Josefa were ordered to be confined separately. A writer of the era describes the scene this way when common soldiers were sent to escort Josefa Ortiz from her home to imprisonment.

"With head held high, self-assured, looking straight ahead, she descended the stairway and crossed the threshold of her home without a single friendly hand raised to offer help. When she was in the street she called to the soldiers. 'Do you know why they're taking me away? For trying to give you a country to honor and respect, for trying to shake off the shame of slavery, for getting rid of the whip that has lashed your backs and those of your children.' The captain who headed the squadron of soldiers, with pistol in hand, said to her, 'Señora, if you insist on trying to incite the troops I will have to kill you.' She answered, 'My life is worth much less than what I have just lost and it would be an honor to shed my blood and give my life in front of my children to teach them that woman knows how to die in defense of her ideals.'"

One of the canons of the church, José Mariano Beristáin when visiting Querétaro said of Doña Josefa that she was "an effective agent, brazen, bold, incorrigible, who never lost a chance nor a moment's opportunity to inspire hatred toward the king, toward Spain, to the causes and fair and legitimate decisions of this realm."

Beristáin ended his tirade by calling her an Anne Boleyn, a strange comparison to be making between cerebral Josefa, faultless wife and mother, and carnal Anne who loved love more than honor.

Incarcerated in the convent of Santa Clara, La Corregidora learned the painful news of the death of the principal figures of the revolution in 1811. The authorities said they would pardon Josefa if she renounced the insurgents and their ideas but she refused. This attempt to make her betray her principles gave her courage to help as much as she could from prison in a new outbreak of rebellion. Because of the customs of the era girls were taught how to read but not to write so that they could not communicate clandestinely with their lovers. The ingenious Josefa, to keep contact with her fellow conspirators, did what she had always done before. She cut words from publications, pasted them on writing paper and was able in this way to send messages to other revolutionaries through a sympathetic connection who was also part of the underground. Because of these activities the viceroy ordered her removed to another, more secure place of confinement, the convent of Santa Catalina in Mexico City where she remained for many years.

Don Miguel had not suffered as hard a fate as his wife. Schooled in obedience to the crown and having served it for many years, he had never been as firm in his desire for a free Mexico as his wife. When the revolution faltered, Don Miguel faltered with it. The viceroy pardoned him and restored him to office. It was a curious situation: the *corregidor* continued working for the man who kept his wife in prison.

In 1816 a new viceroy, Juan Ruiz de Apodaca, took office.

He started a policy of pardoning insurgents instead of executing them if they laid down their arms. Although it was too late, Spain was beginning to see the light. Apodaca was far more humane than his predecessor and when Don Miguel became desperately ill the new viceroy finally released Doña Josefa so that she could attend to her husband but under the condition that she not be permitted to leave Mexico City. When the proud Corregidora stepped outside the convent, she pointed out to those around her that she was leaving to fulfill her duty to her family as wife and mother but would never give up her loyalty to the revolution. When it was brought to her attention that one of her sons was an officer in the army of the royalists under General Agustín de Iturbide she refused to receive him at her home saying:

"No one of my blood can enter here who is capable of throwing away his courage and manliness for such an unworthy cause."

La Corregidora took little part in the political events of the next four years that brought about the brief reign of Iturbide. She didn't approve of him. Generals Iturbide and Guerrero signed an independence pact at Iguala on February 24, 1821 declaring Mexico a constitutional monarchy with Catholicism still the official religion, permitting no other, and allowing Europeans and clergy to keep their land and privileges as before. The quotable Josefa made this bitter comment: "I didn't fight for my personal advantage but for the advancement of my people. Between the Spanish landowners, voracious and thieving, and the Mexican slaves, no compromise is possible. All or nothing. Iturbide represents the interests of the clergy and landowners and Guerrero the insurgents, the slaves. Both are traitors to their causes. In this breast of mine, treason, gentlemen, is not acceptable."

When Empress Ana María, Iturbide's wife, named Doña Josefa Ortiz de Domínguez one of the matrons of honor in her hastily assembled royal court, La Corregidora scathingly refused the dubious distinction using the kind of unvarnished and hardbitten phrases in which she excelled. The exact date of Josefa's death is not certain but there is general agreement that it took place in 1829. Today in Querétaro there is a statue of their most famous heroine in the plaza of Santo Domingo.

Another woman who helped the revolutionary effort was Doña María Fernández de Jáuregui. In 1812 she published a

452-page volume called "El Amigo de la Patria." In March 1813 she released the first issue of "El Curioso Mexicano," an insurgent review, and she was apparently still going strong in 1815 when she put out a monthly, "Las Sombras de Heráclito y Demócrito," devoted to political satire.

The heroines of the independence movement came from all walks of life. One of the most active was a young woman born in Mexico City April 10, 1789, Leona Vicario Fernández. She was the daughter of a wealthy Spaniard Don Gaspar Martín Vicario and a creole mother from Toluca, Camilia Fernández de San Salvador y Montiel. Leona's father, Don Gaspar, was a cultured man who took great care with his daughter's education so that when her parents died and the eighteen-year-old went to live with her mother's brother, Agustín Pomposo Fernández de San Salvador, she was well informed in matters classical and political. She became known for her intellect as well as her beauty.

A young man by the name of Andrés Quintana Roo joined the law firm of Leona's uncle, Don Pomposo. Coming from Mérida in Yucatan, Andrés completed his studies in La Real y Pontificia Universidad where he was a brilliant student. Don Pomposo, rector of the university, had a chance to observe Andrés' talents and was happy to acquire the outstanding youth as a member of his company of lawyers. The delight soon changed to distress.

In the capital city of Mexico the insurgent sympathizers called themselves Los Guadalupes. This group of activists worked secretly to collect money and arms which they gave to the guerillas hiding out in the hills. Don Agustín Pomposo was a conservative and royalist who despised the Guadalupes and wrote pamphlet after pamphlet denouncing them. His pen became even more poisonous when his own son joined up with López Rayón who was chosen as Secretary of State and Communications under the government of the freethinking, rebel priest Miguel Hidalgo. Meanwhile, Andrés Quintana Roo was openly showing signs of interest in the independence movement and Leona Vicario. To make things worse, Don Pomposo's bright and willful niece made no bones about returning the love of the law clerk.

What did one do with a headstrong young woman in the Mexico of the early 1800s? Put her in a convent, of course. The idea did not appeal to Leona for the obvious reasons that freedom was precious to her for its own sake and enabled her as well to see her sweetheart, Andrés Quintana Roo. But there was a third reason. The young woman was sending firearms to the insurgents through an underground station that she was running very efficiently. Proud of her contribution to the cause of liberty for Mexico, Leona tried to conceal her activities but her uncle found out. He immediately popped her into the convent and then the unhappy Tío Pomposo let his strong sense of duty to the Spanish crown rule his emotions and he reported her to the Royal Junta for Security.

The judge who was assigned the case assured Leona that if she named her fellow conspirators he would give her an easy sentence of life imprisonment. If she chose not to divulge their names, nothing could save her from the firing squad. Her uncle who had always been very fond of his niece pleaded with her but her lips clamped down forming a thinner line than before.

The following evening a group of black-hooded and caped Guadalupes, some guarding the entrance, others brandishing pistols and striding into the jail, overcame the guards, rescued the young woman and escorted her to where horses awaited them. They rode off unharmed to a secret spot where they dressed Leona in rags and blackened her face so that she resembled a street girl. A few days later a mule train arrived in Oaxaca with a cargo of crates loaded with oranges and pigskins filled with pulque. But the crates held paper and printer's type and the pigskins were filled with ink for the printing press of the insurgents. The value of the goods was further enhanced by the female ragamuffin who accompanied the load. Upon taking a bath and changing her clothes, the ragamuffin turned into Leona Vicario who would help operate the presses and write material for them to print.

Andrés and Leona were reunited and they married shortly after becoming members of the insurgents. General José María Morelos, head of the insurgent army, was impressed by the patriotism and intelligence of the young couple and when the national congress of Anáhuac met in Chilpancingo Andrés was designated vice-president of the assembly. His name heads the list of the signers of The Act of Independence of November 6, 1813. The group of ten gave power to General Morelos to govern the territory he had conquered so far and to continue fighting while they worked at drafting a constitution for the new nation which would be free of Spain. It took many years before the dream was realized.

Leona lived a dangerous life, taking her daughters along whenever she could accompany Quintana Roo. With her writing ability and grasp of politics she helped write speeches and draft treaties but also nursed the sick and wounded. Her uncle Pomposo and his family continued to reject her because of her democratic beliefs but she never changed her ideals to suit anyone. In thanks for her sacrifices the state of Coahuila decreed on November 15, 1827 that the official name of their capital, Saltillo, be changed to Ciudad Leona Vicario. Her death on August 24, 1842 sent the republic into mourning. The press sang her praises and Don Carlos de Bustamante called her "*orgullo de su sexo y gloria de su patria*" (he glory of her sex and the pride of her country).

In 1814 when the private papers of Los Guadalupes fell into the hands of the viceroy it was discovered that a number of wives of lawyers in the group in addition to Leona Vicario de Quintana Roo and Margarita de Peimbert had been as active as their husbands in the organization. But the capital city had many pockets of insurgents other than Los Guadalupes trying to help the cause of freedom. After Miguel Hidalgo was captured in April 1811 by the royalists in Coahuila a plot was hatched against Viceroy Francisco Xavier Venegas. The leader of the conspiracy was a woman named Mariana Rodríguez de Lazarín. Doña Mariana, wife of a miner from Guanajuato, Miguel Lazarín, held many get-togethers in her home to devise ways and means of helping the revolution. On the Monday evening of *semana santa* (Holy Week) in Mexico City 1811, there was a gathering at Lazarín's house composed mostly of advocates of the revolution.

Suddenly, a little after 8:30 p.m., the bells of the cathedral began clanging violently and a brisk round of gun-play could also be heard, alarming the gathering. The excessive bell-tolling and cannon-fire during the usually quiet *semana santa* indicated unusual happenings and everyone began talking at once. They soon heard that the viceroy's government was celebrating the news that Miguel Hidalgo and other leaders of the insurgents had been imprisoned and that the republican army was completely routed.

The news hit the group like a thunderbolt. The timid forgot they were partisans of freedom and began showing signs of panic. The tenor of the conversation changed among some of the men from resistance to respect tinged with fear as they spoke of the royalist victory. Suddenly, Doña Mariana jumped to her feet and, taking center stage, raised her voice above the din saying:

"Gentlemen, what goes on here? Are there no men in Mexico?"

The cowards in the group dabbed their foreheads with crumpled handkerchiefs and tried to look unafraid as one of their number found his voice and asked:

"But what can we do?"

The flashing eyes of the lady of the house matched the daring of her words as she replied, "Free the prisoners."

There was a shocked silence, then someone asked, "But how?"

"Overpower the viceroy when he's out for his nightly walk and condemn him to be hanged." Mariana Rodríguez de Lazarín looked about her defiantly, daring those present to protest her simple but violent solution. No one did. All knew that a similar fate was in store for Hidalgo and the other revolutionary leaders that had been taken. No mercy would be shown them.

That evening the plot was born that became known in Mexican history as Conspiración del Año Once (the conspiracy of 1811). All plans were made at meetings held in the Lazarín house. One of the group, José María Gallardo, lost his courage the night before the attack was to be made and confessed all to a priest at the convent La Merced. Gallardo was taken into custody shortly after because the priest disclosed the secret to Viceroy Venegas as fast as he could run to the royal palace. Because the details of the plot were never quite clear, the crown officials did not sentence any of the conspirators to death. Although saved from the firing squad, Mariana and her husband were held in prison until 1820.

The rebel chiefs Miguel Hidalgo, Ignacio Allende, Juan de Aldama and Mariano Jiménez were captured in Chihuahua and executed by a firing squad on July 31, 1811. Their heads were hung in an iron cage where they remained on display for ten years. But the freedom movement did not die with its founders. José María Morelos, whose blood was a mixture of Spanish, Negro and Indian, took over the position of leader of the insurgents. Morelos, a short, heavyset man of the people, had worked as an *arriero* and then became a priest. There were many females among the followers who regrouped around him, including a woman called *La Intrépida Barragana* (the fearless concubine) who commanded a company of insurgents, all men, known for their unquestioning obedience to the orders of their commanding officer because of her reputation for courage and daring. She was also sent on missions by herself that required skillful tracking without being detected.

After a series of victories, General Morelos' army established itself at Cuautla and dug in knowing that Calleja, commander of the royalists, was approaching with a heavy force. On the morning of February 18, 1812, La Barragana was sent on a mission of observation. She was ordered to scout out Calleja's army, determine its strength and estimate the length of time it would take the royalists to reach Cuautla where the rebels were entrenched. La Barragana accepted the assignment with pride and began scenting out the movements of the enemy, following them at a distance. Wearing soldier's clothing and armed to the teeth, she traveled light; the only food she took with her was the usual army provision, beef jerky, packed in her saddle bag.

She trailed the royalists without being detected to Tetelcingo where Calleja's soldiers caught sight of her. Having already obtained the information she sought, she turned tail and ran. Some of Calleja's men pursued her, but she was such a skilled horsewoman that she was able to reach Cuautla unharmed where she reported the troop movements of the royalists and other important information to her chief, José María Morelos.

Morelos knew that his only chance against this larger force, which had far better and more modern weapons than his and was reinforced by several regiments from Spain, was to dig in for a siege. He hoped that after a few weeks the heavy seasonal rains would render the enemy's guns useless and that the fever which spread through the area would decimate their ranks. Unfortunately, the rains were late that year. General Morelos, his soldiers and the civilians of Cuautla were forced to hold out for seventy-two days during which no supplies passed through to them through the tight net the royalists drew around the city. After a while, cats, dogs and snakes were considered gourmet fare and finally bark stripped from trees became a kind of Cuautla jerky. There were many brave women in the group, each doing her duty ranging from heroic deeds to humble services. One of the best known and loved was called *La Humana Costeña* (the merciful woman from the coast). No one knows if she was wife, mother or sister of a soldier, or a camp follower, but she is remembered for sacrifices and goodness of heart.

At first, during the siege, she prepared drinks to sell that she concocted from fruit juice or whatever flavorings she could find. She was a poor person herself but her heart went out to the soldiers who guarded the bulwarks day and night despite illness or injury. Knowing that most of Morelos' men were from the coast as she was, La Humana Costeña took the money she made each day from her *refrescos* (soft drinks) and used it to buy the ingredients to make *chiliate*. This was a refreshing and nourishing beverage which had originated on the coast and was prepared from toasted ground corn, honey and water. As long as the supplies were available, she made the *chiliate* and gave it free of charge to the defenders of the bulwarks, not only at the canal at Xochitengo but also to the soldiers at Almeal, a good distance further, where she lugged the heavy *tinajas* (big earthen jars) day after day.

As the siege went on and on and the defenders grew hungrier and gloomier, three sisters provided most of the moments of happiness that the citizens of Cuautla knew. The baby of the group, Luz, was called *La Xocoyota* which means "the youngest" in the Aztec tongue. She tried to dance and sing the troubles of Cuautla away along with her older sisters, María and Teresa. They performed regularly, always smiling, and when the favorite La Xocoyota was thanked for her efforts by Morelos, who was grateful for the diversion brought to his deprived people, she replied gaily, "I shall laugh and sing as long as I live."

It was almost as though the gods were jealous of La Xocoyota's joyous spirit for not long after she was hit by a sniper's bullet. No one knew what had happened to her until they stumbled upon her body in the bushes where she had crawled to die alone so that others would not be saddened.

The year 1813 saw Morelos and Calleja spilling the blood of Mexicans on the battlefield while the people at home starved to death as food prices jumped three hundred percent and scarcities of all kinds began appearing. On the heels of war and famine came pestilence. Mexico City was a perfect breeding ground for disease because of the marshy land on which it was built. There had been much legislation meant to improve sanitation but nobody took the time, money or trouble to enforce it. A typhus epidemic started in Puebla and spread rapidly to Mexico City. By May there were so many dead that they buried them in vacant lots and in the streets. Ultimately, they just dug holes and threw the bodies in one on top of the other.

All food, medicine and sanitation depended upon private funding, as government or civic aid was completely lacking. There were people of good will who tried to help. Doña Ana María Iraeta de Mier was a woman noted for her unceasing concern for the poor and needy and she donated as much food as she could find to buy. The Marques de Valleaseno helped distribute it, caught typhus and died of the disease. Then the charity funds ran out. When the city went bankrupt, they asked Viceroy Calleja if he would grant them 30,000 pesos from the money that had been held by the Inquisition. He refused. When the *cabildo* (city council) asked that the church be required to contribute some of its silver for the purchase of food and supplies, the viceroy turned a deaf ear and let the request die.

Many prominent figures of the revolution, such as José María Morelos, the liberal priest who fought for freedom, and Agustín Iturbide, the loyalist emperor-dictator, were born in the province of Michoacán. But none was more deserving of respect than Gertrudis Bocanegra. Born of Spanish parents in 1765 in the beautiful region of Pátzcuaro she grew up in peace and comfort, devoting herself to her studies until she married Manuel Lazo de La Vega, a second Lieutenant in the royalist army. Many Spaniards who had settled in Mexico and preferred to call it home were disgusted with the representatives sent to New Spain from the mother country and the kind of justice they administered. A large number of the Creole sons and daughters of these Spanish families became ardent revolutionaries when the *Grito de Dolores* was heard.

Forsaking the loyalists, the husband and son of Gertrudis joined the forces of Hidalgo when he passed through Valladolid, Michoacán on his way to Guadalajara. Gertrudis was in complete accord with their patriotism and matched it by keeping the insurgents posted as to the latest moves of the royalist army. She joined the forces commanded by her son-in-law Gaona after the deaths of husband, Manuel, and her son, and she carried out whatever mission was assigned her until she was caught and imprisoned in Pátzcuaro. When asked to inform on her fellow insurgents, she refused; even torture did not wring from her the names of her compatriots. To make an example of her stubbornness, the royalists ordered Gertrudis Bocanegra to be killed by a firing squad November 11, 1818. In gratitude for this woman's contribution to freedom, a statue of her was erected in a garden in Pátzcuaro where she was born.

Manuela Medina, born in Texcoco, was called La Capitana because she raised and captained a company of independents for freedom who saw action in seven battles. She had great admiration for General José María Morelos and, wanting to make his acquaintance, she undertook a journey of 350 miles, saying she would die happy if only she could meet him. She came close to prophesying her own fate because she was badly injured in an explosion en route. Manuela died in her native city in 1822 after a year and a half of being bedridden with severe pain as the result of her combat wounds.

María Fermina Rivera accompanied her husband José María Rivera, colonel of the cavalry, fighting not only the royalists but battling hunger, dangerous roads and miserable weather on the long grueling campaigns. When a soldier dropped in battle, either dead or wounded, she picked up his gun and kept on firing, showing the same courage and daring that her husband did. When Colonel Rivera was killed she kept going until she died in action at Chichihualco in February 1821 where she fought at the side of General Vicente Guerrero.

Another heroine of humble origins who became a martyr for independence was Luisa Martínez, who lived with her husband Estevan García Rojas in the town of Erongaricuaro where they ran a little street stall to earn their living. The greater number of people in the town were *chaquetas* (royalist sympathizers) but Luisa Martínez was on the opposite side and with all her heart believed in and supported the fighters for freedom. She did not merely pay lip-service to the cause, but supplied the army with important news concerning royalist troops, helped find food and supplies for them, and acted as messenger for the chiefs of the insurrection. She was caught in the act of carrying mail for Tomás Pacheco by royalist General Pedro Celestino Negrete. She got away but he captured her again and imprisoned her, telling her that if she paid a fine of two thousand pesos and promised never to communicate again with the revolutionaries she would be released. She met the requirements and was freed, but repeated the offense and was caught and jailed once more. This happened a total of three times until finally, poor as she was, she could no longer raise the money to pay the fine which had been increased to four thousand pesos. Negrete immediately ordered her executed. Before she died in front of a firing squad in the cemetery at Erongaricuaro, she said to Negrete with all the fire and passion a Latina can summon against injustice:

"Why do you persecute me so? I have the right to do as much as I can to help my country because I am a Mexican. I don't think my conduct was wrong in any way; I only did my duty."

Among the foreigners who leant a hand to the cause is a French woman known only as La Mar. She came from Cartagena, a seaport in what is now the country of Colombia. This city had been a hotbed of insurrection against Spain and was also where the liberator of South America, Simón Bolívar, had written his Cartagena Manifesto in 1812. Fired by her own French revolution and the wars for freedom in the Americas, La Mar drifted north and joined up with General Francisco Xavier Mina in Galveston. Mina had been a Spanish officer who sympathized with the insurrectionists. He recruited a company of 500 men in the United States and fought many engagements on the side of Mexican independence until he was captured and killed in 1817. He was the type to appeal to La Mar; they were persons of action as well as conviction who believed in freedom for all.

During the siege of Soto La Marina in the province of Tamaulipas, La Mar cared for the sick and wounded, working day and night. Taken prisoner, she was sent to Veracruz where she was forced to work in a royalist hospital doing the most lowly, strenuous and revolting tasks. She escaped and joined up with a division of General Guadalupe Victoria's army, but she was imprisoned again in 1819 and forced into hard labor in Jalapa. Many letters were sent to Viceroy Apodaca on her behalf but she was not freed and permitted to return to her own country until the viceroy was deposed in 1821 and freedom from Spain was declared.

Doña Francisca Tapia is notable in the history of Mexican women for several reasons. To begin with she took charge of and successfully ran her own hacienda, Pateo, a large holding in the state of Michoacán. Unmarried, she adopted orphans and brought them into her home to live with her and her younger brother as members of the family. There were four orphans at hacienda Pateo when Doña Francisca provided a fifth child of her own out of wedlock--a child who was destined to become famous. The babe was born January 5, 1814 at Pateo and she named him Melchor Ocampo. Present at the birth was Doña Josefa Rufo who helped her mistress with the administration of the hacienda. No one has ever known for sure who Melchor Ocampo's father was. Many men, both political and military sought and were given refuge during the wars of independence at hacienda Pateo. One possible sire was the lawyer Ignacio Alas, friend and confederate of revolutionary leaders Ignacio López Rayón and José María Morelos. Another candidate mentioned was a priest in the nearby town of Maravatío, Antonio M.

Uraga.

Doña Francisca Tapia went to Mexico City to have the child christened, giving rise to the often repeated story that he was born there. However, Melchor Ocampo himself, when elected a deputy, declared that he accepted as a representative of Michoacán because it was his birthplace. Francisca Tapia never divulged the name of the father of her child or from whom he got his name.

Melchor Ocampo was a healthy charming youngster indulged by all members of the family. Doña Tapia recognized his abilities and sent him to Morelia at age twelve where he was fortunate enough to encounter a member of the liberal clergy, Don Angel Mariano Morales, who instructed him in philosophy, law, mathematics and natural science as well as the usual theology and Latin. Melchor Ocampo was fated to be second in prominence only to Benito Juárez in the reforms of mid-nineteenth century Mexico and the two men were lifelong friends. Ocampo not only gave full credit to Doña Francisca Xaviera Tapia for her generosity in providing him a home but also for her great abilities, speaking of her as a person of "marked talent, elevated views, a spirited character of unbounded charity."

Doña Francisca died in 1831 at age fifty-six when Melchor Ocampo was only seventeen years of age. She left the bulk of her large estate to him, although ample provision was made in her will for the orphans. (Her younger brother had died years before.) Ocampo's circumstances enabled him to continue his studies, becoming an expert in law, scientific farming and Indian languages before he entered politics in 1842. Doña Francisca Tapia had dared a great deal and it was not solely gossip she faced. In an era when life expectancy was less than thirty years it took courage to cope with childbirth, married or not, at age thirty-nine for the first time. It took even more courage to add the babe to her nest of orphans so he would not become one himself.

The *Calendario de Las Señoritas Mexicanas* a yearly publication for women, became available in 1839. Published by Mariano Galvan it was the first of its kind. It contained a variety of articles such as the culture and propagation of plants, the history of the shrine of Guadalupe, and colored plates of the latest fashions similar to the American monthly *Godey's Ladies Book*. There was also a calendar which detailed the holy days and saints days. Several years later in 1841 the first weekly aimed at women made its appearance. It was called *Semanario de Las Señoritas Mexicanas.*

What did society women in the big cities do with their time other than fritter it away on dinners, balls, and flirtations? Mme. Calderón de La Barca in her book *Life in Mexico* speaks of a special mass given on the morning of Christmas Eve which was performed entirely by women. These ladies of the aristocracy, all amateur singers, spent long hours that added up to many weeks of rehearsal prior to the performance. A number of them in the group had exceptionally fine voices and were praised not only by doting relatives but by people who had heard the great voices of Europe and had a genuine yardstick of comparison.

One who did become a professional singer was Señorita María de Jesús Cepeda y Cosío. Her career came about mostly because of financial problems in her family, although the stage was frowned upon for young women of the haute monde. At age seventeen she began studying with the Paris-born Mme. Jeanne Anaïs Castellan de Giampetro, prima donna assoluta of an Italian opera company that spent much time performing in Mexico City. In 1845 María de Jesús made her debut and although she sang *Norma, La Sonnambula* and other operas with success, she later suffered unexplained problems and had to give up her career.

A society matron with a trained voice who also sang remarkably well was Señora Margarita de Gorgollo. Although she did not turn professional, she often gave notable concerts and was much in demand to perform at *tertulias*.

Until the mid-nineteenth century many Mexican women of all classes smoked cigars and cigarettes. About 1850 they gave up the habit and no one really knows why. In 1840 a visitor, Albert Gilliam, watching the fancy carriages on the Alameda exclaimed at the ease with which handsome society belles would light their *cigaritos* with a piece of punk and loll back among the cushions exhaling clouds of smoke. The first wife of General Antonio López de Santa Anna, Señora Inés de La Paz García de Santa Anna, a lady known for good works but not for good looks, sent for her tobacco case of gold and diamonds directly after breakfast and began puffing away. She lit up casually along with her husband, the general, and any other men who were present.

The Mexican Christmas *posadas* (festivities) of the nineteenth century seem to have been a specialty of women, although children of both sexes were also involved. The origin of the *posada* stemmed from the nine days of wandering by Mary and

Joseph in Bethlehem as they tried to find lodging for the imminent birth of the baby Jesus. On the last night, Christmas Eve, well-to-do Mexicans would gather in the house of the senior member of their family to begin the ceremony. Lining up in pairs to form a procession, each woman carried a lighted candle in her hand. The children followed dressed as angels in costumes of silver or gold lamé, their white gauze wings tipped with diamonds and pearls, their eyes round with wonder at the mystery and solemnity of the occasion and importance of their role in it. Mothers and children chanted the litanies as they wound through the house which was decorated with fragrant evergreens, and when the procession halted before a closed door, fireworks were set off to represent the sparkling descent of the angels. Then a group of women dressed as shepherds appeared and voices representing Mary and Joseph cried out, imploring in verse for admittance and being refused by a chorus from behind the closed door. This was carried back and forth in rhymed dialogue until finally the doors were thrown open and the holy family entered. Within the room the *nacimiento* (holy birth) was presented on platforms which bore wax figures of the infant Jesus, wise men, and shepherds as well as fountains, trees, and animals to complete the scene. The aroma of roses and violets filled the air, enhancing the beauty of the decorations provided by the women.

Mothers and daughters of the poor paired off and formed outdoor processions that wound from dwelling to dwelling instead of from room to room as they did in the mansions. Although they could not duplicate the expensive clothing and jewelry of the wealthy women, they wore their best finery and were just as devoted to the yearly *posadas* as their more fortunate sisters.

One place where rich and poor women alike were equal was in the cathedrals. Unlike many other parts of the world, in Mexico aristocrat and commoner knelt side by side and concentrated upon their prayers rather than upon the dress of their neighbors as was the custom in countries where families of wealth grouped together in pews. Joel R. Poinsett, first ambassador from the United States to Mexico, himself a Protestant, wrote, "The house of God is open to all and all without distinction stand before the altar." Poinsett was responsible for bringing a flower back to the United States in the 1830s that has been associated with the Christmas season ever since. The plant called the poinsettia is named after him.

Convents were of particular interest because they harbored so many females and because they offered such variations in living conditions. In the nineteenth century there were luxury convents such as La Concepción and La Encarnación. The latter was as large as a palace with great galleries and courtyards, gardens with tinkling fountains, carved stone benches, and a variety of rare flowers ranging from roses and carnations to orchids and gardenias. Each nun upon entering paid a five thousand dollar dowry and brought along two servants. Obviously these ladies came from families with money. Their everyday robes were of fine white cashmere with a black crepe veil and long rosary. The novices wore the same except that the veil was white. The handsome ceremonial habit of the happy sisters was also white but with mantles of sky blue and a gold epaulette or badge worn on one shoulder. From time to time La Encarnación would waive the need for a girl to bring a dowry if she had outstanding natural gifts which might further the prestige of the order. For example, one impoverished applicant possessed a beautiful singing voice which added greatly to the quality of the choir so the girl was admitted without funds.

Visitors to La Encarnación were served supper in an elegant dining room furnished with ornately carved antique armchairs of the heavy, high-backed, Spanish style. The walls were garnished with expensive paintings and the food included all the delicacies found in the finest establishments: fancy cakes, chocolates, custards, jellies, tarts and lemonade. Some of the sweets were decorated with gilt paper cut-outs and presented on silver or fine porcelain platters. During the meal a young girl sang ballads and played the harp to entertain the guests. During the revolution of 1840 soldiers interrupted the nuns' prayers with cannonfire, then penetrated the walls of La Encarnación but fortunately no accidents occurred and the expensive furnishings were spared, although the sisters' patience was sorely tried.

There were other orders where the nuns did not lead the indulgent life just described. One of these was the convent of Santa Teresa. Here, no servants were allowed nor visitors permitted entrance. If relatives wanted to converse with a nun of this order it was necessary, after receiving permission from the mother superior, to talk through a revolving wooden screen which did not permit a clear view of the face of the recluse within. The motto of Santa Teresa was "all or nothing, the world or the cloister." These were the discalced (barefoot) Carmelites with whom Sor Juana Inés de La Cruz associated herself when she first took the veil but from whom she disassociated herself shortly after when she became ill from the life of deprivation.

The ceremony by which one entered the sisterhood of Santa Teresa was an impressive and somber one. In the morning, at her home, the young woman dressed herself in her fanciest civilian clothes for the last time and wore as many jewels as she could muster, topping her costume off with a crown woven of fresh flowers. She passed the day of the ceremony bidding farewell to friends and family and attending parties given in her honor. All the excitement plus nervous tension had often worked the girl into a state of near-frenzy by the time she arrived at the church. Many a young woman, laughing gaily to show how delighted she was at the step she was about to take, fought off hysteria while the smile on her face grew as fixed as the grin on a pumpkin. It seems to have been a tradition that the bride look deliriously happy and not the least bit timid or awed as would have been natural.

As soon as the church doors opened, the crowd burst in and the musicians entered, lining up in rows. The organ boomed out a psalm followed by popular melodies and marches played by the band while rockets exploded outside the church. A black curtain had been hung before the grating through which visitors would be allowed to look into the convent. With a high sense of drama, the curtain was suddenly pulled back, disclosing the scene. Within, the altar was draped in gold and scarlet for the occasion as were the walls, chairs, tables and vestments worn by the priests and bishop. The interior was brilliantly illuminated so that the rich colors dazzled the eye.

In front of the priest's table, a purple rug had been placed encircled by a border of fresh roses, lilies and carnations and in the center knelt the trembling novice clutching a lighted taper almost as big as herself. On either side of the girl, running the length of the room, were prostrate figures dressed in black, foreheads touching the floor, hands holding the same large, lighted tapers. At intervals the nuns of the austere Santa Teresa order arose, chanting as though casting a spell, then falling to the ground and pressing their foreheads to the cold, stone floor. At the conclusion of their incantation, they raised the wan and pale novice from the rug and supported her as she went to kneel at the feet of the bishop who proceeded to question her reasons and the strength of her desire for the vocation. When satisfied as to her sincerity, the bishop gave her his blessing, then the curtain fell.

When the curtain rolled back for the second part of the drama, the bride was prostrate upon the floor but now her finery was gone and she too was covered from head to toe with black robes, surrounded by her black-robed sisters intoning a hymn. At its conclusion she was once again raised to her feet and brought to kneel before the bishop. Making the sign of the cross, he gave her the benediction, at the conclusion of which she made the rounds of her sisters, embracing each as she cemented her kinship. From outside the grating where the spectators sat, a priest delivered a sermon congratulating the bride upon becoming a member of a select group of wise women who had given up the frivolity of the world. When the sermon ended the music started again and the novice came to the grating to gaze out with sorrowful eyes (whether for her fellowmen or for herself it would be hard to guess) upon the world she had renounced. Then the curtain fell, forever shutting her in.

The daily life in this stern order, consisting of only twenty-one nuns, was dreary by any standards. The refectory where the sisters ate had a long narrow table and unvarnished wooden benches. A wooden plate and spoon marked the place of each nun and at the center was a skull to remind the good sisters that no pleasures, even those of a table as spartan as this, last forever. A small pulpit was tucked away in one corner of the room where a nun read aloud from scripture while the others ate their modest servings. At each meal one of the nuns did penance by prostrating herself upon the floor wearing a crown of iron nails with points turned inward to make the scalp bleed. A wooden bit was placed in her mouth and she was served her food in this position, making chewing and swallowing almost impossible.

To insure discomfort the tiny cells contained a wooden plank to be used for a bed. This plank had been deliberately cut short so that when the nun laid down, her feet hung over the end. A wooden block pillowed her head and she was required to clutch a cross placed upon her chest, never permitting the sacred object to slip to the floor. This made sleep an elusive thing. On occasion it was the custom to wear a band of nails around the waist, points inward next to the bare skin, and a cross of nails over the breast. A scourging with a whip preceded the night's rest which ended at 4:00 a.m. The sister's daily robes were made of the harshest materials so that to wear them was in itself a penance.

The women who took the veil at the convent of Corpus Christi had to be of Indian ancestry. They were descendants of the ruling classes of the Aztecs and one of the first nuns of their order was related to Montezuma. Where other nuns donned their finest European-style dresses and jewels for the ceremony, these women proudly wore *cacica* dress, the ceremonial garb of a princess or priestess of pre-conquest days.

There were many opponents to the constitution of 1857 which severed ties between church and state and returned much church property and church men and women to secular life. The convent of Santa Mónica, located on Avenida Cinco de Mayo in the city of Puebla, was one of those which violently protested falling under the ax. Closed by Juárez' laws of the liberal reform, the nuns were ordered to return to civilian life and the convent was sold for individual dwellings. That was that--supposedly. Private parties moved in and the years went by. But now and then there were rumors of strange happenings and spooky things that were hard to explain. Police searches were instituted from a municipal police station located directly across the street, but without ever finding anything of note.

The establishment had been constructed originally in 1606 as a hotel or rooming house for married women of the aristocracy, a chaperoned refuge when their husbands were away from home. But the high society ladies of Puebla turned their backs on it and it was little used until the low society ladies of Puebla inherited the place and it became a shelter where prostitutes were held and forced to reform. In 1762 it changed faces again. Exchanging the profane for the sacred, it became a convent and was named Santa Mónica.

The nuns of Santa Mónica were of a cloistered order; upon taking the veil they were immediately incarcerated within the walls of the convent and nevermore sallied forth. It was whispered that when the edict had been received for them to disperse in 1857, the doughty sisterhood resolved to go underground if they could persuade the new owners of the premises to permit them to dwell beneath the buildings and in odd corners of cupboards and closets. It was even hinted that there was an opening to their quarters behind a revolving chimney through which priests and physicians descended, food was received and refuse was disposed. Perhaps its most important function was that it provided entry for novices who wished to join the order when members began dying off and needed replacement.

Does it sound like a novelist's dream? Well, it wasn't. For seventy years this underground convent functioned covertly, frequently holding its collective breath while the police searched the premises above, having been called in yet again to investigate rumors of strange rappings and squeakings. It contained thirty-nine rooms, two patios, innumerable secret passages, and floors that moved, silently disclosing stairways. Most ingenious of all was a wall facing the upper choir of the church next door. On this wall hung a large painting which covered up an opening through which the nuns, unseen by the congregation down below, could participate in the high mass offered by priests who alone were aware of their presence. There were catacombs below ground that served as graves until the dead became too numerous and the skeletons were removed to a large, dungeon-like room where fifty skulls are still preserved.

How these nuns managed to proselytize and acquire recruits, swelling their ranks from the original fifty to eighty members by the time they were found out, is a miracle in itself. Much of Puebla's population knew of the convent's existence through the years but so well did this city, renowned for its devotion to the Catholic faith, guard the secret that it took a series of freak accidents in 1934 to finally bring about their disclosure. In the midst of the great depression, the nuns of Santa Mónica, like everyone else, needed money. They decided to sell one of their paintings which they sincerely believed to be of much value. The antique dealer who bought it discovered it was worthless. He went on a tequila binge which unhinged his tongue to the extent that, in his drunken wrath at the sisters, he sought out a federal official and told him about the secret convent. In the midst of his informing, he sobered up enough to realize what he was doing and tried to repair some of the damage by withholding the address.

This did not prevent the federal police from instituting a search of the dwellings on Avenida Cinco de Mayo which had been suspect for so long. As usual, they found nothing. But one of the officers, wanting to rest for a moment, leaned against a shelf, upsetting a heavy vase which pressed upon a secret button that caused a bell to ring in the convent. Without hesitation, the mother superior opened the door, thinking that one of the regular visitors such as a doctor or priest was calling and found herself face to astonished face with an officer. This policeman said later that his feeling of cockiness upon pushing his way in soon dissipated in the strangely sacred atmosphere that had been kept secret so many years.

Impressed by the courage of the nuns of Santa Mónica, the police still had no choice but to obey the law and see that the order was dispersed, but the sisters were never prosecuted. Within forty-eight hours they were all gone, leaving furnishings and possessions behind. There is a postscript to the story of the treacherous antique dealer. They say that he went on a business trip to Mexico City, caught smallpox and died.

Santa Mónica was converted into a museum by the government and may be seen today with everything virtually intact, including such gory treasures as the petrified heart of the founder, the pickled entrails of some of the convent's most ardent supporters, and the dried tongue of a famous preacher hanging on a wire. In the same theatre of the macabre, the standard equipment of self-torture is displayed, including the spike-lined belt worn by the mother superior at Lent and the formidable cat-o-nine tails the nuns used to flog each other. Not the least of this graphic display is an Indian painted on velvet whose eyes seem to follow your every move no matter which way you turn. The conducted tours take a long time, a lot of endurance and much squeezing sideways through narrow passages. The final exit takes place in Alice in Wonderland style through a large collapsible looking glass. As government-run exhibits often do, the amusement park aspects are emphasized for the tourist trade. The convent of Santa Mónica is actually a testimonial to the spirit of a group of women determined to live their own lives in their own way despite politicians and police.

Nineteenth century society ladies contributed a great deal to charity in money and time. A favorite was *La Casa de Niños Espositos* (the house of abandoned children) commonly called *La Cuna* (the cradle). Here foundlings were taken in and though most were Indian or Mestizo, there was also a fair sprinkling of Anglo-Saxons. Each lady of the society had a certain number of children assigned to her and was responsible for furnishing clothing and for paying village wet nurses four dollars per month to nourish the babes through infancy. When they were weaned they were returned to La Cuna and could remain under the charge of the organization for life; but usually the children were adopted by well-to-do families who brought them up with their own or gave them status within the household as special servants. In 1840 the president of the organization was a woman known for her good works, the dowager Marquesa de Vivanco, wife of General José María Moran.

Education for women even in the upper classes was a scarce commodity in nineteenth century Mexico. Most so-called ladies could read and write--minimally. They attended a coeducational primary school, then, at age ten, the sexes were separated. The boys went off to academies of learning while the girls were whisked back into the confines of the home. They received private drawing or music lessons until they reached fourteen when they buckled down to the serious business of husband-hunting. Embroidery was popular as an activity for a cultured female as well as the singing of love songs in a caressing voice. A few wealthy families who were well-traveled and had observed European women (other than the Spanish who were kept in a state of educational subservience) made an effort to provide a genuine education for their daughters. Among this select group were three sisters from a family by the name of Fagoaga, daughters of the Marqués de Apartado, a millionaire who had made his money in silver mines and land. These girls, Faustina, Elena and Julia, were educated in French, English, German and Latin and had undoubtedly benefited by the fact that their father had been banished from Mexico several times for political reasons forcing the family into exile in Europe.

Their home was a large hacienda called San Xavier near the village of Tlalnepantla. No matter what the family wealth, rooms in country houses were sparsely furnished in those days. But unlike those of their neighbors, the Fagoagas' shelves contained a treasury of books in many languages on many subjects. In addition to being intellectual, the sisters were most devout and very active in charities that aided women and children of the poor. They devoted much time to teaching the female inmates of the *acordada* (public jail), many of whom were guilty of murdering their husbands in unpremeditated crimes of passion.

Taken on a tour by the Fagoaga sisters, Fanny Calderón de La Barca describes the jail this way:

"Some were lying on the floor, others working, some were well dressed, others dirty and slovenly. Few looked sad, most appeared careless and happy, and none seemed ashamed. Amongst them were some of the handsomest faces I have seen in Mexico. One good looking common woman, with a most joyous and benevolent countenance and lame, came up to salute the ladies. I inquired what she had done. Murdered her husband and buried him under the brick floor! Shades of lavater! It is some comfort to hear that their husbands were such brutes that they deserved little better. Amongst others confined here is the wife, or rather the widow, of a governor of Mexico, who made away with her husband. One very pretty and coquettish looking little woman, with a most intellectual face ... is in jail on suspicion of having poisoned her lover ... We were attended by a woman who had the title of *presidenta* and who, after some years of good conduct, has now the charge of her fellow prisoners, but she also murdered her husband. We went upstairs, accompanied by various of these distinguished criminals, to the room looking down upon the chapel, in which room the ladies give them instruction in reading and in the Christian doctrine. With the time which they devote to these charitable offices, together with their numerous devotional exercises, and the care which their houses and families require, it cannot be said that the life of a Mexican señora is an idle one--nor in such cases can it be considered a useless one."

But the women just described were the fortunates who came from the middle and upper classes. *La Acordada* had another section for *las mujeres pobres* (the poor women) a large communal hall on the lowest floor. Here, hundreds of poor women were herded together in a great unwashed, uncombed horde whose ragged clothes molded from the damp or were constantly scorched from the heat of the ovens where they baked tortillas. The miasma that arose from the slop pails and sweating bodies was enough to chase Mme. Calderón de La Barca away in a hurry.

The Fagoaga sisters were also involved in assisting the institution for insane women on the Calle de Canoa that had been built in 1698. The inmates are said to have been treated in a kindly fashion with the poor being admitted free of charge and the rich paying a modest amount for their keep. Sufficient funds were always lacking and special treatment for special cases, even if much had been known about therapy at the time, did not exist. Most inmates crouched on the floor staring vacantly, some spent their time in endless repetition of woes, and those who were able sewed or sang, although sometimes the same stitch was put in and torn out endlessly and the same few notes were repeated for hours. As with most institutions of its kind, the sights and sounds were melancholy, but judging from chroniclers of similar places in England and Europe, conditions in Mexico seem to have been somewhat better.

In a *finca* (small farm) near Ttalnepantla, not far from Mexico City, an Indian woman named Doña Margarita, described as tall and handsome, was left a rich widow with ample livestock and land. Instead of living opulently and enjoying her good fortune, she chose a life of poverty, preferring to spend her money on the orphans she took into her home. At any given time there might be twelve to twenty boys and girls living with her, many of whom were deformed or ill. They were taught simple skills and if they were able to work, employment was found for them by their benefactress when they were old enough. Doña Margarita was a devout person who had always been renowned in her village for devotion to her faith, but unlike many others her observance of religious rites gave birth to an active concern for human rights.

6
The Lovers

The woman directing the loading of the burros that would carry her eight children, herself and the necessary saddlebags and baskets of food and clothing on the long trip across the mountains from the pueblo of Etla, in the state of Oaxaca, to the port city of Veracruz, looked scarcely older than her oldest child Manuela. Doña Margarita Maza de Juárez, thirty-two years of age, was slight, dark-haired, delicate-featured and had repeatedly proved her mettle in the fifteen years that had elapsed since her marriage to Benito Juárez, who would be known to future generation as the liberator of his country.

The love story of Benito and Margarita was a curious one. Juárez was born in a village called San Pablo Guelatao in the state of Oaxaca on March 21, 1806. His parents, Marcelino Juárez and Brígida García, full-blooded Zapotec Indians, were both dead by the time he was three years old. Benito and his sisters, María Josefa and Rosa, were left in the care of their paternal grandparents. But these elders did not last more than a few years either. Upon their death the children scattered and Juárez went to live with his uncle. When he was twelve years old Benito ran away, trudging many miles to the city of Oaxaca where he located his sister María Josefa. She was separated from her husband and working as cook in the house of Don Antonio Maza, a dealer in cochineal, a widely used red dye made in Mexico. Juárez soon got a job working for a bookbinder, Don Antonio Salanueva, a lay brother of the third order of St. Francis, described by Juárez as "a pious and honorable man" who offered Benito an education in return for service in his house and business. Through Don Antonio, Juárez got his chance for schooling and was a sometimes inspired but always determined pupil who learned to apply the tenacity inherited from his Indian ancestors to the knotty problems of his life and later his country.

Throughout the years Benito Juárez' connection with the family of Don Antonio Maza deepened. His sister María Josefa continued as cook and because he was very fond of her, he visited the household when on vacation from school and returned frequently after he started working. He was twenty years old when the youngest Maza child made her appearance and he dandled the baby on his knee and fussed over her along with the rest of the adults. When thirty-seven-year-old Benito proposed to seventeen-year-old Margarita Eustaquia, youngest daughter of Antonio Maza, he had known her since birth and the young woman was as much at ease with him as she would have been with a member of her own family. But in no way did she look upon him as a brother nor did he consider her a little sister. It was a love match of the most intense and devoted variety and there was never a whisper of gossip after the knot was tied, although Benito and Margarita were doomed to be separated for long periods of time and he was known to have sired a pair of illegitimate children before marriage.

Margarita's mother, Doña Petra Parada de Maza, and her father, Don Antonio, were born in Genoa, Italy. In the Mexico of the 1820s by virtue of ancestry and skin color, let alone money, the Mazas were far above Juárez in social position. It had to be a very broad-minded family that would permit the penniless brother of their Indian cook to marry into it. Don Antonio, as head of household, must have set the example and his educational policy toward his daughter fits in with a liberal view. Although instructed at home, Margarita was taught not only to read but to write, unusual for a Mexican girl born in 1826. The marriage ceremony was held July 31, 1843 in Oaxaca in the church of San Felipe Neri. There was much love between Margarita and Benito but not much romantic nonsense. She called him "Juárez"; he called her "old lady." When asked what she thought about her husband Margarita replied, "He is very homely but very good." Even without Indian tradition, her brevity could equal his.

By 1847 Juárez had become governor of the state of Oaxaca. Bent upon reforms that ranged from building new schools and roads to the establishment of municipal cemeteries to replace burial in churches (an unsanitary practice, especially in periods of epidemic), Juárez had problems inducing the clergy to support some of his changes. He had not yet reached the breaking point that would make him drive hard to bring about the separation of church and state that he had begun to feel would be necessary, but he was giving it a close look. That Doña Margarita shared her husband's liberal ideas was proven by the burial of their two-year-old daughter, Guadalupe, in 1850. As important persons, the governor and his family rated internment inside the church. In accordance with the improved standards of hygiene that he was trying to institute, but unsanctioned by the clerics, Juárez himself, during a cholera epidemic, carried the body of his daughter in its tiny coffin to the public cemetery of San Miguel outside the city of Oaxaca, accompanied by Margarita and other mourners. Benito's advanced ideas caused him to be labeled a dangerous reformer by influential elements of clergy and army. By 1853 he was in exile in New Orleans where he was joined by other Mexican rebels.

At this time Margarita started her peripatetic and often dangerous life. Pursued and persecuted by spies of General Ignacio Martínez Pinollos, one of Juárez' greatest enemies, Margarita and her children had to go underground for a while. They hid out at Hacienda Cinco Señores, owned by Don Miguel Castro, who had been a classmate of Juárez' at the Institute of Sciences and Arts in Oaxaca. Knowing that her husband was penniless, Margarita swallowed her pride and borrowed money, sending her brother, José María Maza, to Benito in Veracruz with the four hundred dollars she had scraped together. When she was able to emerge safely from hiding, she took her family to the pueblo of Etla where she started a tobacco shop and took in sewing in hopes of earning enough money to pay back her debts and put bread on the table for herself and her children.

With the fall of General Antonio López de Santa Anna, the way was clear for the return of Benito Juárez and other reformers who had been in exile in New Orleans. By July of 1854 Juárez was back in his own country and it didn't take long for him to get into politics once more. By 1856 he was again governor of Oaxaca and rising rapidly in national importance as Mexico's first genuine man of the people. It was shortly after that the liberal party, with Benito prominent in the promulgation of its reform laws, set about stripping the Catholic Church of power. Much of its property and revenue were confiscated or curtailed, its separate courts of justice prohibited, and freedom of worship was declared so that other religions could function openly in Mexico. Juárez was next appointed Minister of the Interior under President Ignacio Comonfort and when Comonfort was reelected, Juárez became head of the Supreme Court and simultaneously Vice President of the country.

The liberal reforms were not taken meekly by the clergy. Anyone who swore allegiance to the new constitution was threatened with excommunication. Things grew so bad and Mexico was in such upheaval that Comonfort fled to the United States, leaving the mess to Juárez, who took over as president. It was not to be a peaceful beginning for Benito. Armed uprisings, bloodshed and dissent were still the order of the day. Invited by Governor Gutierrez Zamora to move his government to Veracruz, Juárez, for the safety of all concerned, accepted and at long last was able to contemplate a renewal of family life.

And what of Margarita during this turmoil? Her love for and closeness to Benito continued no matter how little they saw of each other and no matter what hardships and dangers she had to undergo. In all, she bore him twelve children. One son, Benito, and six daughters, María de Jesus, Felicitas, Margarita, Manuela, Soledad and María Josefa, outlived their parents but three daughters died as babies and two sons expired when young children. The strain of constant pregnancy and childrearing alone would have been more than enough to keep several women occupied, but in the early years Margarita had also to supplement the family income and solve all problems without help when Juárez was in exile. The establishment of Juárez and his government in Veracruz was no sign of permanent peace and security for the family but the thirty-two-year "old lady" was still young enough to live in the present and let the future take care of itself. Deciding not to waste one more minute in separation from her husband, Margarita gathered her children about her and told them of the long journey they were to make.

Let us imagine how she would have planned it. First of all, she could not take the most comfortable and convenient way which was to travel the good roads that led to the city of Puebla and from there to Veracruz, even though her youngest child was still a babe in arms. Political enemies of Juárez would be certain to lie in wait on the well-traveled road and the family could be attacked or end up as hostages. Her brother, José María Maza, was going with her to afford what additional protection he could, but there was no way to mask the long caravan of *arrieros*, children and mules. So the alternative road had to be over the Sierra de Cuajimulco (now called Sierra de Juárez) and most of the travel would have to take place at night for further security.

Today, by air, the most direct route from Oaxaca to Veracruz is some 150 miles. To travel the primitive and winding paths by foot and burro in the dark could add half again as many more miles to the journey. Keep in mind that this woman had been a city child and had probably experienced a minimum of forays into wild country. She had also been tenderly reared as the baby of a well-to-do family, indulged if not spoiled. On the basis of stamina alone, Margarita deserves her place in history.

When she had decided on the route and procured the mules and *arrieros*, the next important problem would be clothing. Fashion decreed that the wife of the nation's president and her daughters wear the latest from Europe. No doubt Margarita would possess some of the stylish garments of the day since she had plied her needle for others to earn money in lean times, and it was her hands that always fashioned Benito's fine, white linen shirts. But the tight-fitting bodices, long sleeves that belled below the elbows, and enormous skirts made of a minimum of ten yards of fabric, weighted at the bottom with rolls of scratchy horsehair and frosted with flounces that ran from hem to waist would hardly do, although history tells us that she did not neglect to take her crinolines along. The story goes that when she put them on to be properly dressed before entering Veracruz, the bulky skirt caught on a branch, saving her from a tumble down a precipice proving that the hampering style was good for something.

For the hardest part of the long hike, there were many varieties of long, loose cotton *huipils* worn by the natives of the state of Oaxaca that were a protection against insects and thorns and permitted freedom of movement. There was another advantage to the *huipil*. Traveling at night for greatest security, the caravan would have a good chance of passing as an Indian family taking their wares to or from market should spies be about. By starlight the lighter skins of Margarita, her brother and children would blend in with the darker ones of the tough, machete-armed *arrieros* who had been hired for their survival wisdom, agility with mules and fidelity to the liberal cause.

Doña Margarita must have thanked the Lord many times during the long journey that her oldest children were daughters. Fourteen-year-old Manuela could often relieve the tired mother by herding toddlers and keeping the pre-teens in line so that they would not get lost in the dark. If they were lucky enough to be near a settlement when daylight came, their shelter would be the *choza* (hut) of friendly Indians along the way who offered hospitality while they worked in the fields. In addition to the difficulties in reversing the clock and trying to sleep during daylight, this brave señora must have always rested uneasily, her eyes opening wide every time there was the slightest noise outside, glancing at the small bodies nearby for a reassuring count of their numbers, fearful of assassins or kidnappers.

When Doña Margarita glimpsed the walls surrounding the historic seaport city of Veracruz they must have been the most welcome sight in the world, and to know that her beloved Juárez was there waiting for her must have been the most heartening thought. It didn't matter that the war grew more confusing and that reactionaries governed Mexico City and the central states. Nor did it matter that Veracruz, now the seat of Benito's liberal government, would probably be attacked in the near future. Even the frightful battles that residents of the torrid seaport city had year after year with yellow fever and cholera faded into insignificance. The family would be together and Margarita would have dared any number of mountain treks to have this happy event take place.

Within the year another child was born in Veracruz, a daughter, Francisca. This girl had the honor of being the first birth entered in the civil registry, another reform brought by Juárez and the constitution of 1857. Previously, the Catholic Church had maintained control over the formal recording of births which meant that all infants by registration were Catholics or non-existent. Baby Francisca was unaware of the storm of protest at her civil status and the outcry made by Don Clemente de Jesús Munguía, bishop of Michoacán, who saw a further change in ancient tradition in the defection of this mite.

The next four years were stormy. The war between liberals and conservatives went on with the United States supporting Juárez' cause. Finally on January 1, 1861 Juárez entered Mexico City, but it was a short-lived triumph followed by the assassination of many of his best-loved cohorts. When congress declared him president on June 11 Margarita's emotions must have been mixed. Benito was a man who possessed a fatalistic outlook and was not known for taking precautions. It was not that he was foolhardy; that was no part of his stolid, unemotional style. But rather, he was indifferent to the usual hazards of public office. Knowing the dreadful end of so many of their friends and also of previous attempts on her husband's life, Margarita must have had fear as her constant companion even while taking great pride in Juárez' fame.

Margarita and the children lived a retiring life during these years in the capital. To stroll in the park at Chapultepec was one of their greatest diversions. Judging from the strong bonds of affection that were observed by contemporaries between Juárez and his wife and the open way they wrote of their emotions to each other, it's hard to believe that self-effacement and a meek acceptance of the mother and auxiliary role were the causes of Margarita's quiet existence. This kind of characterization of her as the noble, female self-sacrificer is the one usually presented. Caution would have been a good reason for mother and children to stay out of the public eye at this time. Benito was careless of his own safety but was constantly alert to any threat to his beloved family. The new republic was a shaky fledgling that could fall while trying its wings. Given the opportunity, the circling hawks would attack the whole nest. In a precarious political world filled with assassins and other hazards, it would only have been common sense for the president's wife and children to live quietly.

There were also the eternal pregnancies with their complications and demands upon Margarita's strength and time. In an era when women aged rapidly and died young, Doña Margarita was getting on in years for childbearing and may not have been well enough for a social whirl, although she would prove later that she was, under different conditions, quite capable of having one. We know that she lost an infant daughter in 1862. Also, her father, Don Antonio Maza, passed away July 25 of that year and the mourning observed by Mexican ladies did not permit frivolity, especially when the loss was a parent. During these years we catch a glimpse now and then of Margarita and the girls through the eyes of travelers, in this instance a description given by the Englishman Charles Lempriere from his *Notes on Mexico in 1861*.

"There was no fuss or attention paid them [Juárez' family] except that they were unpleasantly stared at. The mother is a nice-looking, lady-like dame of forty, graceful and dignified. Her three daughters, from twenty to thirteen, were rather tall, rather stout and fairly good-looking."

At the time, Manuela, the eldest daughter was seventeen and Margarita thirty-four years old. Photographs of them bear out the label good-looking. There is a daguerreotype still in existence showing Juárez with his attractive wife on one side and his sister, María Josefa Juárez de López, on the other. María Josefa with her long braids, finely-shaped head and sculptured cheekbones was a handsome woman and some of her nieces resembled her.

The financial problems of Juárez' struggling democracy had necessitated enormous loans whose payments could not be met. The French, British and Spanish debtor governments pressed hard, even landing troops on the coast of Mexico but in the end it was only the French who stayed. Napoleon the third, nephew of the famous conqueror, and his Spanish-born wife, Empress Eugenie, had designs on the young republic. They hoped to make it part of their empire, so the pair ordered French troops to fight the republicans on Mexican territory with the object of establishing a monarchy and taking over the land. There were still strong conservative elements in Mexico who joyously allied themselves with the French and the infant government of Juárez was forced to retreat from Mexico City on May 31, 1863. Juárez sought aid from the United States, which was sympathetic to his regime, but at that time America was fighting its own bloody civil war and could not give much help.

Juárez, his family and government were forced to move again, this time to San Luis Potosí, a city further north. With the toughness and resilience that Benito always exhibited, he never for a moment doubted that this was merely a lull in the permanent formation of the Mexican republic. Doña Margarita probably felt relief to know that temporarily, at least, the threat to the safety of her loved ones was somewhat less. In May, shortly before departing Mexico City, a marriage had taken place between daughter Manuela and a Cuban by the name of Pedro Santacilia. It was a match highly approved of by all members of the family. Juárez was especially pleased. He had met the young liberal when they were both in exile in New Orleans and had the utmost faith in Santacilia as a son-in-law and trusted friend.

Santacilia did not betray the trust. As the war worsened it was he who shepherded the family in November of 1863 first to Saltillo, a hazardous journey of several hundred miles across desert and valley, which would remind Margarita of her experience over the mountains to Veracruz when she bore the sole responsibility for a pack of children. From Saltillo, Pedro Santacilia took the family to Monterrey, where the traumatic decision was made for safety's sake to go to the United States and remain there until the ever-encroaching French were ousted and the republic was restored. Departing Mexico by way of Matamoros, they were escorted by a detachment of cavalry having bid farewell to Benito in the little pueblo of Cadareyta. The journey ended up four months later in New York City where the family lived until a cholera epidemic forced a move to New Rochelle.

The years in the United States would be some of the most sorrowful in Margarita's life. The children, as children always do, became facile in the foreign language, but it remained exactly that to Margarita who acquired no English and missed her home and husband with an intensity that bordered on desperation at times. Two of her three sons died in the strange land. First José, then shortly after, Antonio, age fifteen months, the last born of the twelve children. Almost forty years old now, Margarita's grief helped to undermine her health. The letters she wrote to Juárez from 1865 to 1866 show a state of mind that greatly worried her husband whose devotion never faltered but whose heart was often torn by his inability to be near her and help her. She wrote:

"The loss of my sons is killing me. From the moment I awaken I think of them, remembering their sufferings, blaming myself, and believing it was my fault that they died ... The only thing that calms me for a few minutes is the thought that I shall die and I prefer death a thousand times more than life. My present life without you and without my sons is insupportable ... I do not much blame persons who kill themselves when they have lost all hope of regaining any tranquility. If I had been braver I should have done it a year ago."

Fortunately, there were some happy things to write about too as time went by. Manuela and her good husband Pedro Santacilia had become parents of a baby girl so there was the diversion for Margarita of having her first grandchild. There were also favorable reports on the children's progress at school. In her correspondence with Juárez she commented, sometimes acidly, upon things political. In one letter she describes some of the Mexicans she has seen in the United States as a "roost full of useless specimens."

Another pleasant note was Margarita's debut into society in Washington, D.C. Matias Romero, an old friend of the Juárez family, had been representing the liberal government in the United States capital and had often invited Doña Margarita and her family to visit him, his sister and mother. Finally, in March of 1866, Margarita decided that it was her duty to go because Romero's mother was ill. She took along her second oldest daughter, Margarita, for moral support and help with translation, and also because Romero was married to a New Yorker by the name of Lulu Allen.

The first week of the visit was a quiet one spent in the company of the Romero ladies but by the second week word had spread that the wife of Benito Juárez was in town and there was no escaping. Although she was still under stress from the death of her sons and lacked English skills, Margarita rose to the occasion, attending a reception with Romero given for her by

President Andrew Johnson, his first official function since taking office, followed by a dinner at the home of Secretary of State William H. Seward. A shrewd politician and fine statesman, Seward was reported to have made an enormous blunder when he said to Margarita through her interpreter, the minister of Colombia, "I hope that within a year I shall see in Mexico City my two friends, Juárez and Santa Anna." After a shocked pause, Margarita said quickly, "Tell Mr. Seward he will see one or the other but not both." General Santa Anna was one of Benito's greatest political enemies.

But apparently all was forgiven because a few days later Seward took Margarita on a personally conducted tour through the state department so that she could see the U.S. documents of freedom and liberation and, in a letter written to Juárez dated April 7, 1866, she tells that Seward ended the visit by presenting her with his portrait. He also requested a picture of her to put side by side with Juárez' portrait. She writes her husband in the same letter:

"Who knows how much it will cost, but I must do it because it's enough that he would request it."

Lack of money was always a problem, but Margarita was a stateswoman who knew that her continuing friendship with Seward would benefit Mexico and herself.

Ulysses S. Grant took his turn at entertaining the attractive Mexican lady and decided to round out the previously given dinner and reception with a ball in her honor. President Andrew Johnson made a point of attending. French Minister Montholon and his wife made an appearance that surprised the other party-goers because at that time the puppet-emperor Maximilian had been placed on the throne of Mexico by Napoleon, a most unpopular move in Washington, D.C. Margarita's presence at the ball as official representative of republican President Juárez, backed up by President Johnson's attentions to her, left no doubt as to where the United States' sympathy lay.

While in Washington Margarita had her fortieth birthday which she describes in a letter to Benito as "the terrible day on which I complete forty years." She also protests a report in the *New York Herald* newspaper that she was "elegantly dressed with many diamonds" at one of the social events. She wrote Juárez, "All my elegance consisted of a dress that you bought me in Monterrey shortly before I left ... and as for the diamonds, I had no more than some earrings that you gave me once on my saint's day ... they shall not say that when you were in El Paso in such poverty I was here enjoying luxury."

One detects here a plaintive note at having enjoyed herself while her dear Juárez was in exile in Texas trying desperately to regroup his forces and gather enough money and arms to oust the French invaders. There was also the guilt to cope with that any pleasure was wrong when the two little boys had so recently died.

The tide was beginning to turn in the fortunes of the young republic and its tough, enduring president. On the morning of June 19, 1867, Maximilian, the Austrian emperor imposed upon Mexico, was ordered executed by Juárez. This was the signal for Margarita and the family to return. People in high places in the United States government, including Secretary of State Seward, saw to it that the U.S. revenue cutter, *Wilderness*, bearing dispatches for Mexico was ordered to wait in New Orleans until Señora Juárez and her party of fourteen came aboard. The *Wilderness* sailed July 10 bearing Margarita, her children, son-in-law Pedro Santacilia, granddaughter and servants. It is said that caskets containing the bodies of the two dead boys also were taken aboard to be buried in their homeland, but ship's records do not bear this out.

The date was July 25, 1867 and the port of entry Veracruz, where Juárez and his wife had spent three years and Doña Margarita had become well known for her kindness and charitable works. The good people of the city had prepared quite a reception. The streets in the area where the ship would dock were not part of a neighborhood where gentry lived. This was a humble town and the *gente de barrio* (common folk) poured out of the crumbling woodwork of the *casitas*, happy to wait for hours in the hot sun to welcome the kind lady and her children back to their native soil. Her husband, their president, and the only one so far that had ever resembled them in skin color, would not be present but would await his family in Mexico City where the burdens of state kept him busy from dawn 'til dusk.

In addition to the Veracruz officials and the people, there was a continual welcoming committee that crowded the flat rooftops and perched on the church steeples of the seaport year after year. These were the ugly but necessary *zopilotes* (turkey buzzards) that swooped down and devoured the city's garbage along with any creatures that had the misfortune to be maimed on the streets of Veracruz. If something disturbed the dense black mass of birds on top of a dwelling, the fluttering and undulating made it look as though the roof had torn loose in a sudden gale. A pleasanter part of the population that welcomed Margarita were the doughty little burros, the water carriers who were decorated with gaily-colored feathers and ribbons and whose bells jingled proudly with every toss of the head as they danced along the cobblestone streets vending their wares.

As the *Wilderness* docked with its bright pennants flickering in the breeze, a rumbling came forth from the crowd and bubbled into a cheer. Aboard ship, sailors stood at attention while the band played the *Himno Nacional* (national anthem) of Mexico. Now the people surged forward, impatient to see their own Mexican-born señora and her family and when they emerged on deck the mob went wild. When Margarita descended the gangplank, homemade bouquets were thrust upon her until her arms could no longer hold them nor could her eyes hold the tears that spilled down her cheeks as she smiled and bowed to the good folks who lined both sides of the pathway to her carriage. After shaking hands with the mayor and other officials, she turned once more and waved to the throngs before stepping into the carriage. But the people were not satisfied yet to let her go. As the horses started up a group of men leaped forward, unharnessed the horses and led them away. Then the muscular arms and calloused hands of common workers drew the carriage and its occupants all the way up the long hill to the mayor's house where the party was to pass the night.

Margarita and her family did not sleep much because the whole town turned out for a fireworks display and bands of musicians serenaded Doña Margarita and kept demanding a glimpse of her. The newspapers of the city were filled with stories about her and this excerpt from an article in *La Concordia*, Veracruz, July 17, 1867 expresses the general feelings of the citizens.

"We remember that they had told us that one time not very long ago our streets had been profaned by the cries of a few parasites and a few hired henchmen that acclaimed a foreign woman like she was their guardian angel and it seems to us that our native city has received a complete purification by the passage through its streets and squares of a genuine Mexican woman, the companion of our misfortunes, of whom in the cheers of the town you don't find fake homage, false pride ..."

The *extranjera* referred to was Empress Carlota who had visited Veracruz during her reign, with the French making sure that the usual paid admirers were on hand to greet her. In her voluminous correspondence to Juárez, Margarita mentions Carlota only once and briefly. This was after the empress had gone to Europe and was reputed to be very ill.

Margarita's triumphal train trip to Mexico City was a slow

one. Whistle stops were the order of the day so that the *campesinos* along the way could greet her and her party which included serving maids Juana Arco and María Rivas, and other employees who had been with her in the United States. The cities of Puebla and Cholula paid homage, as did many towns, with bands, speeches and displays of fireworks. After the reign of the foreigner, Mexican women particularly appreciated their own special Mexican woman and Margarita received many letters such as this one dated August 25, 1867, Tapachula, from Concepción and Ursula Escobar, to warm her heart.

"We cordially salute our esteemed señora with fondest affection from our hearts upon your return to the republic. We contemplate with great satisfaction the successful resolution of the country's cause. You have confronted the most bloody, tough and prolonged trials that our sex has suffered ..."

And what was the long awaited reunion with Juárez like? The records do not tell us but you can be sure that the three-year separation and its problems had taken their toll. Margarita, always taller than Benito, was stooped now and the difference in their heights was not as noticeable. The lines in Benito's face were deeply carved, not merely etched. When he clasped his beloved "old lady" in his arms once more he must have been aware of her frailty but in the way of true lovers they looked so good to each other that they could only smile and shake their heads in wonder at the joy of being together at last.

"And they lived happily ever after" would be the proper storybook conclusion, but Margarita and her family had enjoyed more smooth sailing aboard the cutter *Wilderness* than they would ever experience at home riding the ship of state. After the years of warfare, the financial problems, recurring skirmishes, major crimes and divisive individualism of the members of the liberal congress tended to pull apart rather than reconstruct the democracy Juárez was striving to make function efficiently. Badly needed foreign investment shied away from what looked like insurmountable difficulties for the infant republic and Benito, who was more professorial than practical in matters economic, did not find solutions rapidly enough to get the money that was so necessary.

In the autumn of 1869 the Mexican nation had a chance to return some of the hospitality shown Margarita in the United States. One of her Washington, D.C. hosts, ex-Secretary of State William H. Seward, visited Mexico with his son Frederick and daughter-in-law. Though he had served under Abraham Lincoln, Seward declared in a speech made at Puebla that Juárez was the most outstanding man he'd ever known.

Great men expend great amounts of energy and although Juárez, now sixty-four years old, had demonstrated through years of turmoil, exile and repeated attempts on his life that he had the constitution of an ox, he suffered a stroke in October of 1870. For a couple of days his recovery was in doubt and when he hung on, the physicians were afraid he might suffer permanent paralysis. But he fought his way back to a fair state of health and normal activity. Margarita, too, had been unwell for some time. Whether the shock of Benito's seizure hastened her death is unknown, but after enduring what was described only as a "long and painful illness," Doña Margarita, age forty-four, died on the afternoon of January 2, 1871, less than three months after Juárez was stricken. It is only in recent years that her ailment was labeled cancer.

The funeral was held the next day. Speechless with grief and still none too strong after his own illness, Juárez, with all the love and tenderness he had felt for Margarita in the twenty-eight years of their marriage, managed to lift her body into the coffin himself. Unable to bear the sight of the narrow box being sealed, he fumbled his way out of the room, eyes blurred with unshed tears. As a sign that all political differences were suspended during this period of national mourning, two of the leaders of recent insurrections who had been pardoned by President Juárez, Aureliano Rivera and Miguel Negrete, shouldered the plain black box and acted as pallbearers. As the cortege left the little house on Calle Serapio Rendón, the street suddenly filled with people, many strewing flowers as the casket passed by, others openly weeping. All the way to the cemetery throngs appeared like magic joining the river of humanity following the president and his good señora.

The main funeral oration was given by Don Guillermo Prieto, a well-known writer and a member of Juárez original cabinet who had saved the president's life in 1858 by covering Benito's body with his own just as Juárez was about to be fired upon. Journalists throughout the country paid tribute to the Señora Presidente and so did the common people as this excerpt entitled "La Tarde de Martes" shows. It is from the January 5, 1871 issue of the newspaper *La Paz*.

"The legislature, the diplomatic corps, the press, everyone paid homage to the honored wife of the citizen president ... It was touching to see the common people, especially tradesmen, with mourning bands on their arms over their humble clothing."

Even those who disapproved the secular burial and still

resented Benito's liberal policies forgot everything except that they, along with their grieving president, had lost a fine woman who had given as much for her country as any heroine past or future.

The Church of Jesus Christ of Latter Day Saints was founded in 1830 in Seneca, New York by Joseph Smith, Jr. In a series of removals from one state to another the church ended up establishing permanent headquarters in Utah where, in a few decades, the organization and its people flourished and went forth to start other colonies. The Mormons, as they are commonly called, were and are a missionary faith actively engaged in spreading their interpretation. Their first try in a foreign country took place when seven male missionaries set out for Mexico and held Mormon services in Chihuahua in April of 1876. The new and totally alien faith drew a good-sized gathering for any religious group. More than five hundred people attended.

The most sensational and controversial aspect of the early Mormon church was polygamy and it was this practice of a man being allowed to have many wives that was responsible for the first Mormon colonies in Mexico. Various measures were passed in the United States congress for the abolition of polygamy starting with the Edmunds Bill of 1862. None were signed by a president until Chester Allen Arthur scrawled his signature at the bottom of a page, finally making it an offense punishable by law for a man to have more than one wife. This was the signal for many polygamous families to seek refuge outside the United States where they would no longer be persecuted nor prosecuted by those who took offense at the harem system.

Since missionary spade work had already been done in Mexico with some success, it was natural for escaping Mormon refugees in sizable numbers to cross the border. The political climate was right for colonizing because Porfirio Díaz who first became president in 1877 encouraged foreign migration. There were many problems including assaults upon them by Apache Indians who were hiding out in Mexico, but these Mormon families were willing to fight and die for their way of life.

What of the Mormon women who came with their men? Hardship was nothing new to them, nor was religious persecution. If the practice of polygamy can be construed as the tenet of a faith they had often been scorned by other women and hounded from one place to another because of their beliefs. They were industrious, obedient and cheerful and many were well-educated considering the times. In a multi-wife family the offspring of one woman were tended and cared for with equal concern by the other women and in this kind of society where propagation was a must it was expected that if one of the childbearers died young, as was so often the case, the others would care for her baby or babies. Considering human nature, it seemed to have worked out reasonably well and from the male standpoint it must have been ideal. Could part of the welcome of the Latter Day Saints have been the revival of a culture-memory going back to pre-conquest days when polygamy was also an accepted part of Aztec life?

Colonia Juárez was founded in 1886 in the state of Chihuahua along with four other colonies. Some of the burden of being in a strange land was eased for the women by the presence of Dr. Avelina E. Saville, who served for seventeen years as a medical person in Colonia Juárez. Dr. Saville had passed the Utah state medical board examination, practiced for three years in Salt Lake City and was a certified doctor of obstetrics. More than eight hundred babies were delivered by her but her practice was not limited to childbirth. She performed emergency operations on whites and Indians including cataract removals from the eyes of the natives. Her work was aided by three women who were always on call as nurses, Elsie McClellan, Jane Croff and Grandma Hawkins.

The first schoolteacher in Colonia Juárez was Annie W. Romney who held classes in her dugout until the schoolhouse was built. But even when the stockade building was completed there were no supplies available in those early months. The children sat on split log seats without backs and the lucky ones who possessed slates held them on their laps for lack of desks to write on. Paper, pen and ink were unknown and the textbooks were a handful of strangely assorted editions of this and that brought by teacher Annie Romney and parents. By January 1889 a larger, permanent edifice had been constructed and the number of pupils had increased to the point where Sarah Clayson was hired to instruct the younger children. In time the school became an academy and Ella Larsen, a graduate of Cook County schools in Illinois was hired to supervise the primary grades and conduct training classes.

The Mormons have a great love of music, dancing and celebrations. Their adopted country provided many opportunities for fiestas whether it was the Cinco de Mayo, commemorating victory over the French at Puebla, or El Grito de Dolores, Independence Day. Variety was the spice of life in the preparation of the floats, costumes, parades and entertainments but there was one element that always remained the same and that was the presence of Anna B. Hellstrom designated as a "vendor of peanuts, popcorn and lemonade." She is the only woman in a list of fifty-four names showing "Family Head Membership in Colonia Juárez in 1891." The fact that Anna B. Hellstrom, widow, was listed at all among fifty-three men variously described as shoemakers, carpenters, dairy farmers, etc. may have been the result of a statement made by the president of the Mormons, Wilford Woodruff in 1890. His proclamation signified the end of polygamy. This would have made it possible for a woman who had been widowed to remain one by choice and become head of her household.

That Anna's venture into small business made money as well as friends is borne out by Nelle Spilsbury Hatch in her book *Colonia Juárez.*

"Conspicuously on the sidelines was the refreshment stand with Sister Hellstrom ladling out lemonade at five cents a pint and handing out popcorn balls and bags of peanuts for the same price. Nickels hoarded in anticipation of this occasion were soon exchanged for a treat that was too often exhausted long before the demand was supplied. Home grown popcorn made into crunchy balls, roasted peanuts with an exact number placed in each bag and the lemonade made by melting hard sugar in clear fresh water and flavoring it with lemon extract and tartaric acid were a part of every celebration and an attractive feature of every dance."

7
Carlota and Company

Reams have been written about Carlota, the unhappy Hapsburg by marriage who became empress of Mexico, and it is not the purpose here to give other than a brief sketch of her short reign. Of more importance are the Mexican women involved in her court and wherever possible her story and theirs will be told concurrently. Born June 7, 1840 Carlota was the daughter of King Leopold and Queen Louise of Belgium. A brilliant child who read Plutarch's *Lives* at age eleven, the early death of her mother affected her deeply and made her old before her time so that she despised frivolity and lacked tolerance for those less serious and intellectual than she. Her photographs show her to have been most attractive. Tall and stately, this dark-haired woman conveyed majesty by the elegance of her carriage and dress. Her expression is remote but gives no hint of the psychotic personality that would surface under stress.

On July 27, 1857 in Brussels, lovely Princess Charlotte Emily, age 17, married tall, blond, handsome Archduke Ferdinand Maximilian, age 25, younger brother of the powerful emperor Franz Joseph of Austria. The royal couple departed immediately for Italy where Maximilian became viceroy of the northern part of the country. Milan so entranced the impressionable young woman that she announced she would officially change her name to Carlotta which eventually became spelled in the Spanish way: *Carlota*. But despite the enthusiasm of the newlyweds, politics forced Austria to withdraw from the northern Italian provinces and by 1859 Maximilian and Carlota were out of a job.

It was French emperor Louis Napoleon's ambition to restore the glory of his country by building a canal across the isthmus of Nicaragua. The canal would act as an exchange point of the world's great trade routes, owned and run by France of course. Wanting Mexico as a handy chunk of land from which to make further forays into the wealth of South America, it occurred to the shrewd Frenchman to use the political turmoil in Mexico as an opportune moment to kick Juárez out, invade the country and set up a monarchy controlled by France. Louis Napoleon also wanted to have Austria, the greatest power in Europe in his debt, so this combination plus many other complex factors gave Maximilian and Carlota a position which, for all the glorious sound of being emperor and empress of Mexico, would lead to disaster for the royal pair.

The French expeditionary force that seized power was backed briefly by the Spanish and English who had been irritated by Juárez' policies and were also concerned at the size of Mexico's foreign debts and their repayment. Spain and England, unaware that a French puppet was to be put on the newly created throne, withdrew in indignation as soon as France's intentions to own and control Mexico became clear. In the 1840s the United States had bitten off huge chunks of Mexican territory but was violently opposed to having any other foreign power do the same because of its own national security. Although deeply concerned at the French invasion, the U.S. was helpless to assist Mexico against the French. The United States could furnish neither men nor money because it was involved in its own costly and large scale bloodletting known as the Civil War.

There is general agreement that Maximilian was not a brilliant administrator, profound thinker, nor a person of great depth. His big ambition in regard to Mexico before he arrived seems to have been the creation of a flashy luxurious court complete with all the tedious ceremony and protocol of Austria. As younger brother of the most powerful ruler in Europe, Maximilian had been in the shade all his life and a certain amount of preening in his new role was to be expected. This is not to say that the Austrian was completely indifferent to the welfare of his so-called subjects nor a man of evil intent, but he was inept. Perhaps it was lucky for Mexico that France selected a dud instead of a dynamo because a tough thinker-doer might have been harder to get rid of.

The arrival of their imperial majesties in Veracruz, a town whose sympathies were with Juárez, was not riotous. Although the French army had seen to it that triumphal arches and other decorations were erected, a *norte* (north wind) blew in during the night, tore down the decorations and swirled dust all over the streets, making it harder for the *zopilotes* to uncover the garbage and function as the sanitation department. In addition, an epidemic of smallpox was once more sweeping the seaport town, but that was the least of Maximilian's worries. It was not reassuring that the French commander-in-chief, General Francois Achille Bazaine was too busy to meet and escort his emperor to Mexico City, but their majesties' sagging spirits were somewhat braced by the appearance of the suave, charming Mexican General, Juan Nepomuceno Almonte, and his wife, Dolores Quesada de Almonte, who arrived late in true Mexican fashion but nevertheless heartily welcomed the royal pair. Carlota experienced her first *abrazo* from Dolores Almonte which she tried outwardly to accept gracefully while shrinking inwardly from the intimacy. She was never to become accustomed to this physical demonstration of affection and respect, first because such license was never taken with royal bodies in the courts of Europe and secondly because she was by nature reserved.

Doña Dolores Quesada de Almonte was destined to be an almost constant companion to the empress in the year before her husband, Juan, was named minister to France and they departed from Mexico. Described by the United States Minister to Mexico, Gilbert Thompson, in *Recollections of Mexico* as a woman who "would be regarded as an accomplished lady in any country," Dolores Quesada had married Juan Almonte in 1839 when he was Minister of War during the presidency of Anastasio Bustamante. Almonte was an acknowledged though illegitimate son of the mestizo revolutionary priest José María Morelos. Almonte's varied career included education in the U.S. plus diplomatic missions there and in Europe. Described by Fanny Calderón de La Barca in *Life in Mexico* as "a handsome man and pleasant, and an officer of great bravery," his liberal tendencies had turned conservative with time. Highly influential in forming the monarchy, he was a vigorous sixty years old by the time Carlota and Maximilian arrived.

The royal party, consisting of eighty-five people who possessed more than five hundred trunks and suitcases, suffered a long hard trip to Mexico City riding in the bumpy old stage coaches over the rutty old roads. To add to their discomfort was the very real fear of being attacked by the robbers and murderers that operated singly and in gangs, roaming the countryside plundering any likely prospect, Mexican or foreigner, who might be carrying so much as a peso. But when the royal couple finally arrived in the capital, making their official entry June 12, 1864, they were thrilled with the warmth and beauty of the welcome. Throughout the city the mansions were decorated with elaborate wreaths, garlands of flowers, enormous mirrors and carpeted walks. Even humble dwellings boasted palm leaves tied with brightly colored rags. Flags of all nations were flown as well as the French and Mexican ensigns side by side. Driving in a magnificent state coach ordered from Trieste, Maximilian wore the full dress uniform of a Mexican general displaying a dazzling array of male jewelry in the form of medals and decorations strung across his chest. Carlota was garbed in the hoopskirted fashion of the era with a diamond tiara atop her thick black hair and other Hapsburg royal gems sparkling like a million prophetic tears in the brilliant sunlight. A cobweb-fine mantilla of Brussels lace was thrown over her shapely shoulders. They were truly a fairytale couple. Firecrackers popped merrily in this city where bullets had so often rent the air and blossoms were thrown from balconies. Shouts of "Viva el emperador y la emperatriz" rang happily in the royal ears along with myriad church bells. The enthralled mobs broke into the procession in their zeal as it turned into the zócalo where the great cathedral opened its doors to the newcomers for the ceremony that would convert a pair of foreigners into the first family of Mexico.

We can imagine Carlota muttering triumphantly behind her lace handkerchief to Maximilian, whose enthusiasm had never been as great as hers for the job. "See, what did I tell you, Max? These people want the civilization and culture that we bring them. We'll transform them in a few years."

What the bedazzled couple didn't realize was that wily General Achille Bazaine had observed that the pleasure-starved Mexicans would have turned out to cheer the devil himself if given a day of fiesta. They badly needed an occasion to work off some of the frustration and sadness accumulated from years of deprivation and civil war. Also, the French army had policed the city in advance to make sure decorations were put up and that all hands showed on the streets. This kind of trumped-up, enthusiastic welcome would be staged again and again for the emperor and empress throughout their few years in Mexico. But the brilliant uniforms of the Mexican Imperial guard, the Chasseurs D'Afrique and Zouaves plus music, which enchants a Mexican when all else fails, made this an unreal, unrepeatable, unforgettable moment in the lives of the common people who witnessed it as well as the two glamorous young rulers.

Carlota had brought only two ladies-in-waiting with her from Europe, determined to draw her court from the women of the country she was hoping would adopt her with enthusiasm.

Considerable snobbery began to erupt in the Mexican upper classes under the pressure of French chic and Austrian pomp. José Luis Blasio, Maximilian's private secretary, says of the jockeying for position that took place among the blue-bloods:

"In a country like Mexico, which since its independence has been and is essentially republican, and where few possessed legitimate claim to noble titles, there were not many who could prove their descent from the ancient nobility of Spain. But, nevertheless, because of the lure of the splendor of Maximilian's court, everyone was eager to have a position there, and a veritable fever of aristocracy and nobility broke out, so that it was rare to find a Mexican family which did not search out parchments, genealogical trees, or coats of arms to prove their descent from counts, dukes or marquises."

When Carlota announced her choice of ladies-in-waiting, considerable crow had to be eaten by disappointed social climbers. Since, to this day, many of the names rank high in Mexican society the list is presented here:

    Dolores Osio de Sánchez
    Manuela Gutiérrez Estrada del Barrio
    Concepción Lizardi del Valle
    Josefa Cardeña de Salas Varela
    Luisa Quejano de Rincón-Gallardo
    Ana Rosa de Rincón Gallardo
    Rocha de Robles
    Carolina Barrón de Escandón
    Rosa Obregón de Uraza
    Dolores Peña del Hidalgo y Terán
    María Muñoz de Peraz
    María Barrio de Campero
    Luz Robles de Bringas
    Dolores Germandín de Elgüero
    Manuela de Plaizora
    Luz Blanco de Robles
    Guadalupe Cervantes de Morán
    Soledad Vivante de Cervantes
    Concepción de Plowes
    Concepción de Pacheco

Some of the women could legitimately claim nobility including Concepción Lizardi del Valle whose husband's title of Count descended from Hernan Cortés. The most distinguished of them all was Josefa Cardeña de Salas Varela whose royal blood came to her directly from Nezahualcoyotl, the poet-king.

General Francois Achille Bazaine, going on the theory that any Frenchman is a fool who spends his own money for entertaining when he can use somebody else's, gave a huge and lavish ball for the new rulers at San Cosme, the palace he used for his headquarters. No expense was spared and as usual the poor people of Mexico footed the bills for their conquerors. Bazaine had a number of reasons for wanting to be in the good graces of their majesties, the first and foremost being that he, a widower, had fallen head over heels in love with a sixteen-year-old Mexican society girl and desperately wanted the sanction of his rulers for the marriage. The young woman, Josefa de La Peña y Azcárate, came from a distinguished family. Her uncle, Manuel de la Peña y Peña, had been president of the supreme court and on two separate occasions became president of Mexico in the 1840s when the highest office in the land changed hands with alarming rapidity. Josefa's pictures show her to have been a small, piquant, dark-haired beauty. She was a *muñeca* (doll) in appearance but was ambitious, intelligent and courageous although, in the end, she backed a loser. Her fate was much like Carlota's.

Marshall Achille Bazaine is spoken of as the true ruler of Mexico during Maximilian's reign because as long as he remained there heading the French fighting forces, he was able to prevent the Juaristas from taking over. A daring and resourceful general, distinguished in the foreign legion, he rose the hard way through the ranks. He even managed to survive a disastrous first marriage contracted in 1850. Dark-eyed Latinas seem to have been the vulnerable spot in his Achille's heel. The first Mme. Bazaine was a beautiful Spanish girl that Bazaine, the story goes, saw for the first time as a child when he visited her country. Enchanted with the little girl he took her to Paris where he placed her in a convent to ripen and be educated. In 1850, at age 39, he returned to Paris, married her and took her with him to Constantinople. When he received orders to go to Mexico, she returned to Paris until she could join him. There she promptly fell head over heels in love with an actor at the Comédie Francaise, was discovered by his wife and killed herself. Supposedly, the knowledge of her infidelity was kept from Bazaine.

In November of 1863 the marshall held a mass for his dead wife and in 1864 at a ball given at his headquarters he saw Josefa de La Peña, or Pepita as she was fondly called, for the first time. In another romantic tale featuring this short, heavyset, unromantic-looking general, Bazaine was chatting with one of his guests when a lovely young girl stopped waltzing nearby and asked some ladies to help mend a torn ruffle on her hoopskirt. When the repair had been made and the girl danced away, Bazaine, according to Sara Yorke Stevenson in *Maximilian in Mexico*, was heard to murmur: "It's extraordinary how much she reminds me of my wife."

With the same determination he had used to win battles, the Frenchman set about winning the heart of the young woman and in a short time he succeeded. His position and power were dazzling, his Spanish flawless (something which couldn't be said of all the French officers). Josefa-Pepita was said to speak equally flawless French and to have been a bright, ambitious young woman who, along with her family, scented trouble for the monarchs and could imagine that, in time, her bold Bazaine would make an excellent replacement for milksop Maximilian. But all these ambitions were kept under wraps temporarily because Bazaine wanted Carlota to help him obtain the necessary permission from Napoleon and Eugénie for his marriage.

Empress Carlota's tongue could sting when she chose to use it as a weapon. She remarked when watching the chubby, fifty-four-year-old marshall plowing through an *habanera* (Cuban ballroom dance) with his dainty seventeen-year-old fiancee, "He reminds me of a huge lazy fly gloating over that child-like fiancee of his." But eventually she succumbed to the flattery of having Bazaine request her help with his romance. She wrote Empress Eugénie, reporting very favorably upon the beauty, charm and naturalness of Josefa-Pepita and her singular ability with the French language. Then, with the turnabout that a detractor-become-supporter can so easily make, she added, "To tell the truth there is a very decided attraction, for the marshall has even begun to dance again, and gave us to understand he had not missed a single *habanera*."

The wedding took place June 26, 1865 at Chapultepec, the royal palace. Napoleon smiled upon the alliance, believing rightly that this type of marriage helped cement ties between Mexico and France. Maximilian who excelled in grace and charm on social occasions, although he claimed to detest them, put on a magnificent show complete with finest French champagne and for a wedding gift gave the couple a palace called Buenavista, including furniture and gardens, with the stipulation that "when you return to Europe, or if for any reason you do not desire to retain possession of the palace, the nation will receive it and then, the government shall be obligated to give her (Pepita) as a dowry the sum of one hundred thousand pesos."

Of course Maximilian was giving away something that could not belong to him, to Bazaine, nor even to Pepita, although she was born criolla, but only to the people of Mexico. Carlota, who felt the psychological tremors in Mexico City as well as the earth tremors, bestowed upon the bride a set of diamonds and one of her rare embraces. The latter was a sign of greater favoritism than the former and also served as a subtle plea to Bazaine to save Maximilian in the evil days ahead. To be fair to the marshall he tried hard to persuade Maximilian to go with him when he received orders from Napoleon to depart, but the emperor, foolish fellow, felt that his honor was at stake and that he would not show the white feather even though Juárez and his forces were almost upon him.

Pepita left her native land in far grander style than she would return to it. On February 5, 1867 the French army left Mexico City. With bands playing, the well-drilled soldiers marched in perfect step behind their horsebacked leader Achille Bazaine. Pepita was carried in a litter surrounded by guards with one babe in her arms and another well along the way beneath her hoopskirts. The weeping woman, not yet twenty, bade farewell to friends and family. People lined the streets to watch the exodus but there were no tears and no cheers. Sullen faces observed the procession, only an occasional *mujer de la vida* (streetwalker) cautiously waved farewell, saddened more by the loss of ready revenue than by affection.

Many individuals outraged at the Gallic effrontery rejoiced at the departure. Although French enlisted men were generally housed in churches and convents, which they took over forcibly, their officers were billeted at private homes. Among those thrilled at the army exodus was the widow of Manuel Doblado, who had truly felt the lengths to which French thrift could go. The death of her husband-hero, General Doblado, former Minister of Foreign Affairs and a republican who had bravely fought the invaders, made the French high command decide that it would be inappropriate and unpopular for them to billet officers at the widow's house in León, Guanajuato. Instead, they magnanimously decreed that she could avoid the distress of having her late husband's deadly enemies under the same roof with her by locating and furnishing other quarters for them. Of course, the rent and upkeep were to be at her expense. Little quirks like this did not endear the invaders to the invaded. Bazaine had tried to do a bit of last minute pocket-lining by selling the Buenavista palace Maximilian had given him but nobody knew if the returning Juárez government would confiscate private property, so real estate was in a slump. Bazaine was forced to leave the place unsold, although he did squeeze some pesos out by selling all the furniture.

In August of 1870 Napoleon the Third made Bazaine Supreme Commander of the French army. Unfortunately, the marshall engaged in questionable intrigue with the Germans and was tried and found guilty of treason in 1873. He was imprisoned in the Fort de Sainte Marguerite. Unlike Bazaine's first wife, Josefa-Pepita was still loyal to her old man and she boldly devised his escape. The marshall, then sixty-two years old, lowered himself from the walls of the fortress by means of a rope brought to him by his wife. Pepita was waiting for him in a small boat whose oars were pulled by her cousin until the little craft reached a nearby ship that was ready to sail them to Spain and exile. After Bazaine's death in 1888, Pepita returned to Mexico but the republican politicians were hardly inclined to look kindly upon a woman who had married a foreign conqueror who had been courtmartialed and convicted even by his own people of treason. Pepita's sanity was affected and she died impoverished and forgotten in an asylum.

Both Maximilian and Carlota had a good deal of idealism in their makeup and the emperor did try in his feeble fashion to institute measures which would eliminate corporal punishment and bestow a living wage upon the *clases menesterosas* (needy). Carlota had a flair for languages and in no time at all her Spanish was excellent, far better than Maximilian's, and she was able to fill in for him with ease when he was unable to carry through on journeys such as one he had planned to make to Yucatán. The empress also did her duty to the underprivileged by visiting and aiding charitable institutions. But before the end of their first year as rulers of Mexico, the funds for their stipends and expenses gave out and the fancy dress balls and elaborate twenty-course suppers (where it was not unusual for two dozen different rare wines and liqueurs to be served) had to be cut down. The numbers of ladies-in-waiting also had to be cut to reduce the costs of the expensive delicacies and sweets so dear to the palates of affluent Mexican society, along with the curtailment of court ceremonial which called for innumerable lackeys, livery and luxuries.

Carlota and her court ladies were not the only women feeling the pinch of changing times in Mexico. During the French occupation the status of women became increasingly difficult. Because of the civil wars that had torn the country for half a century, the number of women over men was exceedingly large. With the advent of Juárez' reform laws that abolished Catholicism as the state religion and confiscated much church property, the convent life that had provided refuge for so many females had largely disappeared. As yet, jobs for women in business or factory, with the exception of the tobacco industry which had employed females since the eighteenth century, were almost non-existent and available to only a handful from the working classes.

The oldest profession became the outlet for middle class as well as poor women, who also swelled the ranks of *soldaderas* (camp followers). Though the basic function of most of these females was sexual, many doubled as nurses, doctors and pack animals, giving the soldier-lover greater mobility by freeing him from his equipment which the *soldadera* toted along with her belongings and often a child or two. Their reward for services rendered in all departments was that they had a chance at regular rations, palmed a little money now and then and sometimes acquired respectability by legal marriage. There were also the elements of patriotism and adventure, no more to be discounted in the lives of women than in the lives of men, particularly women whose alternative was emptying chamberpots and washing other people's dirty clothes.

Upper class women had their problems, too. Unable to find enough Mexican men to marry and follow traditional family patterns and with convent life fading away, many were seduced or did the seducing themselves. If discovered, they became outcasts and frequently fell into the clutches of white slavers who flourished in Guanajuato, San Luis Potosí and other centers. It was no wonder that all classes of women had many members who opened their arms to French males. Many high society marriages were contracted for political, financial or snobbish reasons. Others were based only upon the age-old attraction between man and woman. French Minister Dano and Count Dubois de Saligny as well as Marshall Bazaine married criollas.

One of the great sorrows of the twenty-six-year-old Empress Carlota was her childless state. Early biographers assumed that she and Maximilian were an ecstatically happy couple but later evidence casts doubt upon their having sustained a physical relationship throughout their marriage. At times Carlota may have felt considerable anger at the out-of-wedlock amors of Maximilian and denied him her bed as punishment. But since she was so distressed at being heirless she must have done a reasonable amount of consorting with her consort to try to obtain her heart's desire. Her lack of young is responsible for a curious interlude in the brief but ever curious reign of this couple and it involves a Mexican child.

Maximilian was not the first Caucasian to carry the title of emperor of Mexico. Agustín de Iturbide, a royalist officer who later became an advocate of Mexican independence in the long struggle against Spain, declared himself emperor in 1822 after freedom was finally secured. He reigned only until 1823 and stayed alive just one year beyond that. His mother, María Josefa Arámburu was Mexican born and came from a well-to-do family. His father, José Joaquin de Iturbide y Arreguí came from noble stock and was born in Peralta, Spain. The birthdate of Emperor Agustín was September 27, 1783 in Valladolid, Michoacán.

In 1805 at age twenty-two, Agustín, now a young officer in a royalist regiment, married nineteen-year-old Ana María Huarte, the daughter of an official, Isidro Huarte, who was in charge of military, judicial and financial matters in his district. Ana María, an heiress and beauty who became noticeably plump in later years, brought a great deal of money and jewels as dowry to the union and, in contrast to the childless Carlota, would bear nine children. Once he had captured the bride of his choice, Agustín went off to the wars and being handsome, strong and dashing, followed the rule of the time and crammed in as many affairs as he could between battles.

Iturbide, round whom controversy has raged for well over a century, did accomplish with his army of the three guarantias a takeover that shed far less Mexican blood than his predecessors had or his successors would. On July 21, 1822 Emperor Agustín and Empress Ana María were crowned in the great cathedral by the bishop of Guadalajara. The ceremony made the old days of the viceroys look almost spartan by comparison. The free-spending Iturbide was doing his part to make money flow from the Mexican treasury for luxuries for himself, his friends and his mistresses. Even Empress Ana María, seeking solace in food perhaps because of her husband's *inamoratas*, is shown as having spent 448 pesos in the month of January 1823 for chocolate, that native delicacy no real Mexican could resist.

It was just as well that she had some enjoyment while she could. When the regime collapsed Iturbide and family were deported and decided on Italy for exile. After thirteen months the ex-emperor thought the political climate favorable enough to risk returning. On July 17, 1824 he disembarked near the town of Soto La Marina; three days later he was dead by firing squad. The unhappy Ana María and her brood were aboard the same ship that had brought Iturbide home to his death. The Mexican government decided that Ana María should establish residence in Colombia but difficulties arose and instead the widow, who had just given birth to her ninth offspring, sailed to New Orleans, then to Baltimore and finally settled in Philadelphia.

In 1861 Ana María died but her sons and their wives and children, along with ex-emperor Augustín's only remaining sister Josefa returned to Mexico City and lived at the old Palacio Iturbide. The decaying mansion was on Avenida San Francisco and the family survived mostly on pride and pennypinching. Josefa, unmarried, was a devoted churchgoer who observed not only holy days but any and all ecclesiastical events with great interest. When Carlota and Maximilian became heads of state, Josefa, during the course of her sacred duties, heard at Churubusco convent that a certain German-born Jesuit priest, Father Fischer, had been assigned the post of court confessor.

The priest spent several days a week at the cathedral and the ambitious Josefa, a wily schemer, devised an opportunity to meet him there and invite him to tea at their family home. Throughout the years the Iturbides had entertained ideas of returning to political life and regaining their royal status. Josefa had kept tabs with avid interest on the childless state of Maximilian and Carlota and the continuing flatness of the royal belly. She now poured into the ear of Father Fischer, who has been called Maximilian's Rasputin, a proposition admirable for sheer audacity and pushiness.

Father Fischer, no mean schemer himself, agreed with the idea and went about putting the bug that had been put in his ear into the emperor's ear. Without so much as a by-your-leave to Carlota, Maximilian consented to the scheme: the Iturbides, willing to exchange their flesh and blood for financial security and future glory, had offered one of their grandsons for adoption as crown prince to succeed Maximilian since he had no heirs of his own. Tía Josefa would be given the rank of princess and allowed to stay with the boy at court as a governess-guardian. The child's mother, father and the rest of the family would depart for Europe where they would live and be supported in proper style. Maximilian announced these plans to Carlota and at least had the grace to give her the choice of which grandson to take. After brooding for several days in hurt silence, Carlota went to the Iturbide home and chose two-year-old Agustín, child of Emperor Iturbide's second son Angel and the United States-born Alice Green.

Alice Green fought for her boy, pleading that she be allowed to stay with him for several more years. Maximilian is quoted as dismissing her appeal as the words of an "hysterical, half-crazy woman" and Tía Josefa called her a selfish mother standing in the way of her son's success. Alice Green de Iturbide gave in after an annual glimpse of the boy was conceded to her as long as she kept her identity concealed. The family then left immediately for France.

The adoption was officially announced September 18, 1865 and was instrumental in further depressing the unhappy Carlota who by this action was publicly proclaimed barren. The royal family now spent much time in Cuernavaca at the Borda estate which Maximilian had refurbished as a country palace. Carlota lost weight and her looks began to fade, although she took some pleasure in Agustín. He amused her with his two-year-old prattle which reflected his mixed background. Grasping a blossom in the garden in his little fist, he would cry "*linda* flower" or run after the kitchen cats shouting, "come here, *gato*." Maximilian enjoyed the retreat at Cuernavaca too, but for different reasons. The Hungarian valet who attended to the emperor's personal needs confided to the emperor's interpreter, José Luis Blasio, that a door in the garden wall led directly to the emperor's suite. Other comments were made on Maximilian's amatory affairs in Cuernavaca by Col. Paul Blanchot, a French staff officer, in his memoirs when he wrote, "Cuernavaca was poisoned for the empress by the knowledge that in those enchanted bowers dwelt an Armida who had cast a spell over her husband's volatile affections." Though the seventeen-year-old wife of one of the Indian gardeners at Borda palace, Concepción Sedano y Leguizano could hardly be compared to the Circe-like heroine Armida immortalized by Italian poet Tasso. The important fact to Maximilian was that she had laid to rest the gossip that it was he who was sterile and not Carlota. Concepción is said to have given birth to the emperor's son in August of 1866.

There were other *queridas* besides Concepción and there is no evidence to show that Maximilian ever acknowledged his illegitimate child or made provision for him or his mother. Rumor has it that Concepción died of grief when Maximilian was executed and that the wealthy *hacendado*, Don Luis Bringas of Orizaba, at whose home Maximilian had frequently stayed, assumed responsibility for the boy's support and took him to France to be raised and educated. During the first world war a man who claimed to be the son of Concepción Sedano by

Emperor Maximilian was accused by France of spying for the Germans and found guilty. Well-educated, he had long had a reputation for being an adventurer and swindler. The execution order as read by the officer-in-charge started with the words, "Sedano, son of the emperor of Mexico ..." It would not be strange for the man to have claimed Maximilian as his father, but to be able to name Concepción Sedano seems more than coincidence.

While Maximilian was adopting other people's children and siring one of his own, Juárez and the republican forces pressed on until the emperor stood almost alone with his adherents dissolving around him. There seemed no choice but to abdicate, but Father Fischer and Carlota urged him to fight on. Then the empress, the gleam of madness already in her eyes, declared that she would go to Europe, see Napoleon and Eugénie with whom she had carried on a voluminous correspondence during her time in Mexico, and obtain money and forces from them with which to put down the republicans. She departed June 21, 1866 with a party of nine who would function as staff. The only Mexican lady-in-waiting who went with her was the Marquesa del Barrio whose husband, Marqués Felipe Neri del Barrio, headed the party with the title of Grand Chamberlain. Manuela Gutiérrez Estrada del Barrio, wife of a long time conservative, had also been born the daughter of one. Her father, José María Gutiérrez Estrada had spent most of his life out of the country, first as minister to Vienna and then Rome. Manuelita's mother was the daughter of Countess Lutzow of Austria who was mistress of the household to Maximilian and Carlota's court. It was Estrada who was responsible for suggesting to Emperor Franz Joseph of Austria that Maximilian rule Mexico. A strong churchman and a snob, he had long dreamed of establishing a true monarchy in his native land.

The empress seemed to trust only the Marquesa del Barrio to be near her. The signs of madness were accelerating and the Mexican lady, who would prove to be a devoted friend, must have had a very trying ocean voyage because Carlota was remote and withdrawn from the rest, depending almost entirely upon her lady-in-waiting for company. When the party landed Manuelita del Barrio must have heaved a sigh of relief when she saw General Juan Almonte on the docks with his wife, Dolores, and witnessed the affectionate welcome the empress gave to Mme. Almonte who had been her first Mexican friend. The Almontes had been in Europe since 1865 where the general functioned in Paris as minister from Mexico. Carlota had expected to make a grand entrance but the Almontes were the whole of the welcoming party. As long as the empress was in France, Dolores Almonte would share the burden of constant attendance with Manuelita del Barrio.

Carlota's several meetings with Eugénie and Napoleon were disasters. At the final encounter on a very hot day, one of Eugénie's court ladies brought Carlota a *naranjada* (orangeade), thinking to please her. Carlota recoiled from it as though she'd been offered an asp on a silver tray, refusing to touch it let alone drink it. This was the first indication of her paranoid belief that Louis Napoleon was trying to poison her.

To add to the empress' burdens in Paris, the American mother of the adopted crown prince insisted upon having an interview with Carlota. Alice Green de Iturbide had been keeping tabs on the dangerous political situation in Mexico and had become frantic with worry about the fate of her son when she heard that Maximilian's government was about to fall. She had also been beating down the front door of the United States minister to France to enlist his support and he had informed Washington of the child's situation. The press got wind of the tear-jerking tale and the indignation of the American public at the boy's plight put pressure on the U.S. government to do something about returning Agustín to his natural mother.

Alice did her part by pleading as hard with Carlota for the return of her son as Carlota had pleaded with Napoleon to rescue Maximilian. This emotionally exhausting get-together helped tilt the precariously balanced sanity of the empress. During Carlota's absence in Mexico City, the pushy Princess Josefa de Iturbide, aunt to crown prince Agustín, had become official hostess for Maximilian. The emperor heartily disliked her because of her pseudo-royal airs and called her, behind her back, "*La Primate*," which means "illustrious person" as well as its zoological connotation. But the court called her "*Doña Pepa*" which translates to Doña Fake or Hoax.

When Napoleon refused to come to the aid of Maximilian, Carlota determined to travel to Rome to implore the aid of the Holy Father, whom she was sure would rather see a royal government that favored the church continue in power in Mexico in preference to the iconoclastic republicans who had severed official ties with the Vatican. Pope Pius IX had ordered that the entire first floor of the Albergo di Roma in the Corso be reserved for the empress and her party. A commission composed of cardinals received her and the Papal Swiss guard was in attendance. At last Carlota felt she was receiving the kind of attention due her rank and mission. Pope Pius received her with solicitude because her distress and illness were written so clearly upon her once handsome face. She mistook his concern as a sign that he would intercede with Napoleon to obtain help for Maximilian. So deep was her delusion that she poured forth all her woes and worries upon the kindly pope who began to regret that he had ever granted her audience. When she shrieked out in Italian, "Napoleon and Eugénie have poisoned me," Pius IX absented himself from the room as rapidly as he could without losing his dignity. He appealed to the Marquesa del Barrio, upon whom the full burden of companionship had fallen once more since leaving Dolores Almonte behind in France, to take charge of her mistress and remove her from the Vatican. The long suffering del Barrios, husband and wife, managed to take Carlota to her hotel where she seemed calmer. But when dinner arrived she refused to touch anything except an orange which she could peel and some nuts whose shells she could crack because all other food might be poisoned, including water.

Back she went next day to the Vatican where she thirstily consumed large quantities of uncontaminated papal water dipped directly from the fountains. With madness now fully upon her, she cleverly talked her way into the pope's presence and extracted permission to make a tour, along with the Doña del Barrio, of the gardens and library where she felt safe from assassins. When it came time to leave she pleaded to remain the night and, when refused, cried out hysterically that she would sleep in the corridor, the only place where she could feel safe. The pope consulted various members of her party including her physician who said that she was indeed suffering a grave attack of something he politely called "mental aberration." Her cries were so piteous that Pope Pius IX succumbed and agreed to permit her and Manuelita to stay. He ordered an apartment prepared for them and they might very well have been the only women to ever pass the night within the sacred walls.

They did not sleep although beds were available. The Marquesa del Barrio told the rest of the party next day that the empress, dressed in black bonnet and black gown, paced the floor all night babbling to herself, refusing to eat or lie down. At daybreak the pope's secretary and physician finally persuaded Carlota to return to her hotel where the exhausted Manuelita collapsed. Empress Carlota's agony was almost at an end, although her life would go on and on.

For the next few days Manuelita del Barrio attended the mad empress twenty-four hours a day, doing without sleep, tasting every dish before Carlota would agree to take a spoonful. In November of 1866, at age 27, Carlota was pronounced incurably insane by Professor Riedel, an alienist from Vienna. The ever faithful Señora del Barrio aided in the transfer of Carlota to Brussels, the city of her birth, and visited her frequently until replaced by a Belgian lady-in-waiting whom Carlota frequently called Manuelita. The del Barrios stayed in Paris as exiles, like so many of the royalists including the Del Valles and Almontes.

In Mexico Carlota Amalia did not go completely unmourned. There were women who defended her memory against detractors, among them the brave and outspoken Concha Méndez. This famous singer, known as the Cuban nightingale, had often appeared in the Teatro Imperial during Maximilian's reign. Carlota, accompanied by Dolores Almonte or Manuelita del Barrio, often went to hear Méndez who provided most of the infrequent moments of unofficial pleasure the empress had by singing her favorite song "La Paloma," which all of Mexico was wild about. It was a new *habanera* which Carlota could never get enough of. Its sentimental lyrics started with:

> *If a dove should hover*
> *At thy window wide*
> *Give it love, my lover,*
> *It is I, thy bride.*

The gifted Cuban nightingale sang it in particularly melting fashion and Carlota sent her a jeweled bracelet in appreciation.

When Juárez became president again Concha Méndez returned. After Carlota's insanity and Maximilian's death, a parody had been written on "The Dove," the song Carlota loved so well. The audience shouted for Concha Méndez to sing "La Paloma Liberal" as it was called. There were innumerable tongue-in-cheek verses like the following and others far more impertinent:

Adios Mama Carlota	Goodbye, Mama Carlota
Adios mi tierno amor	Goodbye, my tender love
Se fueron los franceses	The French have now departed
Se va el emperador	So goes the emperor too.

The plucky singer waved her arms to silence the raucous crowd then said in slashing tones:

"Never shall I do what you ask, señores. I wear on my wrist the bracelet given me by an unhappy princess who today weeps alone, widowed and mad, very far from our country. Neither I nor the Mexican nation, to which I am joined by my heart and my lineage, shall insult the memory of a prince mowed down at Querétaro, nor that of a noble lady who in place of a queenly diadem wears now the martyr's crown."

The Mexicans, admiring this spirited woman who had the courage of her convictions and dared to express them even when they were not in style, generously cheered her and ceased requesting that she sing "La Paloma" or its parody.

Carlota lived on in her demented state until 1927 when she died at age eighty-eight. Young Agustín, the crown prince, was returned to his mother, but this did not end the story of Alice Green de Iturbide's fight for her son's rights. After the death of her husband, Angel de Iturbide, Alice brought suit in May 1878 against José Malo who had once been executor of the Iturbide estate. She asserted among other claims that Malo had wrongfully transferred one of the Iturbide haciendas, Apeo, to a man named Mateo Echais. The result of the decision was highly favorable to the Iturbide heirs. The judge declared September 2, 1878 that the Apeo hacienda rightfully belonged to the Iturbides and that José Malo had to pay all costs connected with the lawsuit. Agustín was educated in Europe, then became a professor at Georgetown University in Washington, D.C. where he taught French and Spanish. He died in 1925.

Another woman born in the United States who looms large in the history of Maximilian and Carlota comes in at the finale but cuts a dashing and romantic figure, even if there is a touch of comic opera about her from time to time. Born on Christmas day 1844 in Swanton, Virginia, plain Agnes Elizabeth Winona Leclerq Joy was one of a family of eight. There was little to indicate her future glory except that she was a fine enough equestrian to perform professionally in the circus. Part of the success of her act must have been her visual qualities in satin tights. Her pictures show a slender, shapely woman with smoldering eyes that went well with dark auburn hair and a sensuous mouth set off by a dimpled chin.

In spite of Agnes Joy's frankness in her memoirs, there is a mystery period in her early life, never explained, that ranges from late childhood to almost eighteen years. During that period she spent a few years in Cuba unaccompanied by any member of her family, which was hardly routine for a girl of that era. Were these the circus years? When she returned to the United States, the civil war was going badly and after visiting with her sister in New York, she traveled to Washington and toured the military camps in the area. General Blenker had gotten together a regiment composed of Germans to fight for the union. One of them turned out to be the man that Agnes Joy would love all her life, Prince Felix Zu Salm Salm, age thirty, whose elegance, grace, courage and skill with a monocle captivated our young sparkler. Prince Félix Constantin Alexander Johann Nepomuk Salm Salm was the younger son of the ruler of Westphalia and went to military school in Berlin. Reckless and extravagant, he enjoyed life in Vienna until his creditors forced him to seek refuge elsewhere. America beckoned with its civil war that had created a demand for professional soldiers, and off went the young prince to seek his fortune in the new world.

Wartime being a great leveler of class distinctions, Agnes and her prince-colonel exchanged vows less than a year after they had met in St. Patrick's Church in Washington, D.C. From the capital the newlyweds went to army headquarters at Falmouth where Prince Salm Salm was appointed commanding officer of the Eighth New York Volunteers after Agnes had wangled the job for him from the governor. Agnes was an instant success at the frequent parties thrown by Major General Joseph Hooker. These events could hardly be called austere since they were catered by the famous Delmonico's restaurant, romantically decorated with Chinese lanterns hung from the hospital tents, and called by contemporary reports a "combination barroom and brothel where no decent woman would go."

Agnes was as spirited as the horses she rode and gossip never bothered her. When President and Mrs. Lincoln came to Falmouth in April 1863 General Hooker held a reception for them. When it came time for Princess Salm Salm to shake the president's hand she electrified the gathering by swiftly reaching up to the heights of the tall president's face and pulling it down to hers so she could kiss him soundly on his whiskery cheek. There is no evidence to show that Mr. Lincoln was the least bit displeased.

Salm Salm's regiment went to join Sherman's army in Chattanooga and Princess Agnes, determined not to be left behind, smuggled herself and her black and tan terrier, Jimmy, aboard a troop train. She designed an outfit for herself to wear during these trying times that bore a red cross insignia on one arm and she was soundly cheered and called the soldier-princess by her husband's troops whenever she rode into view. But it was not merely a costume; she did a great deal of hospital work attending to the wounded.

When the war ended the prince had the rank of brigadier general and was appointed military governor of Atlanta, but this did not suit his love of action and adventure. Knowing of the storm clouds in Mexico and sympathetic to Maximilian's Germanic background which was similar to his own, Prince Salm Salm decided that his next move would be south of the border. Agnes writes of having a six-hour argument with her husband before Félix gave permission for her to go along. He finally relented and the couple set forth accompanied by Jimmy, the traveling terrier.

When the republican armies began closing in on Mexico City, the imperial army unwisely chose the strategy of withdrawal to the walled city of Querétaro, 170 miles distant. After arriving in the capital, Salm Salm persuaded one of Maximilian's Mexican generals, Santiago Vidari, to let him go along disguised as a member of his staff. This time Agnes had to be left behind although she tells us, in her diary, of trying so hard to persuade her husband to let her accompany him that, "I cried and screamed so as to be heard two blocks off ... but Salm stole away and took a street where he could not hear me." But as soon as the prince went off with the imperial army the bouncy young woman started making plans of her own.

The siege of Querétaro lasted seventy-two days starting in February 1867. When Maximilian was taken prisoner, his captor, republican General Escobedo, asked him what members of his suite he would like to have with him. Prince Félix was among the six requested by the emperor. On May 20 the gloomy city of Querétaro was considerably brightened by the arrival of the princess and terrier, Jimmy. Agnes, with characteristic directness went immediately to the commanding officer and demanded to see her husband. She found that Salm Salm and several of the other prisoners had been turning over an escape plan for the emperor but the scheme had died a-borning. Agnes now took over, visiting Maximilian and explaining her plan which was to bribe the top officers in charge of the illustrious prisoner with large sums of gold.

Understanding the power of money, Agnes saw the first obstacle to be obtaining enough cold hard cash. The emperor told her this was no problem but Princess Salm Salm, who could turn a colorful phrase, wrote in her diary:

"The emperor said that money was the least trouble in the affair, for Baron Van Magnus (the Prussian minister) and the other ministers had assured him that money would be at his disposal to any amount. Strange! At the tail of each word of these gentlemen hung a gold ounce but not a miserable dollar at the tip of their fingers."

Maximilian was wrong and Agnes was forced to try and negotiate the escape with two checks signed by the emperor, each for one hundred thousand dollars, payable by his family in Vienna. Though Agnes had little faith in these slips of paper, she insisted on talking to Colonel Palacios at the home of the widow Doña Pepita Vicente where she was staying. Palacios listened to her proposition that he let the emperor escape in exchange for the promissory notes, but he told his superior officer the plot the following morning and Agnes was ordered out of Querétaro. Agnes says of the checks, "A bag full of gold would have been more persuasive." Gossip has it that Agnes also offered her perfectly formed equestrian's body to Palacios for the night but that the strait-laced Indian colonel refused. Although this tidbit may be tasty, it doesn't square with her nature which was more hoyden than whorish, and from the practical side an evening of at-home entertainment would hardly have escaped the notice of her hostess Doña Pepita.

Agnes' next move was to see the president of the republic, Benito Juárez. She had wangled a previous interview with him on behalf of Maximilian but this time she was prepared to plead for the emperor's life and her husband's without regard for dignity, because if she failed, execution seemed certain. Governments everywhere, including the United States, were pleading for clemency for the unfortunate Hapsburg. Private individuals such as Giuseppe Garibaldi and Victor Hugo sent petitions and Mexicans also pleaded for Maximilian's life and that of the two Mexican generals who were to die with him, Miguel Miramón and Tomás Mejía, to be spared.

Among the prominent Mexican women to implore leniency was Carolina Cuilty de Terrazas known for her intelligence and good works. She and her husband, Governor Luis Terrazas of Chihuahua, had long been supporters of Juárez. Carolina as well as other Mexicans including a group of writers from Jalapa were particularly concerned with clemency for Miramón who had been president of Mexico in 1858 and Mejía who was of Indian ancestry. Doña Concepción Lombardo de Miramón, surrounded by her children, also pleaded for her thirty-six-year-old husband's life, but Mejía's wife was unable to do so. Just before the three men were executed, she gave birth to a son whom the general was permitted to see before he died.

We can use Agnes' own pen to describe her second interview

with President Juárez:

"I fell down on my knees and pleaded with words that came from my heart but which I cannot remember ... I said I would not leave before he granted his (Maximilian's) life. I saw that the president was moved; he had tears in his eyes, but he answered me in a low sad voice; I am grieved Madam to see you thus upon your knees before me; but if all the kings and queens of Europe were at your side, I could not spare his life. It is not I who take it away; it is my people and the law, and if I did not do their will, the people would take his as well as my own."

So the princess could do nothing on behalf of Maximilian but she did receive clemency for her husband. Despite her championship of the emperor, Agnes recognized the good qualities of Juárez because she says in her diary that he was a man "who reflected a great deal and deliberated long and carefully before acting." What she didn't add was that once Juárez' mind was made up his decisions were irrevocable. Maximilian's execution took place on June 19, 1866. He measured up to kingly stature during the weeks of his imprisonment and died bravely as befitted his birth and station in life.

The Salm Salms and Jimmy the terrier went to Félix' ancestral home in Westphalia, then to Vienna, but the memory of the prince's creditors was long and they were forced to skip to Switzerland under the alias Von Stein. Agnes was left a widow at age thirty when the prince was killed leading his battalion at Gravelotte. She continued working as a nurse in the Prussian field hospital and was awarded many honors including the Prussian medal of honor. Franz Joseph gave her a twelve hundred dollar a year pension and a relative in America conveniently died and left her some money. She wandered Europe with Jimmy and when she visited Rome asked the pope's permission to become a nun, which he wisely refused. She married Charles Heneage, secretary of the British legation in Berlin, in 1876, but they separated shortly after.

When she returned to the United States in 1899, she presented the standards of the Eighth and Sixty-Eighth New York Volunteers to the survivors of the regiment in a colorful ceremony. Wearing a black hat trimmed with pink roses and a black silk dress, the reporters present were quick to notice that the flashing decorations given Agnes by emperors and kings covered a bosom as trim and curvaceous as ever. She died in Karlsruhe, Germany in 1911.

Although a great number of *zarzuela* (operetta) performers and stock company actresses were from Spain and grand opera singers from Italy and other European countries, increasing numbers of Mexican women joined the performing arts in the nineteenth century. One of the most outstanding was *El Ruiseñor Mexicano* (the Mexican nightingale), Angela Peralta, born July 6, 1845 in Mexico City. Angela came from a humble family and worked for a while as a servant in Puebla even though she had begun displaying her talents publicly at the tender age of eight when she sang *una cavatina* (a short, simple aria) in the opera Belisario with great success. At this time Mexico badly needed a fine singer of its own. The first performance of the *Himno Nacional* was given September 15, 1854 in the Teatro Nacional, it was sung by an Italian soprano and tenor from an Italian opera company that bore the name René Masson. Unfortunately, Angela was only nine years old.

Angela made her debut in 1860 singing *Il Trovatore* in the Teatro Nacional in Mexico City where she was heard and praised by the famous German opera star Enriqueta Sontag. At the same time that Sontag predicted a great future for the young singer, she also said, with the cattiness of a primadonna, afraid the newcomer might displace her, that Angela was "*tan fea y tan desmadrada*" (so ugly and so emaciated) but had amazing talent. A lyric soprano, Angela was only fifteen years old at the time and may have been overly slender at this early stage but later pictures show her to have been well-cushioned with a full face that, though far from beautiful, was pleasant despite a slight cast in one eye.

If there were doubts about her beauty, there were no doubts about the magnificence of her voice. In 1861, accompanied by her father, she left for Europe to continue her studies. She performed in Madrid and Cádiz, then went to Italy for further work. Her voice teacher, Lamperti, said that she was an angel in voice and name and on May 13, 1862 she was presented at La Scala in Milan to great acclaim, receiving wonderful notices in Italy, a country noted for its fine singers and most critical of those with operatic ambitions. This excerpt from *La Gaceta Italiana* is typical of the accolades given her in the press: "The first presentation of Lucía starring the eminent Angela Peralta was a continuous ovation ... the trills, the cadences that poured forth from her throat reminded us of the splendid performance in the same theatre, attended by the same audience, hearing the same opera sung by Adelina Patti ..." To have been put upon an equal pedestal with one of the world's greatest singers was a golden stamp of approval.

Following this, Angela made a triumphant tour of France, Italy and Egypt. Her first return to Mexico was in 1865 during the disastrous Maximilian reign. After several years at home she returned to Europe for more training and triumphs. In 1871 she came back to her own land again when for the first time a truly first class opera company was formed in Mexico City with outstanding voices from all over the world, and the Mexican nightingale the greatest of the group. In addition to singing, Angela Peralta played the harp and piano and composed a number of musical compositions, among them "Un Recuerdo a Mi Patria," "Margarita" and "Ilusión." She married a man named Castera in 1866 and there are hints that the marriage was not very happy, did not last long and that the singer was bitter about it.

On the evening of November 16, 1872 a bust of Angela Peralta was placed in the lobby of the Teatro Nacional. It was a great occasion with the elite of the theatrical, musical and social world present to do honor to their beloved nightingale. The theatre and the streets around it were thronged with admirers on foot and in carriages. Special eulogies were given by famous orators; it was as though fate knew what was in store for her and was determined to give Angela the honors she deserved while she was still around to enjoy them.

Pestilence was raging in Veracruz when Angela went there for a professional engagement in 1883. She had lodgings on the top floor of the same theatre in which she was appearing, a magnificent new structure called El Teatro Rubio. It was there they found her August 3. She had died suddenly of cholera. Only thirty-eight years old, she had barely reached the peak of her powers. Rafael Martinez, a famous journalist known by the nickname "Rip Rip" launched a campaign to urge that her remains be interred in La Rotonda de Los Hombres Ilustres in El Panteón de Dolores. This was done April 11, 1887. El Teatro Rubio in Veracruz was renamed El Teatro Angela Peralta and to this day Mexico still considers this woman to have been their finest opera singer.

Although Mexico loved music and the theatre, it looked askance upon careers in the arts for women, especially behind the footlights. But Mexican born actresses of note began emerging in the nineteenth century, among them Matilde

Navarro, Concha Padilla, Rosa Flores and the queen of the *zarzuela* and can-can, Amalia Gómez. Soledad Cordero, who had been trained by another Mexican first lady of the drama, Agustina Montenegro, was another favorite performer. She was the star of the repertory company of the Teatro Principal, lauded for high moral principles as well as her acting.

An extra touch of theatre involving bullfights took place in 1854. A corrida was given in October of that year in honor of President Antonio López de Santa Ana, no mean actor himself, and his beautiful young second wife Doña Dolores Tosta. The most famous *torero* of the era, Bernardo Gaviño, was appearing and Mexico City went all out for its hero. The most impressive spectacle of a day filled with spectacle was the arrival at five in the afternoon of an elegant open carriage drawn by spirited horses. Two gorgeous young actresses descended from it carefully carrying between them a crown whose myriad overlapping leaves were cleverly contrived from various sizes of solid gold coins. This they set upon the grateful and now glittering brow of bullfighter Gaviño, a little gift from the city of Mexico.

Women poets, musicians and a few novelists emerged, but acceptance wasn't easy. Gertrudis Tenorio Zavala first saw print in the magazine *El Reportorio Pintoresco* published by Father Crescencio Carillo y Ancona in Mérida, Yucatán. There was a note by the editor to the effect that this was the debut of a young compatriot who was called Hortensia. This was the alias used by Gertrudis because a woman who devoted the greater part of her time to poetry or any of the arts was often scorned, not only by men but by many of her own sex. Even a *marisabidilla* (bookish woman) who liked learning for its own sake was considered peculiar and persecuted in small ways. Other Yucatán poets who hid behind pseudonyms were the sisters Luisa and Cristina Hübbe, who used the combination names of Larina Cistis. Then there were Dominga Febles, who signed her work "Julia," and Rosario Sansores, who borrowed the flowery appellation *Crisantema* (chrysanthemum), hoping that eventually she could blossom forth as herself. If over a period of time their work was well enough received, these women dared to poke their heads out and reveal their true identities. The climate of disapproval did not permit females to freely or spontaneously give rein to their creativity. They were forced to write with one eye on the censors, falling back upon the safe themes of religion, children, home and hearth, all expressed in a ladylike manner that would not offend. Patriotism was also allowed and Rita Cetina Gutiérrez wrote epics in celebration of flag and country, also teaching in the Instituto Literaria de Niñas in Yucatán along with Gertrudis Tenorio Zavala.

In Jalapa in the state of Veracruz, Josefina Pérez de García Torres showed an aptitude for poetry from the time she was a child. When she moved to Mexico City she became one of the editors of *El Eco de Ambos Mundos*, a literary magazine. She married a journalist, Don Vicente García Torres. She bore several children, but continued writing poetry, producing several volumes in 1892 and also contributing to *El Renacimiento*, a woman's publication. Some critics considered her the successor to Sor Juana Inés de la Cruz. Like her illustrious predecessor, she died young, passing away in 1894 at age thirty-eight.

Another outstanding woman from Jalapa was María Pérez Redondo, born in 1863. She was given an extensive education when most girls could scarcely read and few could write. She studied history, literature and French along with her major interests of music composition and piano. María made her debut playing a *zarzuela* she had written called "Partir de Ligero" (Leave Quickly) and followed it with the performance of another, "La Amiga de los Niños" (the children's friend) which she directed for the Jalapa cultural society called El Edén. Then she composed several mazurkas, followed by a series of waltzes, dances and polkas. All were written before she had reached the age of eighteen.

Laura Méndez de Cuenca, born 1853 at Hacienda Tamariz, in Amecameca in the state of Mexico, married Agustín F. Cuenca, a notable poet. She wrote what is sometimes called by Mexican critics pessimistic poetry, but her achievements are so many that her poems are just one of the many talents she is known for. She was a professor in the school of Arts and Director of the Normal School. She represented the Mexican government in various international congresses of education in Paris, Berlin, Milan, etc. In San Francisco, California she founded *La Revista Hispano Americana* and did newspaper work in Mexico City. A great admirer and friend of hers in her youth was the poet Manuel Acuña whose brief but brilliant career was terminated by suicide in 1873 at age twenty-four. Perhaps this tragedy had something to do with the mournful note sounded in

Laura's early work. She published a novel, *El Espejo de Amarilis* (1902), and a book of stories, *Cuentos Simplezas*, in 1910. She died in 1928 but her work is, in spirit, a part of the nineteenth century.

There is dissent concerning the place and birthdate of Esther Tapia de Castellanos. Some sources say May 9, 1842 in Morelia, Michoacán, others, Jiquilpan in 1837. She became known as a poet in the liberal newspapers in Morelia before she and her family moved to Guadalajara where she affiliated with the young writers of Jalisco but did not lose contact with her associates in Morelia. A beautiful woman with large, expressive, dark eyes, patrician nose and sensuous mouth, she was an ardent republican who, during the struggles of the Juárez years, wrote verse in defense of national sovereignty and gave recitals to collect funds for the wounded. She published *Flores Silvestres* in 1871 and *Canticos de los Niños* in 1880.

In all of Mexico in 1874 there were only fifteen secondary schools for women, of which several were conservatories of music. A total of 2,300 female pupils were enrolled in these institutions of higher learning and in only three of the schools did they offer physics and chemistry. Otherwise the courses given were simple arithmetic, domestic hygiene, bookkeeping and the so-called womanly arts of cooking, knitting, embroidery, etc. In 1869 the director of a girl's secondary school in Mexico City tried to create courses in medicine, pharmacy and agriculture, but the opposition was so great that she gave up. About this time the press began stirring up a hue and cry over the status of women's education, pointing out that females scarcely had the opportunity to attend primary school, let alone receive advanced instruction. Perhaps the press helped Mexico's first woman doctor to be accepted at medical school.

Matilde Montoya was born in Mexico City on March 5, 1859. Lying about her age, she began the study of obstetrics at eleven years and at age fourteen was practicing midwifery at hospital San Andrés. She also took it upon herself to study Greek, Latin, science and mathematics, showing at an early age that her interests were hardly those of the average young woman of the mid-nineteenth century. Her excellent care of and large practice of women and children in Cuernavaca became so well known that the doctors grew jealous of her reputation and began persecuting this female who dared compete with them. Matilde then went to Puebla and quickly built up just as big a reputation as she had in Cuernavaca with the same unpleasant results. Forced to get out of town once more, this time she went to Veracruz.

When the attacks upon her slowed down, her friends persuaded her to return to Puebla where she entered medical school in the face of renewed opposition that continued throughout her years there. On August 25, 1887 she graduated with honors, the first Mexican woman to receive the title of Doctor of Medicine. She lived well into the twentieth century and was almost eighty years old when she died in 1938.

The yeast of change was fermenting and at the first Congreso Nacional Obrero (National Worker's Congress) in 1876 there were three women representatives out of the total of seventy-two. It wasn't much, but it was a beginning. Also, the status and needs of women were not totally ignored. Enrique Chávarri, popularly known as Juvenal, was an editor for *El Monitor Republicano*, a Mexico City daily known for backing freedom of the press, worker's interests and reforms of all kinds. Writing in regard to the congress, he said:

"Since the woman worker exists, how can you deny her a forum where she can discuss her rights? Woman has ceased to live in isolation. She is no longer a slave, but man's equal. She has already entered the factories. We don't want her to lose heart in her struggle. Let us sustain her in it and give her all her rights."

But despite men of goodwill like Juvenal, the kind of work women did and the pay for it in big cities was minimal. The following ad shows the going rate in Mexico City in 1868:

"A small family needs a chambermaid who will earn three pesos and rations. Also a seamstress who will earn six pesos. Both must be settled persons, reliable and without children. They must have papers attesting to their good character and working habits."

Because the system still exists in the underdeveloped countries of Hispanic America, you can be sure that the salary was monthly, the rations served to the help entirely different from that served to the masters, and that the servants lived in and were on call virtually twenty-four hours a day. The earned pittance often went to aged parents and fatherless children and was supplemented only by pilfered bits and pieces that fell from the master's table.

Bibliography

Adamson, Hans Christian. *Lands of New World Neighbors.* N.p.: McGraw Hill, 1941.

Aguirre, Beltrán Gonzalo. *La población negra de México.* 2nd ed. Mexico: Fondo de Cultura Económica, 1972.

Alatorre, Mendieta. *Margarita Maza de Juárez and María de Los Angeles.* Mexico: n.p., 1972.

Altman, Ida and James Lockhart, eds. *Provinces of Early Mexico.* Los Angeles: UCLA Latin American Center Publications, n.d.

Anderson, Imbert E. *Historia de la literatura hispanoamericano II: Epoca contemporáneo.* Mexico: Fondo de Cultura Económica S.A., 1961.

Anderson, William Marshall. *The Diaries of an American in Maximilian's Mexico, 1865-1866.* N.p.: Henry E. Huntington Libary, 1959.

Angeles, Maria de los. *(Mendieta Alatorre) Margarita Maza de Juáres.* Mexico: n.p., 1972.

Anton, Ferdinand. *Woman in Pre-Columbian America: Aztec, Incan, Mayan.* New York: Abner Schram, 1973.

Arciniegas, Germán. *Latin America: A Cultural History.* N.p.: Knopf, 1966.

-----, ed. *The Green Continent.* N.p.: Knopf, 1967.

Arroyo, Anita. *Razón y pasión de Sor Juana.* Mexico: Porrua y Obregon, S.A., 1952.

Bancroft, Hubert Howe. *Bancroft's Works, Mexico.* N.p.: Bancroft Press, 1888, reprint 1967.

Barca, Fanny Calderón de la. *Life in Mexico.* Garden City, N.Y.: Doubleday & Company, Inc., 1966.

Beals, Carleton. *Mexican Maze.* New York: Book League of America, 1931.

Beckett, Samuel, trans. *Anthology of Mexican Poetry.* London: Thomes and Hudson, 1958.

Bedford, Sybille. *A Traveler's Tale from Mexico.* New York: Atheneum, 1963.

Benítez, Fernando. *The Century After Cortés.* Translated by Joan MacLean. Chicago: University of Chicago Press, 1965.

Blasio, José Luis. *Maximilian, Emperor of Mexico: Memoirs of His Private Secretary.* New Haven: Yale University Press, 1934.

Bobb, Bernard. *The Viceregency of Antonio Maria Bucareli.* Austin, TX: University of Texas Press, 1962.

Boucher, Francois. *20,000 Years of Fashion.* New York: Harry N. Abrams, Inc., n.d.

Brady, Robert LaDon. *The Emergence of a Negro Class in Mexico, 1524-1640: A Dissertation.* Iowa: State University of Iowa, 1965.

Brasch, R. *Mexico: A Country of Contrasts.* N.p.: Longmans, Green & Co., 1967.

Castillo, Bernal Díaz del. *The Discovery and Conquest of Mexico.* Translated by A. P. Maudslay. N.p.: Harper and Brothers, 1928.

Cheetham, Nicholas. *New Spain: The Birth of Modern Mexico.* London: Victor Gollancz, Ltd., 1974.

Clark, Sidney. *All the Best in Mexico.* N.p.: Dodd, Mead, 1970.

Codex Mendoza. N.p.: Aztec Manuscript Productions Liber, S.A., 1978.

Cohen, Martin A. *The Martyr: The Story of a Secret Jew and the Mexican Inquisition.* Philadelphia: Jewish Publication Society of America, 1973.

Collis, Maurice. *Cortes and Montezuma.* London: Faber and Faber, 1954.

Cosío Villegas, Daniel. *Historia moderna de México, Vol.: La república restaurada vida social.* Mexico: Editorial Hermes, n.d.

Costa, B. *Quién es quién en la nomenclatura de la Ciudad de México.* Mexico: Fischgrund Ediciones de Arte, n.d.

-----. *(Jesús Romero Flores) México: Una historia de una gran ciudad.* Mexico, D.F.: Amic Editor, 1978.

Cotera, Martha P. *Diosa y hembra.* Austin, TX: Information Systems Development, n.d.

Covarrubias, Luis. *Trajes regionales de México.* Mexico: Fischgrund Ediciones de Arte, n.d.

Covarrubias, Miguel. *Mexico South.* N.p.: Knopf, 1947.

Coy, Harold. *The Mexicans.* N.p.: Little, Brown, 1970.

Crawford, W. Rex, trans. *A Mexican Ulysses: Autobiography of José Vasconcelos.* Bloomington: L.A. Library, Indiana University Press, 1963.

Dobbs, Jack A. *The French Army in Mexico, 1861-1867.* The

Hague: Mouton and Co., 1963.

Durán, Fray Diego. *The Aztecs: The History of the Indies of New Spain.* New York: Orion Press, 1964.

Du Solier, W. *Ancient Mexican Costumes.* Mexico, D.F.: Ediciones Mexicanas, 1950.

Elkin, Judith Laikin. *Jews of the Latin American Republics.* Chapel Hill: University of North Carolina Press, 1980.

Escobedo, Raquel. *Galería de mujeres ilustres.* N.p.: Editores Mexicanos Unidos, S.A., 1967.

Fehrenbach, T. R. *Fire and Blood: A History of Mexico.* N.p.: Macmillan, 1973.

Fischer, Howard and Marion Hall. *Life in Mexico: The Letters of Fanny Calderón de la Barca.* N.p., n.d.

Flores, Angel. *The Literature of Spanish America: The Colonial Period.* New York: Las Americas Publishing Co., n.d.

Flores, Jesus Romero (B. Costa). *México: Una historia de una gran ciudad.* Mexico, D.F.: Amic Editor, 1978.

Franco, Jean. *An Introduction to Spanish American Literature.* Cambridge: University Press, 1969.

Fuentes, Patricia de, ed and trans. *The Conquistadors: First Person Accounts of the Conquest of Mexico.* New York: Orion Press, 1963.

Gage, Thomas. *A New Survey of the West Indies, 1648.* London: 1946.

Garcia Cantu, Gaston. *El pensamiento de la reacción mexicana historia documental, 1810-1962.* Mexico: Empresas Editoriales, S.A., n.d.

Garcia, Rubén (José Vasconcelos). *Rincones y paisajes del México maravilloso.* Mexico: 1950.

Gibson, Charles. *The Aztecs Under Spanish Rule.* Palo Alto, CA:

Stanford University Press, 1964.

Gomara, Francisco Lopez de. *Cortés.* Berkeley: University of California Press, 1964.

González Peña, Carlos. *History of Mexican Literature.* 3d ed. Dallas: Southern Methodist University Press, 1969.

Greenleaf, Richard E. (Michael C. Meyer). *Research in Mexican History.* Lincoln, NE: University of Nebraska Press, 1973.

-----. *The Mexican Inquisition of the 16th Century.* Albuquerque: University of New Mexico Press, 1969.

Harding, Bertita. *Phantom Crown.* N.p.: Bobbs Merrill Co., 1934.

Haslip, Joan. *The Crown of Mexico.* New York: Holt, Rinehart and Winston, n.d.

Hatch, Nelle Spilsbury. *Colonia Juárez: An Intimate Account of a Mormon Village.* Salt Lake City: Deseret Book Co., 1954.

Henestrosa, Andrés. *Los Caminos de Juárez.* Mexico: Fondo de Cultura Económica, n.d.

Herring, Hubert. *A History of Latin America.* Rev. ed. N.p., 1961.

Herrmann, Paul. *The Great Age of Discovery.* New York: Harper and Bros., 1958.

Israel, J. I. *Race, Class and Politics in Colonial Mexico, 1610-1670.* Oxford: Oxford University Press, 1975.

Jones, Obadiah L., Jr. *Santa Ana.* New York: Twayne Publishers, 1968.

Johnson, William Weber. *Cortes.* New York: Little, Brown and Co., 1975.

King, Rosa E. *Tempest Over Mexico.* New York: Little, Brown and Co., 1935.

Lafaye, Jacques. *Quetzalcoatl and Guadelupe.* Chicago: University of Chicago Press, 1976.

Leies SM, Herbert, F. *Mother for a New World: Our Lady of Guadalupe*. Westminster, MD: The Newman Press, 1964.

Leiva, Raul. *Introducción a Sor Juana: Sueño y realidad*. Mexico: UNAM, 1975.

León Portilla, Miguel. *Pre-Columbian Literature of Mexico*. N.p.: University of Oklahoma Press, 1969.

Leonard, Irving A. *Baroque Times in Old Mexico*. Ann Arbor: University of Michigan Press, 1973.

-----. *Don Carlos de Sigüenza y Góngora: A Mexican Savant of the 17th Century*. Berkeley: University of California Press, 1929.

Liebman, Seymour B., ed. and trans. *The Enlightened: The Writings of Luis de Carvajal el Mozo*. Coral Cables, FL: University of Miami Press, 1967.

-----. *The Inquisitors and the Jews in the New World: Summaries of Procesos 1500-1810 and Bibliographical Guide*. Coral Cables, FL: University of Miami Press, 1974.

Liss, Peggy K. *Mexico Under Spain, 1521-1556*. Chicago: University of Chicago Press, 1975.

Lockhart, James (Ida Altman), ed. *Provinces of Early Mexico*. Los Angeles: UCLA Latin American Center Publications, 1976.

Madariaga, Salvador de. *Hernán Cortés: Conqueror of Mexico*. Coral Gables, FL: University of Miami Press, 1942.

Magner, James A. *Men of Mexico*. Milwaukee: Bruce Publishing Co., 1942.

Mayer, William. *Early Travelers in Mexico*. Mexico, D.F.: n.p., 1961.

Maza, Francisco de la. *Sor Juana y Don Carlos*. Mexico: n.p., 1970.

-----. *La Ruta de Sor Juana.* Mexico: Gobierno del Estado de México, Dirección de Turismo, 1969-1975.

Meyer, Michael C. (Richard E. Greenleaf) *Research in Mexican History.* Lincoln: University of Nebraska Press, 1973.

Meyer and Sherman. *The Course of Mexican History.* New York: Oxford University Press, 1979.

Monti, Laura V. *Sor Juana Inéz de la Cruz.* Gainesville, Fla.: University of Florida, 1958.

Niles, Blair. *Passengers to Mexico.* N.p.: Farrar, Rinehart, 1943.

Nolen, Barbara, ed. *Mexico is People.* N.p.: Charles Scribners Sons, 1973.

Norman, James. *Terry's Guide to Mexico.* N.p.: Doubleday, 1972.

Nuñez y Dominguez, José J. *La Virreina Mexicana.* Mexico: Imprenta Universitaria, 1950.

Ober, Frederick. *Hernando Cortés, Conqueror of Mexico.* New York: Harper and Bros., 1905.

Onis, Harriet de. *The Golden Land.* N.p.: Dallas Press, 1969.

Parker, Henry Bamford. *A History of Mexico.* N.p.: Houghton Mifflin, 1960.

Parkinson, Roger. *Zapata.* New York: Stein and Day, 1975.

Pasquel, Leonardo. *Xalapeños Distinguidos.* Colección Suma Veracruzano. N.p.: Editorial Citlaltepetl, n.d.

Paz, Octavio. *Sor Juana de la Cruz o Las Trampas de la Fe.* Spain: Seix Barral Biblioteca Breve, 1982.

Pere, Foix. *Juárez.* Mexico: Editorial Trillas, 1974.

Pfondl, Ludwig. *Sor Juana Inés de la Cruz.* Mexico: Universidad Nacional Autónoma de México, 1963.

Prescott, William Hickling. *History of the Conquest, Mexico and Peru.* Complete Texts Modern Library Giant. New York: Random House, n.d.

Priestley, Herbert I. *The Mexican Nation: A History.* New York: n.p., 1923.

Reed, Alma M. *The Ancient Past of Mexico.* New York: Crown Publishers, 1966.

Robertson, William Spence. *Iturbide of Mexico.* N.p.: Duke University Press, 1952.

Roeder, Ralph. *Juárez and His Mexico.* New York: Viking Press, 1947.

Romney, Thomas Cottom. *Mormon Colonies in Mexico.* Salt Lake City, UT: Deseret Book Co., 1938.

Rosell, Lauro E. *Iglesias y Conventos de México.* Mexico, D.F.: n.p., n.d.

Ross, Kurt. *Codex Mendoza: Aztec Manuscript, Commentaries.* N.p.: Miller Graphics, 1978.

Saenz Royo, Artemisa, "Xohitl". *Semblanzas Mujeres Mexicanas, Revolucionarias y Guerreras Revolucionarias Ideológicas.* Mexico, D.F.: León Sánchez, n.d.

Sahagun. *Historia General de las Cosas de Nueva España.* Mexico: n.p., 1938.

Salm Salm, Princess Agnes. *Ten Years of My Life.* 2 vol. New York: n.p., 1868.

Scharfman, Rabbi I. Harold. *Jews on the Frontier.* Chicago: Henry Regnery Co., 1977.

Schlarman, Joseph H. L. *Mexico: A Land of Volcanoes.* Milwaukee: Bruce Publishing Co., 1950.

Simpson, Leslie Bird. *The Writing of History.* N.p., n.d.

Smart, Charles Allen. *Viva Juárez.* N.p.: J.B. Lippincott Co.,

1963.

-----. *Juárez*. Spain: n.p., 1971.

Soustelle, Jacques. *Daily Life of the Aztecs*. New York: Macmillan, 1962.

Stevenson, Sarah Yorke. *Maximilian in Mexico: A Woman's Reminiscences of the French Intervention, 1862-1867*. 2 ed. Mexico: n.p., 1972.

Teran, Francisco. "Páginas de historia y geográfica, Quito, Ecuador, 1972." *Américas*. February, 1976.

Terreros, Romero de. *La Vida Social en la Nueva España*. N.p., n.d.

Thomas, Dr. Sandra. *C.I.M. Inter American Commission of Women, Series Studies No. 3*. Washington, D.C.: General Secretariat, O.A.S., 1977.

Toor, Frances. *Mexican Folkways*. N.p.: Crown Publishers, 1947.

Torres Rioseco, Arturo. *New World Literature*. Berkeley: University of California Press, 1949.

Uroz, Antonio. *Hombres y mujeres de México*. México, D.F.: Editorial Lic. Antonio Uroz, 1972.

Vasconcelos, José and Rubén García. *Rincones y paisajes del México maravilloso*. México: n.p., 1950.

Villar, Ernesto de la Torre. *Los Guadalupes y la independencia: con una selección de documentos inéditos*. N.p., n.d.

-----. *Lecturas históricas mexicanas*. Tomo III. N.p., n.d.

Wagenheim, Kal. *Puerto Rico: A Profile*. N.p.: Praeger Paperbacks, 1970.

White, John Manchip. *Cortés*. New York: St. Martin's Press, 1971.

Whitecotton, Joseph W. *The Zapotecs*. N.p.: University of Oklahoma, 1977.

Williams, Mary Wilhelmine. *The People and Politics of Latin America.* Rev. ed. N.p.: Ginn and Co., 1945.

Wong, Kal and Olga Jiménez de. *The Puerto Ricans.* N.p.: Praeger, 1973.

Index

Aguiar y Seijas, Archibishop Francisco de: as woman-hater, 67-68; with rioting women, 68; dislike for Sor Juana Inés de la Cruz, 86.

Aguilar, Jerónimo de: enlisted as interpreter, 4, 6.

Alcázar, María Felipe de. *See* Inquisition: women victims of.

Almonte, Doña Dolores Quesada de: destined to be Carlota's constant companion, 144.

Alvarado, Pedro de: heads up a massacre, 23.

Antuñez, Clara. *See* Inquisition: women victims of.

Anunción, Sister Francesca de la. *See* Inquisition: and treatment of nuns.

Apodaca, Juan Ruiz de, viceroy: releases La Corregidora from prison, 103.

Aragon, Mencía Pérez de. *See* Memorable humble women: mestiza.

Asbaje Ramirez de Santillana, Juana Inés de (Later, Sor Juana Inés de la Cruz) and known to history as La Decima Musa, 72.

Auinime. *See* Aztec women: activities.

Auto de Fé: public court conducted by Inquisition, procedure for, 43-44; grandest spectacle, 46; for Carvajals, 46-48; sentencing, 47.

Avila María de: and tragic love affair, 38.

Azcaxochitzin: target of King Nexahualcóyotl's love, 32; and won by murder, 33.

Aztec warriors: meet Cortés at San Juan de Ulúa, 5.

Aztec women: and first impressions of Conquistadors, 2; given as slaves, 2; baptized, 4; dress, activities and social structure, 2, 17; and polygamy, 18; revered, 17-18.

Barca, Fanny Calderón de la, English writer, praises La Güera, 98-99; describes the public jail, 122-123.

Barragana, La Intrépida. *See* Heroines of the wars for

independence: at siege of Cuautla.
Barrio, Marquesa del: Carlota's trusted lady in waiting, 155, 157.
Bartola, Doña María: daughter of King Cuitlahuac and first historian of Mexico, 37-38.
Bazaine, General Francois Achille: French commander in chief in Mexico, 144; arranges reception for Maximilian and Carlota, 145; power behind Maximilian, 147; and Josefa de la Peña y Azcarate, 147-148; in France, guilty of treason and imprisoned, 150.
Beatas: as female unit of Franciscans, their views questioned, 52-53.
Bermúdez, Beatriz. *See* Spanish women.
Black slave women: favored treatment of, 58-61; tried for sorcery, 59; as Jewesses, 59-60; and heresy accusation, 60; efforts to improve their lot, 61.
Bocanegra, Gertrudis. *See* Heroines of the wars for independence: at Patzcuara.
Bosque, Juana del. *See* Black slave women: as Jewesses.
Briones, Don Mariano, second husband to La Güera, 98.
Bucareli, Viceroy Antonio María, 92-94.
Business women: Aztec, 34; printers, 91-92; hacienda managers, 112.
Calendario de las Señoritas Mexicanas, yearly publication, 113-114.
Calvinists: some tried by Inquisition, 48.
Campos, Catalina de. *See* Inquisition: women victims of.
Camp women: activities and gossip, 11.
Cannibalism: practiced by Aztecs, 6.
Capitana, La. *See* Medina, Manuela.
Carlota, Empress (Princess Charlotte Emily), 136; background of, 142; and ladies in waiting, 145-146; assists General Bazaine, 148; as childless wife, 151-152; and extra marital affairs of Maximilian, 154-155; unsuccessful efforts to obtain help, 155-157; and health decline to insanity, 157-158, 159; last years, 163.
Carmelitas descalzas, 83.
Carvajal family, persecution of by Inquisition: Isabel, 40-48; Luis, Fray Gaspar, Francesca, Leonor, Catalina, Mariana, Anica, 41.
Casa de Niños, La (La Cuna), home for foundlings. *See* Charitable women: as sponsors for orphanages.
Castellanos, Esther Tapia de. *See* Women writers: poets.
Castillo, Bernal Díaz del, famous historian and admirer of Malinche, 14, 30.
Catalina, Doña: and mysterious death, 28.
Cepeda y Cosío, María de

Jesús. *See* Society women: professional and other singers.
Chachiuhnenetzin: Queen to King Nezahualpilli, 33; as a precocious and lustful woman, 33-34; and tragic death, 34.
Charitable women: at siege of Cuautla, 109; in Mexico City, 109-110; as sponsors of orphanages; at Michoacán, 112; at La Cuna, 121-123; help in public jail, 122; help for insane women, 123.
Chávarri, Enrique (Juvenal), backer of reforms, 169.
Chiliate, refreshing drink by La Humana Costeña, 109.
China poblana, description and legend of, 68-70.
Cholula, battle of, 15.
Church of Latter Day Saints: and services in Chihuahua, 139.
Cigars and cigarettes, among Mexican women, 114.
Cimatl: disposes of her daughter, Malinalli, 3; is forgiven, 29.
Cistis, Larina. *See* Hübbe, Luisa and Cristina.
Ciuatlamacazqui. *See* Aztec women: dress, activities and social structure.
Cochineal, 125.
Colónia Juárez: Mormons, 140; nurses serving at, 140.
Concepción, La, luxury convent, 116.
Conquistadors: enter Mexico City, 16; treated well, 18; flee Mexico City, 25-26.
Conspiración del Año Once, plans for, 107.
Convent San Jerónimo, background of, 83.
Convents: variety of living conditions, 116; closing of, 119.
Cordero, Soledad. *See* Women of the performing arts: actresses.
Corpus Christi, convent for women of Indian ancestry, 118-119.
Corregidor, El, center for cultural activities, 100.
Corregidora, La (María Josefa Ortiz), 100. *See also* Heroines of wars for independence: at Queretaro.
Cortés, Hernán: victorious at battle of Tabasco, 1; introduction and description of, 2; and his secret plan, 4; and possible mistake concerning Doña Marina, 6-7; requests meeting with Montezuma, 7; takes possession of all Mexico, 9; takes precaution against desertion, 12; marches to Tenochtitlán, 12-13, 18, 21; emergency march to Cempoala, 22, 23; retakes and rebuilds the capital, 26-27; makes expedition to Honduras in grand style, 28-29; welcomes Franciscan Friars, 35; *see also* Malintzín.
Cosijoeza, Zapotec King, 36; and myths concerning his marriage, 36-37.
Costeña, La Humana. *See* Heroines of wars for inde-

pendence; at siege of Cuautla.
Crisantema. *See* Sansores, Rosario.
Crop failure; and near famine in Mexico, 66.
Cruz, María de la. *See* Black slave women: as Jewesses.
Cruz, Sister Elena de la. *See* Inquisition: treatment of nuns.
Cruz, Sister Inés de la. *See* Determined nuns.
Cruz, Sor Juana Inés de la (La Decima Musa): woman of genius, 70; legitimacy a bitter load, early contact with culture, 71-75; and residence in the royal palace, 76; her genius quizzed, 77-78; her poetry, 79-81; men in her life, 80; brief stay at convent Santa Teresa La Antigua, 82; enters convent San Jerónimo, 83; first volume of poetry published, and denied entry to University of Mexico, 84-85; and the Inquisition, 86; at climax of her career, age 42, and self-imposed tragic intellectual decline, 88-89; *see also* Women writers: poets.
Cuenca, Laura Méndez de. *See* Women writers: poets.
Cuna, La. *See* Charitable women: La Cuna.
Decima Musa, La. *See* Cruz, Sor Juana Inés de la.
Determined nuns, 63-65; open new convent, 65; and their underground convent, 119-120.

Diego, Juan, and miraculous visions, 53-54.
Discalced Carmelites. *See* Determined nuns.
Discontented women, 66-68.
Domínguez, Miguel: destined for importance, marries Josefa Ortiz, 100.
Elizalde, Juan Manuel, de: third husband of La Güera, 99.
Elvira, Doña. *See* Women spoils of war: Tlaxcalan battles.
Encarnación, La: luxury convent, 116.
Encarnación, Mariana de la. *See* Determined nuns.
Enríquez, Juana. *See* Messianic hope, failure of.
Erazu, Doña Catalina de (nun-ensign): spectacular mule driver and adventurer, 49-50.
Escalante, Juan de: and first indication of trouble with Aztecs, 18.
Estrada, María de. *See* Spanish women.
Eugénie and Napoleon, 155-157.
Fagoaga, Faustina, Elena, Julia. *See* Society women: as believers in education for women. *See also* Charitable women: help in public jail.
Febles, Dominga "Julia." *See* Women writers: poets.
Fernández, Leona Vicario. *See* Heroines of wars for independence: at Oaxaca.
Fischer, Father (Maximilian Rasputin): assists in adoption scheme, 153.
Flat house: as jail for Inquisi-

tion prisoners, 40; description of and existence in, 42.
Flores, Rosa. *See* Women of performing arts: actresses.
France: land troops in Mexico, 132.
Franciscan Friars: bring Christian gospel to Mexico, 35.
French forces: departure from Mexico, 149-150.
Gage, Thomas, 63.
Galve, Conde de, Viceroy, fails to quell 1692 riot, 67.
Gallardo, José María: reveals plan for Conspiración del Año Nuevo, 107.
Galvan, Mariano, publisher, 113.
García, Torres, Josefina Pérez de. *See* Women writers: poets.
Gómez, Amalia. *See* Women of performing arts: actresses.
Gorgollo, Señora Margarita de. *See* Society women: professional and other singers.
Grant, Ulysses S.: entertains Margarita Juárez, 134.
Grito de Dolores, 110.
Guadalupes, Los: insurgents in Mexico City, 104-105; and rescue of Leona Vicario, 105.
Guatemala, Ana María. *See* Women protestors: at expulsion of Jesuits.
Guerra, Fray García: target of determined nuns, 64-65.
Guerrero, General: declared traitor by La Corregidora, 103.
Guitérrez, Rita Cetina. *See* Women writers: poets.

Hellstrom, Anna B.: and unique Mormon status, 141.
Hernández, Catalina: as a Beata, speaks up, 52-53.
Heroines of wars for independence: in Querétaro, 99, 100-103; as writers, 103; in Mexico City, 104-106; at Oaxaca, 104-106; at siege of Cuautla, 107-109; at Pátzcuara, 110; at Texcoco, 110; at Chichihualco, 111; at Erongarícuaro, 111; at Soto la Marina, 112.
Hidalgo y Costilla, Father Miguel: fires opening shot of insurgent movement, 99; a strong influence on Doña Josefa Ortiz, 101; as a free-thinking priest, 104, 106; imprisoned and executed, 106-107.
Hogal, Doña de. *See* Business women: printers.
Huarte, Ana María, beautiful and fertile heiress, 152.
Hübbe, Luisa and Cristina (Larina Cistis). *See* Women writers: poets.
Huexotzincatzin: put to death by his father, 35.
Huipil, native dress worn by Margarita Juárez, 129.
Human sacrifice, practiced by Aztecs, 6.
Inquisition: torture by, 42; sentences by, 44; and treatment of nuns, 50-52; women victims of, 48-49; torture and hangings of black leaders of riots, 58; and milder moments, 60; tightens hold, 65; outwitted by La Güera, 97.

Iturbide, Agustin de: loyalist emperor-dictator, 110; and La Güera, 97; subject of gossip, 98; declared as a traitor, 103; exiled and death by firing squad, 152-153.
Iturbide, Josefina, sister of Agustin: and adoption scheme, 153.
Iturbide, Alice Green de: and adoption of her son, 154, 156.
Jáuregui, Doña María Fernández de. See Heroines of wars for independence: as writers.
Jesuits, expulsion of, 90; reaction to, 91.
Johnson, Andrew, President of U.S., 134.
Josefa, Doña. See Ortiz, María Josefa.
Joy, Agnes Elizabeth Winona Leclerq; romantic and professional equestrienne, 159; and Prince Salm Salm, 160; as nurse, at siege of Querétaro, 160-162; attempts to free husband from prison, 162-163.
Juárez, Benito: destined to be Liberator of Mexico, 125-126; returns from exile, 127; declared president, 130; orders execution of Maximilian, 135; refuses Carlota's pleas, 162-163.
Juárez, Benito and Margarita: a deep love, 125-126; early financial and political problems, 127.
Juárez, Doña Margarita Maza de: and many children, 128; journeys to Veracruz to join Benito, 128-130; a hazardous life, 130-131; and sorrowful life in the U.S., 132-133; debut in Washington society, 133; reunion and heart swelling reception, 135-137; homage paid, 138-139.
Judaism: and Carvajal family, 40-45.
Juvenal. See Chávarri, Enrique.
Ladino: language of insurgents at secret meetings, 44.
Lady of Tula, King Nezahualpilli's talented and favorite concubine, 34; and intrigue, 35; see also Business women: Aztec; and Women writers: poets.
Lazarín, Mariana Rodríguez de. See Heroines of wars for independence: in Mexico City.
Ledesma, Fray Bartolomé de, Inquisitor at first nun's trials, 50-51.
Lempriere, Charles: and "Notes on Mexico 1861," 131.
Léperos: teenage hoodlums join rioting women, 67.
Lincoln, Abraham, President and Mrs., 160.
Luisa, Doña. See Women, spoils of war: Tlaxcalan battles.
Lutherans: and the Inquisition, 48.
Magdalena, María. See Black slave women: as Jewesses.
Malinalli: as slave girl, 2-3; see also Malinche, La; Marina, Doña; Malinchista.
Malinche, La: exceptional personal attributes, 3; and

Women of Mexico

women of Cortés camp, 10; pregnant, 19; as interpreter, 19-20; and mixed acceptance in Montezuma's court, 23; son Martín born, 26; accompanies Cortés to Honduras, 29; remembrances of, 30. *See also* Warrior women: Aztec; Malinalli; Marina, Doña; Malinchista.

Malinchista, a misnomer, 31.

Malintzín (Cortés), 12.

Mar, La. *See* Heroines of wars for independence: at Sota La Marina.

Margarita, Doña. *See* Charitable women: as sponsors of orphanages.

Marín, María. *See* Inquisition: women victims of.

Marina, Doña: destined to be indispensable to Cortés, 2; given as wife to Alonso Puertocarrero, 5; as interpreter, 6; begins intimate relationship with Cortés, 12; and hazardous march to Tenochtitlán, 12-13; as realist, 13; and faith in Christianity, 16; as Totoloque interpreter, 20-21; concern for her unborn child, 22-23; saves the Conquistadors, 15; married off to Juan Jaramillo, 29-30. *See also* Warrior women: Aztec; Malinalli; Malinche, La; Malinchista.

Maroons: black agitators, 57.

Martín, Don: Cortés and Doña Marina's son, 30.

Martín, Juana. *See* Spanish women.

Martínez, Luisa. *See* Heroines of the wars for independence: at Erongarícuaro.

Maximilian (Archduke Ferdinand Maximilian): description of and background, 142-143; refuses to leave Mexico, 149; executed, 163.

Maximilian and Carlota: made emperor and empress of Mexico, 143; and reception in Mexico, 143-145.

Maximilian's Rasputin. *See* Fischer, Father.

Medina, Manuela (La Capitana). *See* Heroines of the wars for independence: at Texcoco.

Memorable humble women: mestiza, 39; weavers, 39.

Méndez, Concha, Cuban Nightingale, 158; favored by Carlota, 158-159.

Messianic hope, failure of, 49.

Mexican nightingale, the. *See* Peralta, Angela.

Mexico: and beginning of changes, 90; in political turmoil, 128; returns U.S. hospitality, 137-138; financial problems, 150; and effect of diminished convent life, 151.

Mexico City, a boom town, 56; racially mixed, 57; and unrest among blacks, 57-58.

Mier, Doña Ana María Iraeta de. *See* Charitable women: at siege of Cuautla.

Mociuaquetzque. *See* Aztec women: revered.

Mock battle, staged by Cortés,

8.
Montenegro, Agustina. *See* Women of the performing arts: actresses.
Montezuma: status of and description, 5-6; aids Cortés, 13; and Cortés' possible godly status, 16; living style, 16-17; presents mask of Quetzalcoatl to Cortés, 18; as prisoner in his own home, 20; a historical puzzle, 21; dies of broken heart, 24-25.
Montoya, Matilde. *See* Professional women: medical doctors.
Montúfar, Archbishop Alonso de: conducts first trials of nuns, 50-52.
Morelos, General José María: advised by La Capitana, 110; assumes leadership of insurgents, 107.
Mujer emplumada, punishment for street walkers, 97.
Mulatta of Córdoba: legendary black beauty, 61; seized by Inquisition, 62; and mysterious jail break, 62-63.
Navarro, Matilde. *See* Women of the performing arts: actresses.
Noche triste: evacuation of Tenochtitlán by Conquistadors, 25-26.
Negrete, General Pedro Celestino, royalist, executes Luisa Martínez, 111.
New Christians, status of, 40-41.
Nezahualcóyotl, poet king of Texcoco, 32-33, 147.
Nezahuapilli, successor of Nezahualcóyotl, 33; and incessant amorous problems, 33-35.
Nun-ensign. *See* Erazu, Doña Catalina de.
Nuñez, Ana. *See* Inquisition: women victims of.
Nuñez, Captain Felipe and Isabel de Carvajal, 41.
Nunneries, basic function of: in Mexico City, 56.
Nuns, and vida común, 92-94.
Ocampo, María. *See* Inquisition: women victims of.
Ocampo, Melchor: son of Doña Francisca Tapía, 112; and great destiny, 113.
Ochoa, mayor of Querétaro; and secret revolutionary meetings, 101-102.
Olmedo, Fray Bartolomé de: baptizes slave girls, 4; conducts mass, 7.
Olid, Cristóbal de: sent by Cortés to explore Honduras, 28.
Oroz, Fray Pedro de: befriends Carvajal family, 44.
Ortiz, María Josefa (Doña Josefa). *See* Heroines of wars for independence: at Querétaro.
Otumba, battle of, 26.
Padilla, Concha. *See* Women of performing arts: actresses.
Palacios, Beatriz de. *See* Spanish women.
Pelaxilla, Aztec princess: and myths concerning her marriage, 36-37; saves the Zapotec kingdom, 37.
Peimbert, Margarita de. *See* Heroines of wars for independence: at Oaxaca.

Peña y Azcárate, Josefa de la (Pepita): and General Bazaine, 147-150.
Pepita. See Peña y Azcárate, Josefa de la.
Peralta, Angela (The Mexican Nightingale). See Women of the performing arts: singers.
Peréira, Inés. See Inquisition: women victims of.
Pizárro, Leonor, Cortés' illegitimate daughter, 4.
Poinsett, Joel R., first U.S. ambassador to Mexico, 115.
Polygamy. See Aztec women: polygamy; as practiced by Aztecs, 33; outlawed in the U.S., enters Mexico, 139.
Professional women: medical doctors, 140, 168; teachers, 140.
Puertocarrero, Alonso, Hernando: marries Doña Marina, 5; sent to Spain by Cortés, 111-112.
Quetzalcoatl: great god of Aztecs, 5, 8, 13; myth of, 20.
Quintana Roo, Andrés: and independence movement, 104-105; marries Leona Vicario, 105.
Redondo, María Pérez. See Women of performing arts: composers.
Reforms, liberal: as taken by the clergy, 128.
Riot of 1695: a preview of things to come, 68; see also Discontented women.
Rivera, Blanca de. See Inquisition: women victims of.
Rivera, María Fermina. See Heroines of wars for independence: at Chichichualco.
Rivera, Doña María de. See Business women: printers.
Rodríguez, Esperanza. See Black slave women: as Jewesses.
Rodríguez, Isabel. See Spanish women.
Rodríguez, La Güera. See Velasco y Osorio Barba, María Ignacia.
Romney, Annie W. See Professional women: teachers.
Salanueva, Don Antonio, lay brother: benefactor of Benito Juárez, 125.
Salm Salm, Prince Felix Zu: and Agnes Joy, 160.
Sanbenito, garment of penitents, 30-40.
San Joaquin, Sor María Ana. See China Poblana, legend of.
Sansores, Rosario (Crisantema). See Women writers: poets.
Santacilia, Pedro: escorts Juárez family to the U.S., 132-133.
Santa Ana, Dolores Tostade, wife of President Antonio López, 166.
Santa Mónica, convent of: early history and closing of, 119; existence disclosed, 120-121; see also Determined nuns.
Santa Teresa, La Antigua: austere convent, 82-83; founded by Carmelitas Descalces, 116; ceremony for entering, 117-118; a dreary life, 118.
Saville, Dr. Avelina E. See

Professional women: medical doctors.
Seward, William H., U.S. Secretary of State: entertains Margarita Juárez, 134; visits Mexico, 137.
Siege of Cuautla, 108-109.
Siege of Querétaro, 161.
Sigüenza y Góngora, Don Carlos de: consults Sor Juana Inés de la Cruz, 84-85; and strong influence on Sor Juana, 81-82.
Slave girls, accept pseudo marital status, 5.
Smallpox: in Mexico City, 26; kills Cuitlahuac, Montezuma's successor, 26.
Society women: professional and other singers, 114; as sponsors of festivities, 114-115; and social inequality, 115; as believers in education for women, 121-122.
Soto La Marina, siege of, 112.
Spanish women: as nurses; guards; in combat, 27.
Tabasco, battle of, 1.
Tapía, Doña Francisca. See Charitable women: sponsors of orphanages; see also Business women: hacienda managers.
Tecuichpochtzin, Montezuma's daughter, and Cortés, 22.
Tendile, chief emissary of Montezuma: presents Cortés with many gifts, 7; and the great god Quetzalcoatl, 8.
Tenochtitlán (Mexico City): description of, 16; and Cortés' plan, 8; battle for, 24-26.
Texcoco, description of, 32.
Three performing sisters. See Heroines of wars for independence: at siege of Cuautla.
Tlacochuatzin, mother of King Ixtlilxochitl, refuses baptism, 36.
Tlaxcalans, and battles with Conquistadors, 13-14.
Tsipaqua, Christina. See Inquisition: women victims of.
Uluapa, Marqués de: son of, marries La Güera's sister, 95.
Unconventional women, 94-99.
United States: and Juárez' liberal government, 143.
USS Wilderness, returns Margarita Juárez and family to Veracruz, 135.
Valle, Marqués del, Cortés' legitimate heir, 30.
Velasco, Don Antonio Rodríguez de, father of unconventional sisters, 95.
Velasco y Osorio Barba, María Ignacia (La Güera Rodríguez). See Unconventional women.
Velásquez, Diego: governor of Cuba, 10; and plans for Mexico, 7; sends fleet to Cempoala, 21-22; and plot to overthrow Cortés, 28.
Venus and the three graces, 96.
Vida común, 92-94.
Villar Villamil, José Jerónimo Lopez de Peralta de: marries La Güera, 95.
Virgin of Guadalupe: founding of the cult, 53; importance

of as unifying symbol, 54-55.
Viscaínas, La, orphanage school, 100.
Vivanco, Marquesa de. *See* Charitable women: as sponsors of orphanages, La Cuna.
Von Humboldt, Baron Alexander: fascinated by La Güera, 96-97.
War, famine and pestilence in Mexico City, 109.
Warrior women: Aztec, 13-14, 26-27.
Women of Mexico: some not born in the new world, Introduction.
Women protestors: at expulsion of Jesuits, 91; of vida común, 93-94.
Women: and changing roles, 70.
Women of performing arts: singers, 164-165; actresses, 165-166; composers, 167.
Women, spoils of war: at Battle of Tabasco, 1; at Tlaxcalan battles, 14.
Women writers: poets, 34-35; 166-168.
Women's rights, growing, 169-170.
Xuárez, Catalina, Cortés' wife, 4; arrives in Mexico City, 27; and mysterious death, 28.
Xochitl, Doña María Castilan. *See* Memorable humble women: weavers.
Ynaga, Maroon leader, 57.
Zavala, Gertrudis Tenorio. *See* Women writers: poets.
Zócalo, central plaza, 56.
Zopilotes, 135, 144.

Zumárraga, Archbishop, 53; accepts a miracle, 54.
Zuñiga, Doña Juana de, Cortés' second legitimate wife, 30.

Other Books by Floricanto Press

La Mujer Latina Series

The Broken Web
The Educational Experience of Hispanic Women

Edited by Teresa McKenna and Flora Ida Ortiz
Co-published with The Tomás Rivera Center

ISBN 0-942177-00-2. 1988
Hardbound $32.00
Paperbound $23.95

A revealing anthology of essays on the failure of the institutions to provide for and encourage the educational achievement of Hispanic women, thus adding to the inequalities they face in U.S. society today.

Maravilla

By Laura del Fuego

ISBN 0-915745-15-1. 1988
Hardbound $25.95
Paperbound $12.95

From the housing projects of East L.A. to the lively scene of San Francisco's Haight-Ashbury district in the 1960s, Laura del Fuego's first novel tells the absorbing tale of a young Chicana making her way through turbulent times.

Women of Mexico
The Consecrated and the Commoners

By Bobette Gugliotta

ISBN 0-915745-16-X. 1988
Hardbound $32.95
Paperbound $19.95
Illustrated

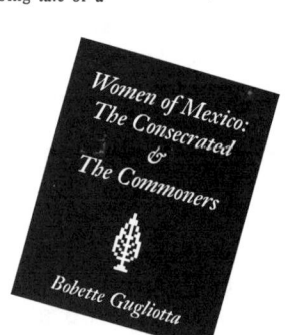

This collective biography not only offers insight into the more famous and infamous women in Mexican history, but weaves a fascinating tale of how the ways and deeds of Mexico's unsung heroines have shaped both a culture and a nation.

La Mujer Latina Series

Between Borders
Essays on Mexicana/Chicana History

Edited by Adelaida del Castillo

ISBN 0-915745-14-3. 1988
Hardbound $45.00
Paperbound $32.00

The first serious, comprehensive history of U.S. Latinas of Mexican descent prior to the 20th century. Written by a team of Mexican and U.S. scholars and based on copious documents and sources from both countries, this book sheds light on the traditional leadership of the modern Latina that is both ignored and little understood.

Fiction

Bring Me A Story

By Sally Benforado

Hardbound $14.95 1986
ISBN 0-915745-08-9

Softbound $9.95 1986
ISBN 0-915745-11-9

In the eleven short tales of *Bring Me a Story*, author Sally Benforado weaves together the oral history of a family of Sephardic Jews, from their close-knit home in Turkey to their new lives in America. They are stories of a heritage that spans the globe, of centuries-old traditions transported to a different world, and of a people who held on tightly to the ways of their ancestors, who, like them, left their homes to settle in a strange new land. *Bring Me a Story* stands as a living testament to a people born of their Hispanic ancestry, Jewish tradition and immigrant experience.

Collection Development

The Chicano Public Catalog
A Collection Guide for Public Libraries

Compiled by David Gutierrez and Roberto G. Trujillo

ISBN 0-915745-03-8. 1986 $39.00 300 p.

An authoritative guide to the best and most significant writings for public, academic and professional Chicano collections with full descriptive annotations. It includes indexes, annotations and bibliographic data. An important tool for collection development and evaluation.

Literatura Chicana
Creative Writings Through 1984

Compiled by Roberto G. Trujillo and Andres Rodriguez
Introductory essay by Luis Leal

ISBN 0-915745-04-6. 1985
$23.00
210 p.

More than 750 bibliographic citations of creative and critical literary works in print and nonprint form on the Chicano experience. Organized by genre and indexed by title and author, the bibliography covers poetry, fiction, theatre, oral tradition, and other subjects and includes listings of literary periodicals, dissertations, bibliographies, anthologies, and video and sound recordings.

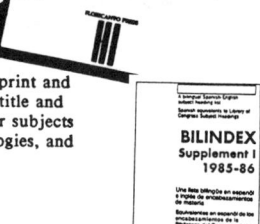

Bilindex & Bilindex Supplement 1
A Bilingual Spanish-English Subject Heading List

Standardized Spanish equivalents to Library of Congress subject headings including: an explanatory preface; cross references; scope notes; children's subject headings; standard subdivisions; and English-to-Spanish index; regional variants of authorized Spanish subject terms; and hard-to-find technical items.

Bilindex: ISBN 0-915745-00-3. 1983. Hardbound $65.00. 533 p.
Bilindex Supplement I: ISBN 0-915745-02-X. 1986. Softbound $55.00. 334 p.

Mexican American Studies

El Libro de Caló
The Dictionary of Chicano Slang

Edited by Harry Polkinhorn, Alfredo Velasco and
Malcolm Lambert

2nd edition
ISBN 0-915745-10-0. 1986
Hardbound $32.00
Paperbound $17.95
100 p.

This is an indispensable dictionary that is easy to use; it is a guide to understanding the dialect popularly spoken by Mexican Americans in the regions of the Southwest. Includes an English-Caló concordance.

Mexican Americans in Urban Society
A Selected Bibliography

By Albert Camarillo

ISBN 0-915745-12-7. 1986
$29.95
250 p.

A specialized but comprehensive bibliographic study documenting the contemporary and newly acquired urban experiences of Mexican Americans living in the U.S. cities as they migrated from the crop fields of the Southwest to the newly emerging post-war industries. The most updated and complete bibliographic control effort on writing on regional urban developments by Mexican Americans.

Online Information on Hispanics & Other Ethnic Groups
A Survey of State Agency Databases

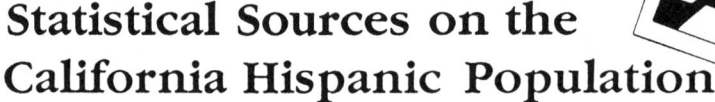

Edited by Roberta Medford and Eudora Loh

ISBN 0-915745-07-0. 1986
$45.00
200 p.

This is the most complete directory of state agency databases, located in the 10 states with the largest Hispanic populations, with a listing of their names, addresses, and phone numbers. This includes a wide range of statistical and other pertinent data on Hispanics, Blacks, Asian-Pacifics, and other ethnic groups living in the U.S. Complete with indexes, this book is a guide to the myriad of data collected and maintained by state agencies on ethnic groups.

Statistical Sources on the California Hispanic Population

Edited by Eudora Loh and Roberta Medford

ISBN 0-915745-01-1. 1985
$22.00
210 p.

A comprehensive directory of state documentary sources on the Hispanic population of California on a wide range of subjects, from consumer patterns to population, health and housing. This directory describes and evaluates the data sources. Includes index.

Lector

PLACE OF THE HERONS:
Small Press in Texas
JAMES M. CODY

MAKING THE VISION TANGIBLE:
A Talk With
LUIS VALDEZ

CUENTISTAS, MYTH & MAGIC:
Interview with
RUDOLFO ANAYA

PALABRAS HERIDAS
from
FRANCISCO X. ALARCON

LIVING UP THE STREET:
New From
GARY SOTO

CHICANO BIBLIOGRAPHY:
An Overview by
LUIS LEAL

REVIEWS
NANCY ROBINSON

Lector: The Hispanic Review Journal
Lector: Mexican American Writers

$45.00

Focus on Mexican American Writers

Floricanto Press • 16161 Ventura Blvd., Suite 830 • Encino, CA 91436

LA RED/THE NET

The Hispanic Journal of
Education, Commentary and Reviews

1989

Volume 2, Number 2

Announcements & News: Page 2
Feature Article: Page 7
Film Review: Page 11
Statistics: Page 13
Point of View: Page 19
Job Market: Page 25
Feature Report: Page 36

Published by Floricanto Press, 16161 Ventura Blvd., Suite 830, Encino, CA 91436-2504 (818) 990-1885

Giselle K. Cabello, Editor
University of California, Los Angeles
Roberto Cabello-Argandoña, Publisher
Translation, Typesetting & Graphics, Production
IAD, Inc., Exclusive Distributor
17337 Ventura Blvd., Suite 203, Encino, CA 91316-3905

All book titles reviewed and/or listed in this journal are available through Inter-American Development. Send orders to Inter-American Development, 17337 Ventura Blvd., Suite 203, Encino, CA 91316-3905 • (818) 990-1885

LA RED/THE NET (ISSN 1043-3321) is published as two separate publications for the price of one: a journal and a hotline publication. La Red/The Net: The Hispanic Journal of Education, Commentary and Reviews is published to inform and report on general issues affecting the education, and particularly the higher education, of Hispanics

Lector

VOLUME 5, NUMBER 2

SAN FRANCISCO'S
CHICANO MURAL
MOVEMENT
by
MELISSA PEABODY

SAN FRANCISCO'S
MEXICAN MUSEUM
by
ROSAINES AGUIRRE

CALEXICO:
An Essay in Images
*Photography
and Text by*
Harry Polkinhorn

SELECCIONES
DE LIBROS
offered by
HISPANEX/I.A.D.

BOOKS REVIEWS

Floricanto Press • 16161 Ventura Blvd., Suite 830 • Encino, CA 91436